A
Lifetime
of
Words

FABAUS LANDRY

LUCAS
PARK
BOOKS

ST. LOUIS, MISSOURI

Themes

Introduction   1

  1   Where Is God?   3

  2   What Is the Church?   23

  3   Worship and Prayer   41

  4   Community   53

  5   Stewardship   73

  6   Role of the Minister   93

  7   Social/Political   109

  8   Time   127

  9   Lent and Easter   139

10   Thanksgiving   153

11   Christmas   159

Notes   167

Introduction

The letters in this book are a small representation of those written by Dr. Fabaus "Bob" Landry to his congregations over a span of 43 years. He wrote monthly letters while at Berea Christian Church (Logan County, KY) and bi-weekly letters while serving at Collierville Christian Church (Collierville, TN). Although he wrote letters to members of his congregation while in Dover, Tennessee, these letters were more personal in nature so they are not included in this book. During his twelve years at the First Christian Church in Knoxville, Tennessee, he began his weekly musings. Some of these pieces were adapted and printed in the local newspaper, *The Knoxville Journal*. Others were also printed in the Christian Church Disciples of Christ magazine, *The Disciple*. Dr. Landry continued to write weekly letters to his congregation in Austin, Texas, for almost twenty years until his retirement.

One of his Austin parishioners said that Bob was a minister who "didn't send people to heaven, but rather brought heaven to the people." Bob truly lived the life of one dedicated to social justice and equality for all people. His writing style remained "folksy," whether dealing with daily matters or events of great importance in the community and the nation. Many people encouraged him to publish his theology throughout his ministries, but he never took the time to sit down and write his manuscript. We are the poorer for that. We can, however, share the letters he wrote, which provide a glimpse into Bob's theology and philosophy of life.

Bob wrote everything in longhand, even his sermons and prayers. His many quotes, stories, and illustrations came from years of extensive reading, studying, and conversations, during which he would pull out a 3 x 5 index card, sheet of notepaper, or scissors and tape, and collect the nuggets he wished to save. Though Bob's organizational system was meticulous, in order to combine them into a book, all the printed newsletters had to be reviewed, organized into topics, scanned, converted, typed, compiled, and then edited. Of course, none of these documents were footnoted or referenced. Sometimes the quotes were not exact and sometimes the quotation marks were used for emphasis or reflective of what might have been said. The endnotes for this publication required extensive research of books and papers, trips to the library, and the use of other research techniques to create the best references possible.

May these words of a lifetime be uplifting and valuable to each of you,

Judith Landry, Adena Landry Patterson, Tamara Landry Bell,
Shana Landry Chandler

1

Where Is God?

August 15, 1963

From the Minister's Pen:

Novelists and playwrights often preach more gospel in one book or play or movie than is heard from a thousand pulpits on a given Sunday. The demands of the gospel that we Christians treat our fellow men as brothers is often muted when delivered as part of a theological harangue from behind a pulpit. We hear the Word -- and yet we don't. But the novelist and the playwright draws a picture -- holds up a mirror -- from which we cannot turn aside. We are judged and condemned when we see ourselves in the picture or in the mirror. So was my experience 10 days ago when I saw *West Side Story* at a Nashville theater. I left bemoaning "what man has made of man"[1] -- and decrying my own inability to communicate the gospel of love in a world of hate.

Then last week one of our young deacons gave me a copy of *The Vixens* by Frank Yerby, a novel of post-Civil War New Orleans. My reaction was the same. The novelist and the playwright are saying something about the problems of our age. Meanwhile, we Christian ministers palaver about the sentimentalists of heaven, of strolling in a dew-dampened flower garden, of the riches of Christian fellowship. Our world is one vast Samaritan road and we priests and Levites travel it daily. What have we done to heal the sick, to lift the fallen, to help the downtrodden, to bring justice to the discriminated against? Very little! And who then will God send to do what we won't? He will send the notably irreligious -- the novelist, the playwright, the actor, the poet. I heartily recommend both *West Side Story* and *The Vixens* to your attention.

January 30, 1974

Dear Fellow Finders of Nice Things:

Serendipity has reference to the fortunate, though unintentional, result of an unusual coincidence of circumstances -- as *Webster's Seventh New Collegiate* puts it: "the gift of finding valuable or agreeable things not sought for."[2] For instance: A dairyman was driving out to the milking barn with a trailer load of feed. The racket made by his tractor flushed a pair of pheasants out of a hedgerow. In their excitement the two birds flew into the rear wheels of the tractor. So -- dairyman and his family had pheasant-under-glass for supper. Serendipity!

The energy crisis has been the occasion of a number of "serendipities." The speed limit has been lowered, a lot of folk are "car-pooling" it, more people are staying home over the weekends. So, the intended result of gasoline conservation has been achieved. Coincidentally, tires are wearing better, insurance premiums are going down, neighbors are getting to know each other in car-pools, and families are rediscovering the warmth and intimacy of the home and hearth. Serendipity!

A lot of "serendipitous" things happen at church. For instance: a couple of 40-year-old men reluctantly back into the business of teaching a Sunday School class of 8- and 9-year-old children. A frightening prospect! A terrifying responsibility! Coincidental to getting the job done, these two men rediscover the youthful glow, become excited about children again, establish friendships that will last a lifetime! Serendipity! Another for instance: A sweet young thing with a cup of hot chocolate in her hands stumbles in the church courtyard and dumps her hot chocolate all over herself and the new suit of a complete stranger. What a mess! But that stranger turns out to be the handsomest and most wonderful fellow who ever brought a bride to the marriage altar. Serendipity! Finally: The classic case is that of the sour skeptic who came to church to scoff and stayed to pray. Serendipity!

Has it happened to you? It certainly has! In the workshop, while cooking, at the store, driving home from work, in Sunday School -- and so on! The appropriate response to a "serendipitous" happening is that of joyful gratitude. To help you express your thanksgiving for your personal "serendipities" our hymn of praise next Sunday will be: *When Morning Gilds the Skies*! See, the sun has been getting up sorta late since the beginning of the energy crisis. And we have been enjoying a most fortunate, though unintentional, result of an unusual coincidence of circumstances -- that is, sunrise over the Smokies! What a splendid, what a magnificent, what a grand display of nature's beauty! And next Sunday we will be celebrating those serendipitous sunrises! And we will be celebrating Sunday School classes for 8- and 9-year-old children and new dimensions of life for men in their 40s. And celebrating spilled chocolate. And happy marriages. And pheasant-under-glass. And a whole lot of other serendipitous things that have been taking place at the church and elsewhere! Come! Your joy will be more intentional than happenstance!

With a happy smile on the outside -- but an intense seriousness on the inside, I am, <u>coincidentally</u> as well as <u>intentionally</u> your pastor and fellow seeker and finder of nice things.

February 16, 1977

Dear Fellow Disciples and Learners:

Am just back from nine days of continuing education leave spent in New York and Washington, D.C. Several have asked about the details of this "time away." (It can hardly be called "time off" because the pace is so demanding, the schedule so packed, the work so heavy.) Well, the details could not be managed in a 300-page book! But, in broad strokes:

> Two days in "The Big (and Dirty) Apple" -- the University Club, the Riverside Church, the Union Theological Seminary -- conferences, reading, writings, books, etc. The peak of that 48 hours was one hour spent at the Andrew Wyeth exhibition at the Metropolitan Museum of Art. Ah!
>
> Took AMTRAK to Washington, D.C., for seven days at the College of Preachers of the National Cathedral -- America's oldest and finest continuing education center for ministers. Reading extensively in the sermons of Frederick W. Robertson and the poems of William Wordsworth. Visits with Edward L. R. Elson, Chaplain of the United States Senate; with George Docherty, recently-retired pastor of the New York Avenue Presbyterian Church; and with Charles Trentham, for 23 years pastor of the First Baptist Church, Knoxville, and now the President's pastor at the First Baptist Church, Washington, D.C. (Please forgive all this name-dropping.)

Now -- that just touches the high spots! The details will have to wait for the unwritten 300-page book.

For those who were not sure about last Sunday's sermon: "A Letter to a Nine-Year-Old" -- those remarks were a first-hand report of Amy Carter's baptism -- and reflections on the meaning of her baptism for her, for her parents, for us. Observed it and reflected upon it from a "seat on the 50-yard line" -- just two pews behind her Mommy and Daddy. Yes. The letter and/or sermon will be sent to Amy at 1600 Pennsylvania Avenue. A typed copy and the cassette.

My soul is still vibrating from the readings, the insights, the conversations, the worship services, the inspirations of this "time away." I am living again at the trembly edge of ecstasy. The borders of the infinite and the ultimate seem not so far away anymore. If your pastor appears a bit nervous, over-stimulated, hyperactive -- what you see is what is there.

Walter Kerr wrote of a friend who expressed two fears:

> One was that, if he did not slow down, he would have a heart attack. The other was that, if he did not hurry up, he would not be able to accomplish enough that was useful before he had his heart attack.[3]

Bob Landry is like that, caught somewhere between those two fears. And a lot of other folk are caught right there with me. Fine company!

This is a great time to be alive! And I am deeply grateful for the privilege of it all!

- for the privilege of living and moving and having my being in the 20th century;
- for the privilege of thought and of speech and of touch;
- for the privilege of travel and of study and of continuing growth;
- for the privilege of making my pilgrimage toward spiritual maturity in the company of the splendid fellowship of Disciples and Learners who are within this church;
- for the privilege of spending "time away" so that "time at home" becomes more vibrant, productive, satisfying, fulfilling.

Thank you! Thank you! Thank you!

May 7, 1980

Dear Friends:

It was a thoughtful thing to do. He brought me a gift. Indeed -- he brought me ten gifts! And for no special reason. He just wanted me to enjoy some of the things he enjoyed most. So -- he had climbed his hill behind his house -- where the leaves of a thousand Smoky Mountain autumns had formed a rich, moist mulch. Ferns and mosses were in abundance. And wildflowers, too! Delicate mountain orchids -- lady's slippers, both pink and yellow. Bird's-foot violets. Dwarf-crested irises. Trillium, too -- some white, some yellow, some maroon. He had gotten down on his knees -- dug them up by hand! Carefully he had held the soil intact -- protecting the sensitive roots and the more sensitive blossoms that drew their life and color from those roots. These he had put into plastic bowls. Each bowl he had filled to the lip with velvety moss. All ten plants he had then put into two cardboard cartons and brought to church. With a wave of the hand he gave them to me -- all ten! It was a generous, thoughtful thing to do.

The five dwarf-crested irises I arranged in a semi-circle on the outer edge of our rose bed next to the back gate. The two lady's slippers I set out on our patio on the opposite side of the maple tree from the tulips. The three bird's-foot violets I replanted in a naturally shady area near the front wall of Tammy's bedroom.

Now -- every time I open the back gate I am reminded of his thoughtfulness. When I look out my east window onto the patio first thing each A.M. a pair of lady's slippers wave a greeting to me -- and I know why. The bird's-foot violets near the front wall of Tammy's bedroom I will see less often -- but when I do -- I will remember who gave them to me.

Gifts do that for us -- they remind us of persons who are thoughtful, who care, who love, who give. The pen with which I am writing these lines was a Christmas gift. She left it on my desk one December day with a tiny card which read: "Thanks for being my friend." I never put this pen to paper but that I think of her. The full lead crystal paperweight on my desk -- the one with a fine line etching of a lamb lying down with a lion -- the word "Shalom" inscribed above that etching -- that paperweight was a gift from one of my dearest friends and fans. Rarely do I get to see her -- but six or eight times a day I reshuffle the stacks of paper on my desk -- and there's that paperweight -- and I remember....

The tie I am wearing was given me by one of my older brothers. Most of my neckties were gifts. And each time I slip on a gift-tie the memory of the person who gave it to me flashes across my consciousness. A rich purple tie I especially enjoy wearing. It matches nothing -- it clashes with everything! Folk sometimes do a double-take because this purple tie just does not coordinate with my blue or brown suits. Still I wear it -- and proudly, too! Why? Because Paw Paw Landry gave it to me -- and I love to remember my father! A key ring -- a conch-shell -- a pair of salt and pepper shakers -- a watch -- a coffee cup -- a table cloth -- a scarf -- a brooch -- a lamp -- a belt -- a painting -- a vase -- a book -- a jar of apple-butter -- a ticket stub -- a magazine subscription -- a picture -- Ah! We are surrounded with mementos from thoughtful and kind and generous persons. What is it that you have in your pocket -- or on the end table -- or next to the flower stand -- or on the mantelpiece that is a reminder of the thoughtfulness and kindness and love of a friend? Or, to reverse the question -- what is it that someone else has that is a reminder to him of your thoughtfulness and kindness and love? "It is more blessed to give than to receive!" (Acts 20:35 RSV)

June 27, 1986

Dear Fellow Missionaries:

David Livingstone -- born in Scotland -- spent most of his life in Africa -- buried in the company of England's poets and statesman and artists in Westminster Abbey. Livingstone's biography tells of his travels for the Gospel -- through jungles, through swamps, over mountains, across deserts. His wife and his child died. He buried them together in an unmarked grave on the edge of the Kalahari Desert. Then he hiked across that desert to the east coast of Africa. Weakened by malaria, forsaken by his porters, threatened by hostile tribes -- still he pursued his work of bringing the light of the Gospel to the Dark Continent.

Once Livingstone was attacked by a lion whose teeth tore into his left shoulder. Ever after, his left arm hung limp at his side. He returned to Scotland to tell of his sufferings as a missionary. He appealed to others to join in this work with these words: "In the light of the morning sun I have seen the smoke from the breakfast fires of a thousand villages where the Gospel of Christ has never been heard."[4] Thousands of young people followed Livingstone's footsteps to Africa -- to Asia -- to India -- to China -- to the Islands of the Sea!

Livingstone's greatest monument is said to have been a white clapboard church house in Zanzibar. That church house was built on the spot where he had first seen slaves being sold to the highest bidders! Once, there was an auction block where persons were treated like merchandise. But through the work of David Livingstone there now stands a church house on that spot where persons are treated as sons and daughters of God!

Overworked -- exhausted -- unrewarded -- without support -- still Livingstone did not give up. What was it that kept him faithful to his missionary endeavor? Livingstone began each day by repeating to himself a verse from Matthew 28 -- the final line in that Gospel -- the last recorded words of Jesus: "...and, lo, I am with you always, even unto the end of the world." (Matthew 28:20 KJV) And each evening -- as he slumbered on his cot he repeated those words: "...and, lo, I am with you always, even unto the end of the world!" Anybody looking on might have concluded that David Livingstone had pursued his missionary work alone. But he was not alone. The Christ who gave us the Great Commission was Livingstone's constant companion: "...and, lo, I am with you always, even unto the end of the world!" That one line -- repeated morning and evening -- put courage in his heart and strength in his soul.

It is a good line! It is a great line! We, too, would do well to use it -- and to use it often! To say it when first we awaken in the A.M. To repeat it as we lie down to sleep in the evening. To be mindful of it throughout the hours between: in our work -- when we face troubles -- before we undertake major tasks -- as we deal with persons in need -- in moments when we feel threatened. We are not alone. Christ is our constant companion: "...and, lo, I am with you always, even unto the end of the world!" It is a good line! It is a great line! Use it! Often!

For the high privilege of being in good company at all times we should be grateful.

September 18, 1987

Dear Christian Readers:

We subscribe to the *Austin American-Statesman* -- six months at a whack. Our last pay period started April 1-- ends September 30. Our subscription is up for renewal October 1. But we may just let it slide. Why? Will we be able to get along without it? Can we stay in touch with what's happening now if we don't daily read the daily? Don't know -- but we may try not reading the newspaper for the next six months! We may find it hard to decide about umbrellas if we don't see the weather report. But with 265 days of sunshine guaranteed by the Chamber of Commerce, do we really need to know the forecast? Besides, some 40% of the time it is in error!

How about the daily gyrations of the stock market: IBM, Unisys, GM? Since our stock of stocks is nil, will our not-knowing matter? There's 'leventeen pages of want-ads -- thousands of things we might get a bargain on -- if we needed them. And houses for sale and/or rent. And boats. And lots of offers for employment. And dogs to adopt. And all the display-ads, too: beau coups of cosmetics and jewelry and formal wear. And the Sunday edition comes with loads of inserts from Sears, K-Mart, and Montgomery Ward. Will we be able to survive without the knowledge of how much we can save if we buy now and pay later? Maybe. Maybe not.

Can we live without the chuckles à la Cathy and Garfield and Hagar? Will we miss Erma Bombeck and Ann Landers and Miss Manners? Will our days dullen without the headlines about bankruptcies and mortgage rates and the latest episode in the life of the hottest rock star? Will we be greatly impoverished if we do not read Lee Kelly's bold print list of Austin's bluenoses, or John Kelso's lampoonery of our not so sacred cows, or William Buckley's put-downery of all things unreactionary?

Of late we have been blanketed with coverage of Pope John Paul's marathon around the good ole U.S. of A. "Blanketed" is the right term. We've been force fed the whole nine yards! Reporters have noted that His Excellency JPII uses 2% over his Raisin Bran, that his jeweled tiara is insured for $700,000.00, that his boot size is 10-D, that the Pope-mobile has Michelin tires. We have high regard for the man. And especially for his office. But all this square-footage of newsprint has been too much. We feel a bit like the fellow who was told more than he wanted to know about the penguin. He regretted having asked. We are suffering from information overload. To the Nth.

The media: newspapers, magazines, television, radio -- the media take a slice of life, throw the spotlight on it, magnify its significance, serve it up as though it is the latest and greatest. But it all is a distorted view of the real world. And we have to sift through an awful lot of chaff to salvage a few kernels of the real thing. Indeed, the media (and especially the newspaper) can blind us to the real thing. And what is that real thing? In my case, the real thing is my wife, Judie. We get to see each other over a cup of coffee at 7:15 A.M. before she rushes off to her students at Westlake High School. Should we let the newspaper come between us during that five minutes? Or the latest issue of *Time*? Or the *Good Morning, America* show? Or the radio reports of the previous night's temperatures and rainfall? Hardly! Much better it is to see the real thing close at hand -- together to offer thanks for the soggy Shredded Wheat -- together to watch the blue jays at the bird feeder -- and together to check signals for the rest of the day.

Well -- we may try it for 30 days or so. Even for six months! Let the newspaper subscription slide, hide the *Time* magazine, switch off the TV, unplug the radio. Having blanked out the news and noise of the world outside we then may discover a calm and sane universe inside. "Be still," the Bible says. "Be still and know!" Know what? "Be still and know that I am God!" (Psalms 46:10 RSV) Tune out the racket and distraction without. Tune in the still small voice within.

May 6, 1988

Dear Friends:

She brushed her hair back with her right hand. It was not a fast movement. Rather deliberate. The dark strands fell into place as she slowly brought her hand to rest on the arm of the wheelchair. I leaned over and whispered to her, "Michelle, it is great that you can fix your own hair. You are not fast at it, yet. But 10 days ago, your Aunt Wanda was having to brush it back for you." She looked up with bright eyes and a watermelon-slice smile. She sounded out a hopeful note, "I am getting better every day. My fingers are still clumsy -- but at least I can feel them now."

Michelle is recovering from a severe case of Guillain-Barre Syndrome -- a viral disease of the nervous system. This disease progressively paralyzes the body. It begins in a numbing of the extremities: the hands and feet. It moves into the arms and legs. Sometimes it goes on to total paralysis so that even breathing is curtailed. If that happens, the patient has to be put on a respirator. In Michelle's case, it did not get that extreme. The illness (G-BS) reaches a peak after which its effects subside gradually. Patients recover their ability to breathe. Their torso muscles are rejuvenated. The abdominal muscles are restored. Then the arms and legs. Finally, the hands and feet. The recovery period varies from a matter of weeks to as long as a year -- even two years. Therapy continues until the patients are 100% healed. In most cases, it is "110%" because the patients compensate. That is, they go beyond healing to wellness -- and they go beyond wellness to excellence in health and strength.

In Michelle's case, she is grateful for being able to brush her hair back with her right hand -- slowly -- deliberately -- studying the movements because her fingers are still without feeling. Once fully recovered, she will never again take for granted the joy of fixing her own hair. Two weeks ago, she couldn't prop herself up in bed on her elbow because her arms were paralyzed. Instead, any movement she made depended on her use of abdominal and shoulder muscles. Have you ever tried to roll over in bed without the use of your arms and legs? Try it! Michelle had to do that for one month. She now has the strongest stomach and shoulder muscles at Church! Her legs and feet are still motionless. She can see her feet -- but she cannot wiggle her toes. She can use her hands to push her knees together -- but her knees don't feel each other. Since her legs and feet are paralyzed, she has to get around in a wheelchair. She can do "wheelies"! Someday soon she will graduate to crutches. Some weeks from now -- maybe months -- she will carefully make her way down the church aisle on her own -- reaching from one pew to the next until she gets to the one where Grandpa Bartie always sits -- fourth pew, center-left. When Michelle does that, the entire congregation will sing a doxology of thanksgiving. Not a dry eye in the house!

We take so much for granted! What a pleasure it is to brush back one's hair -- even if it takes just one quick flick of the hand and wrist! How nice it is to roll over in bed to get more comfortable -- even if it takes just a shove of the elbows and a push of the knees! It is a delight to stroll out to the curb to pick up the mail -- even if it just takes a few quick shuffles of the feet! To raise a cup of coffee to the lips! To fluff up a pillow! To flip the light switch! To turn the ignition key! To empty the dishwasher! To slice a banana! To sign a check! To pour sunflower seeds into the bird feeder! To push a grocery cart! To lift a hymnal! To mow the lawn! To crack a pecan!

Life is a great gift -- a great gift filled with thousands of smaller gifts -- voice, movement, touch, fragrances, friends, music, books, sight, memory, church, colors, plants, tools, holidays, pets, in-laws, etc., etc., etc. But we often take these many good gifts for granted! For instance, can you brush your hair back with a quick flick of your hand and wrist? If so, don't take that movement for granted! It is a gift! Lift up your heart in thanksgiving: "Praise God from whom all blessings flow!"[5]

June 3, 1988

Dear Friends:

One of our favorite themes is that of "Making the Best of a Bad Mess." We can put un-good things to good uses. Remember the folk who discovered that their formula for soap produced a product that was so light it floated?[6] What a peculiar thing! Soap was not supposed to float! Such an oddity would never sell! But an enterprising salesman probably said, "Let's transform this liability into an asset. Let's capitalize the notion that our soap floats!" They did! And Ivory Soap became as common in the bathroom as Vick's Salve and Bayer Aspirin and Old Dutch Cleanser!

Are dandelions good for anything except to make more dandelions that spoil a neat lawn? Adrian Wells thinks so! He considers dandelion greens a delicacy! He has a dandelion plantation in Wilton, Maine. He has earned his fortune cultivating dandelions, canning them, shipping them nationwide to folk who share his taste. Seems to me that Mr. Wells deserves an award for putting un-good things to good uses![7]

So does the lady who brought a blossoming prickly pear cactus to the church a couple weeks back. Appropriately arranged, that obnoxious and dangerous bit of desert flora became the prettiest centerpiece in the room. As a somewhat-newcomer, I consider this plant the real "Yellow Rose of Texas"! All of which reminds me of the lady from Minnesota who did a very unusual thing. She won the grand prize in the floral arrangement competition. But her "flowers" were all weeds! Right! She took Queen Anne's Lace and giant foxtail and turkey foot and wild sumac berries. Arranged them so uniquely and attractively that she won over all those who had entered real flowers! That's "Making the Best of a Bad Mess"!

Often, what we see in things is more important than the things themselves. The perceptive eye can see good uses for un-good things. With an artistic touch, things of small value become sentimental treasures. Rightly marketed, a bar of soap that floated became a best-seller! Dandelions became a source of wealth! A cactus became the prettiest thing in the room! Weeds, gracefully arranged, won the grand prize!

In terms of "Making the Best of a Bad Mess" nothing quite surpasses the Christian gospel that Paul summarized in these lines:

> For consider your call, brethren; not many of you were wise according to worldly standards, not many were powerful, not many were of noble birth; but God chose what is foolish in the world to shame the wise, God chose what is weak in the world to shame the strong, God chose what is low and despised in the world, even things that are not, to bring to nothing things that are, so that no human being might boast in the presence of God. He is the source of your life in Christ Jesus, whom God made our wisdom, our righteousness and sanctification and redemption; therefore, as it is written, "Let him who boasts, boast of the Lord." (I Corinthians 1:26-31 RSV)

Ivory Soap -- dandelion greens -- prickly pear cactus -- winning with weeds -- un-wise, un-powerful, un-noble who became the children of God, citizens of the kingdom of heaven! That's Good News!

June 10, 1988

Dear Friends:

In a made-for-TV-movie, Katherine Hepburn plays the role of a wealthy, world-travelled writer. But her editor feels she is out of touch with the real world. To convince her editor that she is still in touch, Hepburn agrees to live with a supposedly ordinary family for one week. By the third day, she discovers she can't stand the family. And the family can't stand her! It is a complex situation, but to make a short-story shorter, by the end of the week Hepburn has become friends with one of the teenagers. But the teenager is discouraged, depressed, wants to give up. During a serious conversation with Hepburn, the teenager says, "I can't do it! I can't do it! I give up!" But Hepburn responds, "Well! You can't give up! You <u>can</u> do more than you can do!"[8]

"You can do more than you can do!" That is a great line! Deserves to be put on a bumper sticker. It is a "booster"! Makes you feel better: better about yourself -- better about your circumstances -- better about your resources -- better about your future! It boosts your self-esteem. It pumps adrenalin into your arteries! Your heart beats faster! Your lungs breathe deeper. Your muscles become stronger! Your confidence rises!

"You can do more than you can do!" That is a great line with which to start the day. The alarm jangles you out of your slumber. You stumble to the bathroom. You brush your teeth. You splash cold water into your face. You push back your hair. You look into the mirror and see somebody who is already running to catch up before the day has even started! You must throw breakfast together -- hustle Junior and Sis off to the car-pool -- clear the dishes -- dress for success in less than six minutes -- speed off to a full day's work at an Indy 500 pace: sales letters, reports, interviews, committees, phone calls, research -- pick up the kids at the day-care -- get dinner on by 6:30 -- concert at 8:00 -- so it goes until you collapse at midnight. You can't do it all. Or can you? It is an impossible dream! You splash colder water into your face. You push back your hair again. Who is that in the mirror? Somebody on the edge of exhaustion -- behind before the day has begun. You have given everything you had. And you have no more to give. So, now you are ready to give up. Then, you repeat the words: "You can do more than you can do!" And you don't give up! Instead, you attack your responsibilities with fresh energy -- confident you will make it -- grateful for your health and for your children -- hopeful for tomorrow! "You <u>can</u> do more than you can do!"

I discovered the same sentiment in a book of *Great Quotes from Great Women*. "You gain strength, courage and confidence by every experience in which you must stop to look fear in the face. You are able to say to yourself, 'I have lived through this horror. I can take the next thing that comes along.' You must do the thing you think you cannot do."[9] The great woman who said that was Eleanor Roosevelt. Paul expressed this notion in Christian terms, "I can do all things in him who strengthens me." (Philippians 4:13 RSV) And 800 years before Paul, the great prophet Isaiah said it for all religious persons:

> [T]hey who wait for the Lord shall renew their strength,
>   they shall mount up with wings like eagles,

> they shall run and not be weary,
>> they shall walk and not faint! (Isaiah 40:31 RSV)

Tomorrow, when the alarm jangles you out of your slumber -- you stumble to the bathroom -- you brush your teeth -- you splash cold water into your face -- you push back your hair -- you recognize the gal in the mirror who is facing another impossible day, say to yourself, "You can do more than you can do!" Better yet, as a Christian, open yourself up to receive strength from beyond yourself. With Paul say, "I can do all things in him who strengthens me!" (Philippians 4:13 RSV)

> Do not pray for easy lives; pray to be stronger men.
> Do not pray for tasks equal to your powers; pray for powers equal to your tasks.
> Then the doing of your work shall be no miracle, but you yourself shall be a miracle.
> Every day you shall wonder at yourself,
> At the richness of life which has come to you by the grace of God.
>> -- Phillips Brooks[10]

August 14, 1998

> O, these truants from home and from heaven,
> They have made me more manly and mild,
> And I know now how Jesus could liken
> The kingdom of God to a child!
>> -- Charles Dickens[11]

> "Truly, I say to you, unless you turn and become like children, you will never enter the kingdom of heaven!" (Matthew 18:3 RSV)

To be like a child -- fresh -- innocent -- trusting -- curious -- unburdened by prejudice -- without guilt or anxiety or fear: "to such belongs the kingdom of God." (Luke 18:16 RSV) To be like a child -- to lay no demands on others other than to be warmed and filled and dried and cuddled: "to such belongs the kingdom of God." To be like a child -- uninhibited -- spontaneous -- honest -- unaware of the boundaries in the games people play: "to such belongs the kingdom of God." To be like a child -- having no past -- remembering no "good ole days" -- thus, living intensely in the present and wide open to the future -- and having a lot of future: "to such belongs the kingdom of God." "Let the children come to me, do not hinder them; for to such belongs the kingdom of God. Truly, I say to you, whoever does not receive the kingdom of God like a child shall not enter it." (Mark 10:14-15)

What memories flooded Jesus's mind as he likened the kingdom of God to a child? Did Jesus remember clinging with his chubby fingers to his father's much larger finger as they walked to the orchard? Was he remembering the first time he touched a dandelion puff and watched the tiny seedlings parachute to the ground? Did Jesus have in mind the night when his uncle raised a finger to the dark sky and showed him how to find the North Star? Surely the tender and gentle caresses of his young mother were unforgettable! Was it early -- or was it late -- that a teacher pointed out to Jesus the complexities of a lily of the field: stamen -- pistil -- calyx -- petal -- sepal -- stem -- leaves -- roots? More recently, who were the children with whom Jesus lived -- brothers and sisters, cousins? Who were his nieces and nephews? Who were the neighbor children with whom Jesus played ball, fetched water, went to synagogue school?

As we grow older, our eyes develop cataracts. Cataracts form when the normally clear fibers that make up the lens become cloudy, somewhat like the white of an egg that becomes opaque when boiled. When our eyes develop cataracts our sight becomes blurry, foggy. We walk around with caution. We bump into things. We stumble. We read -- but only the large print. We see -- as "through a glass, darkly." (I Corinthians 13:12 KJV) The colors of the rainbow fuzz into grey.

This happens not only with the sight of the eyes. This happens also with the vision of the heart!

- We no longer notice the love between a mother and her child.
- Spiritual cataracts blind us to the endurance of a soul who must bear the burdens of two!
- The grief of the folk who hang a black bow on the door no longer touches us.
- The child across the street has within itself a spark of divinity but we do not fan that spark to a flame!

The infant, the toddler, the kindergartner, the schoolgirl look with clear eyes on a brand-new world every day! To them this universe is as fresh and as refreshing as vanilla ice cream. They have not been this way before. For them each step is a first! They want to investigate the inner workings of a clock. They smack their lips as they slather heavy jam on light toast! For children it is the first morning after creation! Would that we who are older could see things through the unclouded eyes of a child! Would that we could touch things with a child's fingertips! Or relish the taste of a July peach with the tongue of a child! Or tune in with a child's ear to the lullaby of heaven! Or smell the things only a child can smell!

"Truly, I say to you, unless you turn and become like children, you will never enter the kingdom of heaven!" (Matthew 18:3 RSV)

May 8, 1992

Dear Christian Friends:

An old friend of mine, "Hop" Bailey, greeted me with a question, "Well, Preacher, how are things going?" "Hop" had been an amateur baseball player in his younger years. My answer to his greeting led off this way, "Well, Hop, I feel like I am in a batter's practice cage with a steady stream of baseballs coming at me. I don't have the energy and I am not quick enough to swing the bat at all the balls." "Well, Preacher," Hop responded, "you don't have to hit all of them. You just have to hit the important ones." Since that greeting I have let a lot of "balls" of lesser significance fly past me so I would have the energy and be quick enough to hit "the important ones."

I read somewhere that Alfred Tennyson was strolling one day in a lovely garden where many flowers were in full bloom. A friend strolling alongside Tennyson asked him, "You know you write a lot of poetry about Christ. Can you summarize for me what Christ really means to you as a poet?" The great Tennyson stopped, and pointing down to a magnificent blossom answered something like, "What the sun and rain and soil are to that flower Jesus Christ is to my soul!"[12] That is how it is with the influence of Jesus Christ on us. Christ has been to us the sun and rain and soil -- nurturing us, encouraging us, giving us warmth and sustenance so that we could blossom into our best selves. And we pause in the midst of our heavy and hectic schedules to give thanks for his example and inspiration.

A bit nearer at hand, there are a number of persons who have had wholesome influences on us. They have been like the sun and rain and soil to our souls. They have been encouraging, helpful, kind to us. We ought not be too busy to tell these persons that we appreciate what they have done for us. They have cultivated within us our best sense of who we are and have helped us along the way to become better persons! And saying thanks to them is one of "the important ones."

So -- take the time right now. Pick up the telephone, call one such individual, and say, "I appreciate you for what you have done for me." If not the telephone, write a note to express your gratitude. If not the phone or a note, the next time you are near a gift shop, pick up a memento, a souvenir, some precious thing to express to them your sincere appreciation. Do not be so busy -- do not jump on the treadmill and run so hard all day -- and for so long -- that you fail to do one of the most important things in life. And that is to let persons who have had significant influences on you -- to let them know that you appreciate what they have done for you!

February 18, 2000

REQUIESCAT
CHARLES SCHULZ
1922 – 2000

Charles Schulz died just hours before the publication of his last *Peanuts* comic strip. Quite a coincidence! He worked right up to his final deadline! Felt good about his efforts. Laid down his pen just before he laid down his life! We don't really believe that "timing is everything." Yet, in this case, timing was a whole lot!

Schulz disliked the notion of retiring to a life of leisure: drawing a Social Security check, relaxing with a fishing pole, hunting the forests for feathered and furred things, chasing the white ball of cow-pasture-pool,[13] cruising on a Norwegian liner, sipping Scotch with the codgers at the City Club. He never enjoyed such activities so much as he relished drawing his "family" of round-headed kids speaking words that were always funny, often profound. Schulz stuck to what he enjoyed most! Right to the last! He got his greatest satisfactions from his creative work. It was inconceivable that he might be put out to pasture to be pampered like a has-been thoroughbred on alfalfa and clover!

What a treasure he gave our world! Journalists, professors, educators, playwrights, cartoonists, literati, and philosophers will be mining diamonds of delight, emeralds of insight, rubies of wisdom from his oeuvre of over 50 years! His "family" (Charlie Brown, Lucy, Snoopy, Linus, Schroeder, Peppermint Patty, Pigpen, Marcie, Franklin, et. al.) ran the gamut: simple to sophisticated -- glad to sad -- bright to dark -- ecstasy to agony! We liked the Schulz "family" because the Schulz "family" was like the Smith "family," like the Jones "family," like the Landry "family."

In the creation story God said, "Let us make man in our image, after our likeness." (Genesis 1:26 RSV) The "image and likeness" of God in that story is that of a laborer at work: bringing order out of chaos -- separating the light from the darkness -- forming oceans and mountains -- planting forests and orchards -- setting the sun and the moon and the stars in the heavens -- evolving birds and sea monsters and creeping things and beasts. By the time God said, "Let us make man in our image, after our likeness," he was a confirmed workaholic! Finally, God crowned his creation by creating a fellow laborer and workaholic! God was exhausted by his efforts, but was happy with the results: "And God saw everything that he had made, and behold, it was very good!" (Genesis 1:31 RSV) Then he took the next day off. God rested.

Here, in this latest generation, a man created in the image and likeness of the Creator toiled all of his life -- right to the end! Then, weary and worn, he ended his labors and he ended his life at the same time. Now, he, too, is at rest.

March 17, 2000

Dear Fellow Seekers:

We sometimes discover the Divine in unexpected places. Abraham did near the Oaks of Mare. Moses did in a desert. Elijah did in a cave. Jesus did in the Wilderness.

We expect to discover the Divine when we enter Michelangelo's Sistine Chapel for the first time. We expect to discover the Divine on hearing Beethoven's *Ninth Symphony* for the ninth time. We expect to discover the Divine while driving through the bluebonnets on the Bastrop Highway for the umpteenth time. Ofttimes we are disappointed.

Still, there are "moments, sure tho' seldom"[14] when we sense the presence and the power and the peace of the Divine:

- "The still, small voice" of an infant speaks of the genius of the Creator Who eons ago started this magnificent experiment in light and life and love.
- A patient with fevered brow and weak knees who still believes the hand of God wears the glove of the surgeon confirms our confidence that we are not alone.
- The saint who has gone the second mile -- and the third -- and the fifteenth! -- her eyes shine with the brightness of Heaven.

Close encounters with the Spirit are ofttimes unexpected, unplanned, unprogrammed. How colorless our lives would be without the sensitivity of soul to discover: "What no eye has seen, nor ear heard, nor the [human heart] conceived, what God has prepared for those who love him!" (I Corinthians 2:9 RSV)

During a dark time in Frederick Buechner's life he was sitting by the side of the road. He was full of anxiety, full of fear and uncertainty. The world within seemed as shadowy as the world without. In *Telling Secrets* he said:

> I remember sitting parked by the roadside once, terribly depressed and afraid about my daughter's illness and what was going on in our family, when out of nowhere a car came along down the highway with a license plate that bore on it the one word out of all the words in the dictionary that I needed most to see exactly then. The word was TRUST. What do you call a moment like that? Something to laugh off as the kind of joke life plays on us every once in a while? The word of God? I am willing

to believe that maybe it was something of both, but for me it was an epiphany.[15]

Just one word: "T-R-U-S-T." On one of those license plates that you can get by paying a little extra. It was a license plate with a word on it instead of just numbers and a letter or two. And of all the words the license plate might have on it, the word that it did have was the word T-R-U-S-T: TRUST. Spoke eloquently to one in need. Some would say: "A discovery of the Divine in an unexpected place." Makes good sense to most of us!

Where? When? How? What? Who? Many would tell us to seek the Divine in a cathedral -- at a concert -- in a field of flowers. Jesus shifted the search from sight to insight, from yonder to here, from later to now: "The kingdom of God is not coming with signs to be observed; nor will they say, 'Lo, here it is!' or 'There!' for behold, the kingdom of God is in the midst of you"! (Luke 17:20-21 RSV) Makes good sense to most of us!

Your Friend and Fellow Seeker.

September 7, 2001

Dear Friends:

The grocer would tuck the carton of eggs into the top of the brown paper sack. Then with a smile, he would point to a goodie of some sort and say, "Lagniappe." The goodie might be a peppermint stick, a ball of bubble gum, a Tootsie Roll, a jaw-breaker, a coconut cookie in the Jack's Cookies container.

"Lagniappe" (lanyap) was the "something extra" the grocer gave to each of his customers, somewhat akin to the 13th donut in the "baker's dozen." This was his way of adding a toothsome touch to shopping chores, and of saying "thank you" for coming to his store. "Lagniappe" was good public relations. It was an immediate and tangible and tasty expression of appreciation. Made for repeat customers. "Lagniappe" -- "something extra" -- "a gift above and beyond" -- "a favor undeserved" -- "a grace note." Into every life there should fall at least a little "lagniappe."

It's good to receive "lagniappe" -- sweet, tasty, refreshing, encouraging. But to give "lagniappe" is even better. "Lagniappe" is to be compared with mercy, which, according to Shakespeare, is "twice bless'd":

> The quality of mercy is not strain'd.
> It droppeth as the gentle rain from heaven
> Upon the place beneath, it is twice bless'd:
> It blesseth him that gives and him that takes.
> 'Tis mightiest in the mightiest; it becomes
> The throned monarch better than his crown;

It is an attribute to God himself;
And earthly power doth then show likest God's
When mercy seasons justice.[16]

Indeed! "Lagniappe," too, is "twice bless'd" -- "It blesseth him that gives and him that takes."

Have you received a bit of lagniappe lately? A couple of weeks back I greeted one of our Trustees with this familiar line: "How are you feeling?" He responded with a hearty: "I'm feeling a lot better than I deserve." There's a fellow who has a high "L.Q." (Lagniappe Quotient) What is your "L.Q."?

Have you given a little lagniappe lately? Like dropping in to see old man Kowalski -- not because he deserved your visit -- but because you knew it would "make his day." And then you came away feeling he had "made your day." That's double lagniappe: "It blesseth him that gives and him that takes."

God laid out his work of creating and outfitting the universe. Figured it would take him about seven days in all. But he finished it and furnished it in only six days -- and had this tag end of the week left over. God leaned back on his lawn chair, put his hands behind his head, smiled, and then said, "Lagniappe" (which in Hebrew is pronounced "Sabbath"). There it is. A gift. Something extra. Above and beyond. Free. Gratis. What are you doing with God's weekly "lagniappe" to you?

All this scribbling about an unusual word and a delightful custom remembered from childhood times in the Cajun country is more than mere scribbling. Actually, this "lagniappe" thing is not unlike the Gospel which speaks of God's giving to persons who were undeserving. Of course, God's greatest gift to us we remember on Sunday. So then -- COME! Join the great congregation every Sunday when we rejoice in the light and the love and the life that are ours by the grace and mercy of God.

Lagniappely yours.

July 5, 2002

Dear Lovers of the Mountains, Finders of Fishing Holes, Combers of Gulf Beaches, Etc., Etc., Etc.:

The summer slumped in on us a couple weeks ago. The Sunday School classes were thinnish. The Congregation was less than robust -- both in numbers and in singing power. May have been the early morning sprinkles dampened some folk's intention to be in church. More likely they were doing what they had intended -- they were elsewhere. A long weekend has a way of transforming the mountains and lakes into magnets that draw people out of the concrete and asphalt jungle into the great outdoors. That's why there were so many empty pews. The "Summer Slump" is measured by the proportion of empty pews at 11:00 A.M. on the Sabbath during the months of June-July-August. It is a high-odds bet that many a well-worn pew will be vacant several Sundays between now and Labor Day. So what? Shall we be unhappy? Shall we frown? Wring our hands? Whimper? We shall not!

In years past we have read the laments of other ministers who whined the blues because of the "Summer Slump." And they did everything in their capacity (and some things that ought not have been in their capacity!) to reverse the mid-year exodus to the highways and high hills. They browbeat their congregations. They threatened. They fumed. They stormed. They begged. They cajoled. They pleaded. They whipped up attendance contests. They laid guilt on absentees. They passed out bubble gum and balloons. One pastor gave genuine cotton-candy puffs to his champion "pew packers"!

Such ministers behaved as though it were the Lord's will that the ebb-tide in summer church attendance not occur. Sometimes they succeeded -- but in what? They maintained the facade of "churchianity" under a gloss of carnival gimmicks. Inflated attendance records are dubious indicators of genuine Christian commitment. Such ministers also succeeded in making millions of devoted religious folk feel miserable about being in the woods or on the oceanside or "down by the riverside" on Sunday. That kind of success is failure!

There is an opposite perspective from which to view the "Summer Slump." Empty pews in June-July-August represent families spending vacation time together. The days are longer. The kids are out of school. Dad gets his annual leave. Why should the family not escape to the Gulf Coast for an extended time of togetherness and refreshment? According to the Bible, the Sabbath was made for relaxation and re-creation. Therefore, let us not complain and cry because of empty pews. Rather, let us rejoice that our people have the time and the resources and the freedom to rediscover themselves as persons within the family! This pastor is convinced that the revitalization and rejuvenation of family togetherness during the "Summer Slump" is crucial for authentic Christian living around the rest of the calendar.

Most church families will be away two Sundays or more during the summer months. Pastors truly care for their people. So let your pastor know when you are leaving -- where you are going -- how long you will be away. Thus, he will be aware of your journeyings and will pray for a full and happy time for you. Then, report in when you get home -- and the pastor and all the congregation will rejoice in your summer pleasures and in your homecoming. And your well-dusted pew will welcome you back.

The synagogue in Jesus's day probably had something like a "Summer Slump" -- folk in Nazareth off to the Mediterranean coast to enjoy the sea breezes, up to Lebanon to shade among the cedars, down to Galilee for sailing, over to

Jerusalem for shopping. Though Jesus never penned a minister's message like this one he did say something that parallels this new slant on an old issue. It was a simple statement -- but so very significant! "The sabbath was made for man, not man for the sabbath"! (Mark 2:27 RSV) Jog around that one for a while -- and you will enjoy your summer vacation and long weekends a bit more!

Your Pastor and Friend.

2

What Is the Church?

December 19, 1973

Dear Christians:

Fylma and Ab Witt drive 90 miles each Wednesday for the privilege and joy of singing with our Church Choir -- all the way from the top of Bluff Mountain to 211 West Fifth Avenue and back again! And they do it every Sunday, too! <u>Every</u> Sunday! Karen and Frank Hutton and little Eric journey 75 miles round trip from Jefferson City each week -- <u>every</u> week -- merely to be a part of the gathered fellowship of First Christian Church! By rough guess-timate about 60% of our membership must travel from 8 to 40 miles to share in what's happening at Fifth and Gay. Last Sunday such "commuters" forced our crowd to overflow into the balcony. And that overflow crowd was rewarded by a service of worship beyond the superlative!

What a setting: wreaths, candles, evergreens, the Chrismon tree, poinsettias, carnations! What a day: orchestra, organ, choir, soloists, and Handel's *Messiah*! What a climax: "The Hallelujah Chorus"! And then an even greater climax when 11 youths made The Good Confession and one adult transferred her membership into our growing congregation. It was worth driving 8 or 40 or 75 or 90 or more miles to be a part of all that! A memorable day! Plus!

And there is "More to Come" next Sunday with the Handbell Choir front and center, with a Baby Dedication Service, with our Children's Christmas Cantata: "Lo! A Star!" with a Baptismal Service for 12 new members. Friends -- it is, indeed, a privilege and a joy to be a part of an exciting and expanding community that gathers each Sunday for praise and prayer and preaching!

Now -- a word about all this gathering and scattering as it relates to a very pressing social issue, namely, the energy crisis. Our national leaders have asked us to turn down our thermostats, drive more slowly, to cut out unnecessary and "luxury" travel, etc. And to all this we offer an emphatic, "Amen!" But, if we are to make it through this energy crunch -- we will need <u>more</u> church, not less! -- we will need <u>more</u> spiritual strength, not less! -- we will need <u>more</u> moral courage, not less! -- we will need <u>more</u> individual and community uplift, not less! Religion is not one of the electives in the university of life. Rather, religion is one of life's indispensables! And in critical times like these, the <u>church is a necessity, not a luxury</u>!

So -- yes -- we will turn down the thermostats, we will drive more slowly, we will cut out unnecessary and "luxury" travel, etc. Nonetheless, on Sundays we will pack in our churches with overflowing crowds because in this crucial decade we need most of all what the church has to offer!

If you are a bit frightened over the cold months ahead; if you are discouraged over matters domestic or international; if you are despondent because of your own inability to stretch restricted resources over greater demands; then, friend, you need the insight and the uplift and the encouragement of such a service of worship as last Sunday's. Or of the one we will have next Sunday. And the next! And the one after that! The best investment you will ever make for your personal good and for the community benefit will be the energy you burn to and from the gathered fellowship each and every Sunday. Ask Fylma! Ask Ab! Ask Karen! Ask Frank! Ask Eric!

With my thermostat at 68 and my speedometer at 50, I am, your friend and pastor.

June 5, 1974

Dear Christian Friends:

God sometimes seems a slow poke! For instance, millions have been praying:

> Thy kingdom come,
> Thy will be done,
>   On earth as it is in heaven. (Matthew 6:10 RSV)

-- and they have been praying for 19 centuries! But the "kingdom" has not yet come. It seems to be hidden somewhere in an ever-receding future. Still we must wait another day -- another year -- another century. We pray for the "kingdom" -- but God leisurely takes his time about it all.

The New England preacher, Phillips Brooks, was known for his poise and imperturbability. But his friends knew that he sometimes suffered moments of frustration and irritability. Finding him pacing the floor one day, a visitor asked, "What is the trouble, Dr. Brooks?" "The trouble is," Brooks responded, "that I am in a hurry but God isn't!"[17] Well -- friends -- sometimes, "Them's my sentiments."

But we have this matter backwards! God is not dragging his feet. We are! God is not a slow poke. We are! God is way out ahead of us. We have a lot of catching up to do! With beckoning lures, he draws us forward. But we reluctantly, hesitatingly bring up the rear -- the far rear! God already has opened up tremendous possibilities for the kingdom. Meanwhile, we pray about it! "Back to God?" That's not it at all. It's forward to God -- for he is way, way out ahead of us!

Why is the church not what it ought to be -- that triumphant fellowship of earth-changers? God is not to blame. We are! Why must every local Christian community fall at least two notches below the superlative? Because the possibility for excellence is not there? No! Rather because we prefer to get along at the C+ level than to put in that over plus of effort that merits an A. Why does the achievement of kingdom goals always run about six months behind schedule? Because God is a slowpoke? No -- because we are!

Some folk are inclined to think: "We really have something big going!" So -- they pat themselves on the back and coast along at a mediocre pace. They may be right in their observation. They definitely are wrong in their response to that observation. Admittedly -- we have been moving ahead -- but hardly as well as we might! Admittedly -- some programs have been cranked up and are proving an uplift to the fellowship -- but still we have a long way to go before the church engine is humming along on all six cylinders. Admittedly -- there is a vitality and joy and thrill in the atmosphere here, but friends: "ya ain't seen nutin' yit!" Far be it from your pastor to encourage contentment with yesterday's accomplishments. Always we must lean into the future praying, thinking, working for that elusive kingdom. Always we will keep the pressure on -- set goals beyond our capacity -- call for an extension and expansion of our ministry in this time and in this place. Robert Browning summarized the matter in a couple lines:

> Ah, but a man's reach should exceed his grasp,
> Or what's a heaven for?[18]

Folks, if you see me smiling, it's because we are headed in the right direction. But underneath the smiles, if you detect a touch of discontent, that discontent is there because we aren't moving fast enough! So c'mon friends -- let's hurry on! Encouraged because of a lot of nice things -- but doomed to perpetual dissatisfaction with anything less than our very best, I am, your pastor and friend.

June 20, 1978

Dear Church Friends:

That word "church" carries a load of freight: high steeple topped with a gold cross, stained-glass windows, heavy pulpit with open Bible, soft-shoed ushers, deep-throated organ, worship bulletins, pews, Communion Table. "Church" is a notion identified with a building and things that take place there, mostly on Sunday morning. But we need to expand, stretch, enlarge the concept:

"Church" is folk gathered at the mortuary in loving remembrance of a fellow pilgrim. These folk cry openly. Tears that tell eloquently that they care, they feel <u>with</u> the bereaved.

"Church" is 70-80 persons enjoying close communion over potluck in the Fellowship Hall -- awaiting the Judge's report of a trip to Russia and his 600 slides!

"Church" is a stack of get-well cards on a night stand.

"Church" is a real estate agent managing 600 apartments for the elderly, mindful of Jesus's words: "...I was a stranger and you welcomed me." (Matthew 25:35 RSV)

"Church" is folk gathered in the Hyatt's "Country Garden" for "soup and salad" -- but also for mutual encouragement in the Christian pilgrimage.

"Church" is a scholarship for a young person who otherwise would not make it into -- or through -- college.

"Church" is four antsy twelve-year-olds discussing with the Pastor their future.

"Church" is five dozen Disciples gathered at local picnic grounds -- taking in the beauty of the Smokies -- sharing news, hopes, frustrations, concerns -- loving each other as Christ taught them to love.

"Church" is a cup of coffee shared with a friend in the hospital lounge -- a friend whose spouse is in surgery.

"Church" is a gaggle (or a giggle) of teenagers off to Bethany Hills camp for a week of study, fellowship, play.

"Church" is a gift of cash -- dimes, dollars, hundreds -- for one in need.

"Church" is a teacher on the University Campus, an engineer at the City, a worker in the Court House -- each a vital cog in making our community more wholesome, more just, more free, more caring, more enlightened.

"Church" is any Christian anywhere at any time giving a cup of cold water in the name of Christ to any thirsty soul.

The visibility of "church" is most apparent on Sundays when the <u>gathered</u> flock joins in praise and prayer and preaching. There 'tis: steeple, <u>stained-glass</u> window, pulpit with Bible, ushers, organ, bulletin. "Church" is indeed closely identified with a building and a worship hour. And it would be extremely difficult to be "church" without a place and a time for coming together.

But "place and time" are mere means to a nobler end. "Place and time" are but the setting in which we are affirmed, inspired, enthused to <u>scatter</u> into the highways and byways. The "highways and byways" from -- Monday through Saturday -- that's where the "church" follows the footsteps of Christ in love and in service!

Your friend -- "in Christ" and "in church" -- wherever and whenever.

October 18, 1978

Dear Church Friends:

Found a wilted sprig in the courtyard this A.M. Broken from one of Carolyn's geraniums. Victim either of an unkind predestination -- or of a stray football caromed off the Fellowship Hall by one of our church youth. Picked it up. Held it lightly twixt thumb and forefinger. A pathetic casualty in the struggle for existence in a world of harsh weather and stray footballs. Much the worse for last night's frost. Once a blossom of lipstick red. A thing of beauty. But <u>not</u> a joy forever! Rather, fated soon to be a twist of fiber and a smidge of dust. 'Minded me of Tennyson's lines:

> Flower in the crannied wall,
> I pluck you out of the crannies,
> I hold you here, root and all in my hand,
> Little flower -- but <u>if</u> I could understand
> What you are, root and all, and all in all,
> I should know what God and man is.[19]

Church is a lot of things to a lot of people:

- Church is a boy and a girl holding hands in the chapel, trembly with passions and dreams.
- Church is a newcomer discovering a friend from way back yonder!
- Church is a janitor mopping coffee stains off the kitchen floor.
- Church is a stumble of children hustling out the door near the Christian flag -- a light interlude in a serious service of worship.
- Church is a hug and a kiss on the porch steps. Sometimes for one who is happy. Sometimes for one who is bereaved.
- Church is a pair of deacons stepping lively to the Doxology.
- Church is the organist improvising a meditative piece on the communion hymn tune -- with chimes.

- Church is a widow -- writing a check for 1/10 of her Social Security check -- and dropping that check into the offering tray.
- Church is a whisper -- or a poke in the ribs -- when the preacher makes a point that applies to one's spouse.
- Church is teenagers pitching a football where a lot of people think they ought not!
- Church is a sprig of geranium -- now faded -- but one that raised big questions -- for the poet -- and for the preacher, too!

Friends -- let's have more boys and girls holding hands in the chapel. More newcomers discovering old friends. More coffee stains on the kitchen floor. More children stumbling their way to Junior Church. More hugs and kisses on the porch steps. More happy deacons enjoying their weekly waltz down the aisle! More compliments to our organist for her super-good renditions of the great music of the church. More widow's mites cast into the treasury. More whispers and pokes-in-the ribs when the preacher steps on your spouse's toes (and on yours, too!). And more kids pitching footballs where "they ought not"!

Carolyn will be moving her geraniums indoors soon. Safe from winter's freezes and from stray footballs. Safe until April 1979 when once again she will bring them out into the spring sunshine to add splotches of green and red to the brown brick and buff stone and beige columns of the church courtyard. Coffee in the courtyard 'tween Sunday School and Worship -- with boys and girls and newcomers and janitors and children and hugs and kisses, etc. -- with or without geraniums -- that's church, too.

June 7, 1991

Dear Christian Friends:

One rose is enough. Two roses are more so! I arrive at Twelfth and Guadalupe on Sundays at about 9:00 A.M. -- plus/minus a few. Drop my sermon manuscript and the copy of my pastoral prayer on the couch. Stroll back into the kitchen to greet a group of early arrivals. Maybe a couple others. Pick up two of Opal's milk-glass vases (purchased at garage sales for two-bits each). Snitch the scissors out of the volunteers' desk. Amble out to the front lawn to clip a couple of long-stemmed beauties. One is for the sideboard in the Adventurer's Classroom -- just below the Menn mirror. The other claims the window sill in the hallway that leads from the parlor to the sanctuary. Both of these roses are seen by 80% of the folk who are in the worship service on any given Sunday. They brush past these roses twice: once on the way to the Sanctuary for the Worship Service, again on their way to the Community Room for the Fellowship Half Hour. A couple touches of beauty -- colorful -- with healthy green leaves -- in two-bit vases -- set in strategic spots. These roses call to mind the story told by Frederick Fisher about Alfred Tennyson strolling with a friend in his garden. The friend is said to have asked Tennyson what he thought of Christ. Lord Tennyson probably pointed down to a lovely rose in mid-blossom "and said simply: 'What the sun is to that flower Jesus Christ is to my soul.'"[20]

One on the sideboard, the other on the window sill -- these are much more than just two roses. First, an investment when they were planted way back about Valentine's Day. Then, weekly nurturing, pruning, fertilizing, watering, spraying for mildew and aphids. Now, blossoms beside our pathway to and from the Sanctuary -- from and to the Fellowship Hall. Those blossoms turn our frowns into smiles. We whisper a prayer of thanksgiving for those roses -- and for all things bright and beautiful.

Church is a garden where things bright and beautiful blossom:

Parents dedicate their infants.

Toddlers discover kind eyes and friendly smiles.

Children learn to sing "Jesus Loves Me."

Teenagers blossom in self-confidence.

Graduates receive bouquets of best wishes.

Brides and grooms make their vows of love and loyalty in a setting of many roses.

Young families are nurtured, encouraged, supported.

Folk who are bruised by unfortunate events are helped to recovery and to find a measure of hope for the long haul.

Mothers and fathers give thanks for the fruit of their labor, the harvest of their years.

Church is a lot of things:

- A life raft for those whose ship has sunk
- A lighthouse showing the way to the harbor
- A confessional where sinners are forgiven
- A school for learners, followers, disciples of Christ
- An oasis for pilgrims on the journey to spiritual maturity
- A filling station for the soul that needs to be pumped up

Church is a lot of things. Church is a garden -- a garden where bright and beautiful things blossom at their best!

September 25, 1992

Dear Friends of Little Children:

A gaggle of giggly girls on one side of the Sunday School table -- an adult who cares on the other side -- in between, a supply of construction paper, several pairs of scissors, glue, crayons, pictures, and a Bible story book. That is all it takes: a half-dozen bright-eyed youngsters -- an adult who cares -- a table with supplies. That is all it takes in hundreds of thousands of Sunday School rooms. And in those hundreds of thousands of Sunday School rooms some of the best things that ever happen take place:

> A child is welcomed! She feels at home! Cared about! Others are there. They all become friends for life! Teachers sense curiosity, readiness, desire, energy. They realize what a great privilege it is to share time and space with these great persons yet in bud.

> Together, they follow Abraham and Sara. Together, they memorize The 23rd Psalm and The Lord's Prayer. Together, they see "the light of knowledge of the glory of God in the face of Christ." Together, they hum "Jesus Loves Me" -- "Silent Night" -- "This Little Light of Mine."

> The girls discover that not all Bible heroes were men: Noah, Joseph, Moses, Paul. There were many great women, too: Rebekah, Miriam, Deborah, Esther, Lydia. The boys find that they can find their way through the books of the Bible -- all the way from "Generations" to "Revolutions." Genesis 11 -- The Tower of Babel; I Samuel 17 -- David and Goliath; Matthew 5-6-7 -- The Sermon on the Mount.

To some folk, all that seems like so many small potatoes. To an outsider, yes. But for those who have had their lives shaped by the stories of David's sin and his repentance, of Esther's courage, of the Prodigal Son's return, of the Good Samaritan's goodness -- for those who have had their lives shaped by such stories, that table with a gaggle of girls on one side and a caring face on the other and a Bible story book in between -- that is not "so many small potatoes"! The soul of the church is won or lost at that table! Little feet are turned to the upward path. Little hands learn gentleness and generosity. Little hearts discover they can forgive as well as be forgiven. Little eyes recognize the face of Jesus reflected in the face of their caring teacher. That's not "small potatoes"! That's big stuff. Real BIG! With great consequences! For a long, long time!

You can help! All it takes is a caring heart and an hour or two each week. We will provide the room, the table, the supplies, the gaggle of giggly girls (and boys)!

April 30, 1993

Dear Church Members:

It takes some fancy footwork to walk the tight-wire of church priorities. "Tight-wires" (the plural) would be more correct. For there is not just one "church priority" -- there are many "church priorities"! And each "church priority" has a different face, another schedule, a greater necessity, a more compelling urgency than all other "church priorities" put together. Or, so it seems!

What is the most important thing in the life of the church? What is the church's number one priority? For some it is worship. One hour -- around the Table -- with inspiring music -- loving prayers -- insightful scriptures -- encouraging preaching. That moment at the end of the week when we drag our depleted souls into the sanctuary -- look at our lives in the light of eternity. That same moment when we leave the sanctuary -- refreshed and renewed and strengthened to do God's work in our time! The hour of worship -- a number one "church priority"!

For others it is study -- serious study! With friends -- opening the Bible -- discovering those saints and prophets who triumphed over troubles -- sharing insights garnered over long years -- listening to the Word -- both in the words of Scripture and in the words of our friends. And from the still, small voice within, too! Whatever enhances our serious study of the Christian faith and life -- that is a number one "church priority," too!

Outreach! That's a number one "church priority," too. Reaching out to draw our friends and neighbors close to Christ. Reaching out to support the fallen, to guide the young, to encourage the broken, to forgive the sinner, to weep with the bereaved. Outreach! A number one "church priority."

Caring for the building of the Church -- and caring for the church building -- each a number one "church priority." Leading young couples up the path toward happiness in marriage. That's a number one "church priority." Setting a table -- coffee at one end, tea at the other, cookies in between -- to enhance the Fellowship. That's a number one "church priority." Feeding the hungry -- clothing the naked -- visiting the sick -- ah! -- the list is a long one! Could fill a notepad. A thick notepad!

Church Priorities on my mind.

September 3, 1993

Dear Fellow Christians:

The hillside was a light olive -- a bit nearer brown than green. They have had less of a drought in Oklahoma than we have had in Texas. The sun was warm -- but not as warm as the sun in Austin. The flowers had survived the 340 miles in an air-conditioned Suburban. In a couple hours they would be arranged over the fresh-turned mound of earth. By the next morning they would be limp. By the next afternoon they would be dry. By the week's end they would be removed by the caretaker.

The sentiments of the 23rd Psalm were so right: "The Lord is my shepherd, I shall not want." (Psalms 23:1 RSV) The last lines were especially right: "Surely goodness and mercy shall follow me all the days of my life; and I shall dwell in the house of the Lord forever!" Three graduates of the Lindsay High School Class of 1929 were seated with the family. Tears -- the overflow of grieving, but grateful, hearts -- tears brimmed the eyelids, washed trails down heavily powdered, rouged cheeks. A breeze moved the flaps on the low green tent. What a magnificent privilege to feel that breeze and to hum:

> ...when the wind comes sweepin' down the plains...
> O-K-L-A-H-O-M-A, Oklahoma! O.K.!"[21]

Lots of such little things are likewise magnificent privileges, such as:

> Having finished the dishes, to dry the hands, then squeeze a spot of Ivory lotion into one palm and rub it into the other. To lift the top half of a hamburger bun -- shake salt and pepper on the lettuce and tomato, to relish that first bite -- follow it with a potato chip and a sip of Coca-Cola. To reach - for the phone and recognize the voice of a friend -- either new and near or old and far away.

> To guide the cart up and down the aisles of the supermarket -- pass up the cabbages and rutabagas -- clutch a mess of beans -- feel the fuzz on the Fredericksburg peaches -- sort out the bananas -- grind some vanilla flavored coffee -- get a carton of Blue Bell Butter Pecan on sale!

> Touch the cheek of a child -- feel tears fill the eyes as we try to sing the National Anthem -- offer a prayer at the Communion Table -- turn up the thermostat in November and turn it down in June -- fold tea towels and fluff up pillows -- read a greeting card twice!

Lots of little things! But beside an open grave such little things are not so little! Rather, they are great and magnificent privileges for which we are doubly grateful. I fumbled my way through the lines Mary Lee had asked me to read for her family and friends. The last lines summed it up:

> O say of me when my last hour slips;
> Like one bright leaf to softly rest among
> The others -- Life was honey on the lips;
> Of one who died believing she was young![22]

After a prayer I turned toward the casket and offered the benediction. The family and friends lingered. One of the nieces pulled a few roses out of the floral blanket on the casket. Folk said farewell, began to scatter. At Speed's house I changed into my riding clothes. A second niece drove me to the Oklahoma City Airport. Southwest Airlines Flight 51 was on schedule despite a cloudburst. An hour layover in Dallas. Touched down at Robert Mueller Airport five minutes ahead of schedule ready for home. I lay my limp limbs on the mattress. My pillow was softer than usual. My eyelids were heavier than ordinary. It had been a good day!

The last words spoken in that hillside cemetery (as the winds were sweeping down the plain) were words from the heart of the congregation. They were words of affection and appreciation:

> We share each other's woes, Each other's burdens bear,
> And often for each other flows, The sympathizing tear.
> When we asunder part, It gives us inward pain;
> But we shall still be joined in heart, And hope to meet again![23]

January 5, 1996

Dear New Year's Congregation Members:

A ship is mighty complicated: hull, deck, keel, bow, stem, mast, engines, rudders, wheelhouse, galley, quarters, pumps, fans, vents, tanks, lifeboats, hawsers, anchors -- much more! Much, much more! In my teen years, I read most of C.S. Forester's *Hornblower* novels. Became familiar with nautical talk: quarter deck, mains'l, bo'sun, foc'sl, bulkhead, first mate, quay, gig. Forester knew how mighty complicated a ship is. He knew it first-hand. He had been a sailor. I learned it third-hand -- reading.

A church is mighty complicated: narthex, nave, crossing, sanctuary, choir, altar, communion table, pulpit, pews, stained-glass windows, organ, baptistry, etc. A congregation is mighty complicated: parishioners, ministers, music director, Sunday School, committees, Trustees, Elders, Deacons, Deaconesses, fellowship groups, weddings, funerals, baptisms, prayers, youth meetings, missions, General Board, treasurer, etc. A church, a congregation: mighty complicated! I grew up in the church. Learned about the Bible, God, Jesus, Disciples/Apostles, the Gospel, sin, salvation, saints, forgiveness -- much more! Much, much more! I learned all this! First-hand! Not by reading. I have been involved in it for 59 years! And I feel a bit like Millie, the cook at the church. I asked her whether she wanted her funeral in the church or merely have a service at the graveside. Millie answered: "In the Church! I'se been in it all mah life. An' when I goes out -- I wants to go out 'in the Church.'" Millie knows the Church first-hand!

Many of our folk had repeated causes for joy this past year. New babies came into their homes. Teenagers graduated from high school. Several continued -- some finished -- their college/university work. Some had beautiful weddings. Family life was rich. Business was booming! For the most part, our folk were more healthy than otherwise! All of us have reasons for thanksgiving!

However, some in our congregation had a very hard year! Death invaded their homes. School was a disappointment for some. Marriages were under stress. Business was not good. Accidents and illness made their lives a thicket of thistles and briars. All such folk are happy that their "hard year" is past. And they look with hope for a much better next year!

Some saintly soul observed: "Joys shared are doubled! Sorrows shared are halved!"[24] The Congregation is a "mighty complicated" network where we share both our joys and our sorrows, both our delights and our despairs, both our successes and our failures, both our triumphs and our tragedies. "[We] rejoice with those who rejoice! [We] weep with those who weep!" (Romans 12:15 RSV)

It is an immense joy to share in the "mighty complicated" life and work of the Church. It is a choice privilege to put in words Sunday after Sunday the Gospel that transforms sinners, strengthens the weak, gives guidance to youngsters, lifts up the discouraged, offers hope to the bereaved. I am grateful to all of you for this privilege! And for all your support of this "mighty complicated" congregation.

God bless us, every one!

January 16, 1998

Dear Church Members:

"Love at first sight!" You might call it that. When Burnell Waldrep ushered me into the Central Christian Church sanctuary for that first time over fourteen years ago I fell in love! The sentiment of the Psalmist suffused my soul: "How lovely is thy dwelling place, O Lord of hosts"! (Psalm 84:1 RSV) I slipped into a pew two-thirds of the way back. Burnell took the pew immediately behind me. We were silent. My eyes swept down the aisle to the carved Communion Table. On the left panel, the deer at the water brook: "As a [deer] longs for flowing streams, so longs my soul for thee, O God. My soul thirsts for God, for the living God"! (Psalms 42:1-2 RSV) On the right panel, the birds in the birdbath: "Even the sparrow finds a home, and the swallow a nest for herself, where she may lay her young, at thy altars, O Lord of hosts, my King and my God"! (Psalms 84:3 RSV) And above the center panel, the victorious Lamb: "Behold, the Lamb of God, who takes away the sin of the world"! (John 1:29 RSV)

My eyes lingered on the extraordinary combination of Elders' Chairs and Pulpit. Later, I would read the burnished brass plaque on the back of the Minister's Chair: "Honoring the Ministry of Dr. John Barclay: 1941-1969." Beyond the Pulpit I saw the Baptistery and above it the descending dove and higher yet the half-dome and the curtain of heaven: "And when Jesus was baptized, he went up immediately from the water, and behold, the heavens were opened and he saw the Spirit of God descending like a dove, and alighting on him; and lo, a voice from heaven, saying, 'This is my beloved Son, with whom I am well pleased.'" (Matthew 3:16-17 RSV)

The wrought iron chandeliers, the crusaders on the capitals of the pillars, the soft colors in the side windows, the magnificent stained-glass window of the risen Christ surrounded with the shields of the twelve disciples -- I drank it all in. Burnell leaned forward. He whispered: "It's beautiful, isn't it?" -- a statement of fact, not a question for response. I said nothing. Nothing needed to be said. The tears in my eyes spoke eloquently of the joy in my bosom. It was "love at first sight"! And it has been "love at second sight," too! And "third" as well! I have walked into that sacred place a thousand times -- and still the feeling 'whelms me: "How awesome is this place! This is none other than the house of God, and this is the gate of heaven"! (Genesis 28:17 RSV) Indeed! Beautiful? Beyond words! "Love at first sight"? Yes!

Others, too, have a long love affair with this house of God:

> Elders who preside at the Communion Table.
>
> Children who sit in pews where once their great-grandparents sat.
>
> Brides and grooms who repeat vows: "...to love and to cherish, till death us do part."
>
> Deacons who serve the Bread and the Wine.
>
> Mature persons who remember where they were baptized. And when. And by whom.
>
> Architectural students and young artists with pads and pencils.
>
> Musicians who have filled the room with the echoes of Handel's *Messiah.*
>
> Grief-stricken parents, bereaved widows and widowers, distraught sons and daughters who have wept at the words: "Dear friends, we are gathered in loving remembrance of..."
>
> Anxious, troubled folk in search of inner peace.
>
> Some who came to scoff and stayed to pray.

For these, too, and for many others as well, it was "love at first sight." And at "second sight," too.

This inspiring building was a gift to us from a previous generation. They built it. They paid for it. They gave it to us. We did not have to build it. We did not have to pay for it. We received it -- gratis! Ours is the privilege of using it to the best advantage for "the glory of God and the service of man." Ours, too, is the privilege of caring for it -- and then, later on, passing it on to the next generation in at least as good a condition as that in which it was when we received it.

June 14, 2002

Dear Fellow Christians:

Incredible Victory is the story of the daring battle of Midway that changed the course of World War II in the Pacific. In some 300 pages Walter Lord detailed the plans of Admiral Yamamoto to invade Midway with a Striking Force and to lure the U.S. fleet into an all-out battle which the overwhelming armada of 190 Japanese ships was almost certain to win. Lord also detailed Admiral Nimitz's work with Task Force 16 (aircraft carriers *Enterprise* and *Hornet*) and Task Force 17 (aircraft carrier *Yorktown*). Secrecy -- surprise -- code-breaking -- submarines -- PBYs (Patrol Bombers) -- cruisers, destroyers, battleships -- dive-bombers -- torpedo planes -- ship repairs -- weather -- communications -- Lord put a thousand items on the Pacific panorama as Yamamoto and Nimitz risked everything on one strategic battle. The climax of that battle came in six minutes from 10:20 A.M. to 10:26 A.M. on June 4, 1942. In those six minutes American dive bombers crippled three Japanese aircraft carriers: the *Akagi*, the *Kaga*, the *Soryu*. All three sank. A fourth Japanese aircraft carrier, the *Hiryu*, escaped from the sea battle, but was sunk the next day. The American fleet lost only one aircraft carrier, the *Yorktown*. Task Force 16's aircraft carriers, the *Enterprise* and the *Hornet*, were unscathed! The advantage now lay with the American fleet. The author summarized the outcome of *Incredible Victory* in these lines:

> The second-guessers were soon at it too. Strategists argued, perhaps correctly, that the submarines were badly deployed...the scouting was poor...that communications were slow and overly complicated... that there wasn't enough coordination between Task Forces...that the *Yorktown* might have been saved...that Task Force 16 was too slow in following up the first day's success.
>
> In ticking off the things that weren't done, it was easy to forget the big thing that *was* done. Against overwhelming odds, with the most meager resources, and often at fearful self-sacrifice, a few determined men reversed the course of the war in the Pacific. Japan would never again take the offensive.[25]

There are times in the life of the church when we do some "second guessing." We play the games of "what if" -- "supposin' that" -- "should have" -- "if only." Those games tend to be nit-picky. And they distract us from seeing the BIG picture. Anybody can check off a punch-list of a lot of things that have gone wrong! Meanwhile, such folk overlook the one BIG thing that has gone right!

Our list of disappointments and setbacks and frustrations and fumbled opportunities adds up to a heavy and weary burden. But -- BUT! -- what about the great BIG thing that has gone right? Moreover, when all has been taken into account and we march down to the climactic six minutes of the battle, we know the ultimate outcome: "Hallelujah! The kingdoms of this world have become the Kingdom of our Lord and of his Christ! And he shall reign forever and ever! King of kings! Lord of lords! Forever! Hallelujah!"[26]

The church needs all that we have to offer -- and more! Come! Lend a hand! We are in this struggle to the end. Don't miss the battle! We need you! And, yes, you need us! Keep your eye on the BIG picture!

June 21, 2002

Dear Long-Time Friends:

Eighteen years ago -- June 1984 -- I flew back to Knoxville to pack up our furniture for the move to Austin. While there I played the PR role as though I represented the Heart of Texas Chamber of Commerce. In a braggy tone I said, "Jack -- there's enough arable land in West Texas -- and enough sunshine and warmth -- that we could raise enough wheat and corn to feed half the world -- if we just had a little water!" Jack rubbed his chin a bit and drawled back to me, "Bob, 'a little water' is all that hell needs." Which may have been Jack's way of balancing my perspective!

Whatever, eighteen years ago, Judie and I loaded up our furniture in a 26-foot U-Haul truck. With our two dogs in the truck with me -- with Judie following in "Ole Blue" (our '57 Pontiac Star Chief) -- with Shana trailing behind in our Honda, we headed west. Away from the Great Smokies. Toward Big Bend. Since then, we have had 18 years of some fast-lane traffic mixed with potholes! Some scenic vistas mixed with dark valleys! Some celebrations mixed with some disappointments! Both pluses and minuses! Overall -- more good than otherwise! Perspective!

Spent Thursday-Friday-Saturday in Monroe for a family reunion. When I drove in to 1801 Stone Ridge Circle, the lawn was lush! Only 96 hours before it had been dry as barley straw. From January through May we had had a record-breaking drought. Three heavy rains in one week had transformed our desert into an oasis! All our lawn needed was just "a little water"! Some drought. Some rain. Perspective!

Life is not just the same old seven and six! We have much variety in our days, weeks, months, years. Ups and downs! Straightaways and detours! Mountaintops and swamps! Jungles and deserts! Heaven and hell! Summers at church sometimes seem to be mostly downs -- detours -- swamps -- deserts -- hell. Nonetheless, let's keep our perspective on things. We shall survive the long, hot, dry, dusty June and July and August. And we shall not only endure -- we shall prevail! Soon comes September and new life. Meanwhile, "a little water" helps. Keep in touch. When you are away -- send us a card. When you are in town -- fill your pew. The doors are open! The Table is spread! The Gospel is free! COME!

Your Long-Time Minister and Friend.

June 13, 2003

Dear Friends:

WELCOME TO THE CHURCH! Please sign the "Friendship Pad" and pass it on to the next person in the pew. After the benediction please join us in the Community Room for coffee or punch and cookies and conversation.

This greeting is printed in each week's worship bulletin. It is intended to help newcomers feel at ease in our midst, experience an uplifting time of praise and prayer, and follow that with a half-hour of good fellowship in the Community Room. Most of our first-time guests read it as it was intended. Others might read it otherwise. Some first-time guests may be afraid this is a subtle way of discovering their names and addresses for a mailing list. Still others may suspect that after the benediction they will be shanghaied to the Community Room for a coffee cup pep rally and hard-sell recruitment session. The words may be identical, but the eye of the reader will revise the message to suit herself. Beauty is in the eye of the beholder -- as is understanding -- or fear -- or suspicion.

We who are old-timers should help all our first-time guests interpret this greeting in the best possible light! No matter how friendly the welcome may be intended in black and white print, that friendly intent must be confirmed by a personal word and a gentle touch. A warm greeting in the bulletin cannot thaw an iceberg reception. Of course, our congregation has a sterling reputation for love and compassion and affection. A total stranger, one who does not even understand English, can still sense that church fellowship is made up of folk who genuinely care. It shows in the happy hand clasps, in the great bear hugs, in the pleasant chatter, in the way the children are cared for, in the manner our older folk are attended to. The printed greeting and the established reputation and the actual experience are consistent. Occasionally a visitor may slip through the welcome network and leave feeling left out in the cold. But that is very rare! Even so, two such persons is too many! Indeed! One is too many!

Next Sunday, search the sanctuary for an <u>un</u>familiar face -- someone who appears to you to be a stranger -- possibly a first-time guest. At the last note of the closing chorus, go to that person, reach out your hand, and say, "My name is Jane Doe -- but I don't know your name. Are you a newcomer to Austin?" After you have discovered her name, a bit about her work, school, family, then gently lead her over to the Community Room for coffee and cookies and conversation. When that new friend of yours leaves, she will feel in her heart what Jesus meant when he said, "I was a stranger and you welcomed me." (Matthew 25:35 RSV) Let's roll out the red carpet for all our first-time guests!

July 11, 2003

Dear Fellow Disciples:

My work as a Christian minister sometimes seems to be a solo affair. It is not! Rather, my work is dependent upon and is supported by the efforts and gifts of dozens of others -- even hundreds! Their resources and time and prayers enlarge and enhance and extend the ministry of this congregation far beyond the work of its minister. Some 300 members generously give of themselves to make our ministry together as a Congregation "a thing of beauty -- a joy forever"![27]

So! Every hospital call the minister makes has behind it the support of 300 members.

The same goes for every wedding held in the sanctuary. When a bride and a groom exchange their vows of faith and fidelity, that ceremony has behind it the support of 300 members.

The same goes for every baptism that takes place under the church half-dome.

And for every funeral when a bereaved family is embraced by the family of faith.

And for every committee meeting. And for every communion service. And for every pastoral prayer. Every choir anthem. Every issue of the newsletter. Every personal conference. Every infant dedication. Every fellowship dinner. Every worship bulletin. The list is a very long one!

The overall work of this church may seem to funnel primarily through the minister. But -- the minister knows very well that there are 300 other members out there -- doing their part, too! The minister's task is not a solo affair -- not a lonely matter -- not a solitary effort. "I am not alone!"

Morning and evening, midday and midnight, we all must be mindful of the many who make this a fellowship of folk who "rejoice with those who rejoice" and who "weep with those who weep." (Romans 12:15 RSV) And there have been many such folk in times past -- 150 years past! And there will be many more such folk in times future -- 150 years future!

The loves and the labors of many souls -- Past -- Present -- Future -- make a church where: The memory of Jesus Christ is honored; His teachings are shared; His ministry is continued; His presence is real. "We are not alone!" And at dawn and at dusk -- at noon and at night -- we are grateful! The life of this Congregation is the accumulation of the words and deeds, the gifts and sacrifices, the hopes and prayers of hundreds of kind and caring and compassionate Christians!

Your Fellow Disciple and Minister.

3

Worship and Prayer

September 3, 1975

Dear Christian Friends:

It is that time of shifting of gears again. Labor Day is past. Travels to Myrtle Beach, Disney World, Timbuktu in search of Eldorado or Shangri-La are behind us for another year. Weekends in the Smokies, on the lake, with the in-laws are almost ended for 1975. Summer gardens are playing out. The kids are back in school. Collegians are crowding "The Hill" again -- dormitories filled to capacity! Only ten days and the Big Orange will take on the Maryland Terrapins at Neyland Stadium. Fall sneaks in on us in September. And the first frost will come shortly thereafter, making October the most beautiful month on the calendar. Then November with Thanksgiving and the trimmings followed by the gentleness and joy of December. With things like that to anticipate there is no regret over summer's going and September's coming! Here at our church we intend to have a great 120 days for the four months ending December 31, 1975.

In some of our congregations September is "Church Loyalty Month." Perfect attendance at Church School and Worship is urged for all members -- including especially our C-E members ('C' for Christmas, 'E' for Easter). We should not "drag" people anywhere -- not even to church. It is much better to "draw" them. In that spirit we encourage you to be part of the church for the next four Sundays. You will be happy you were "drawn" to try it. And it may even prove to be habit-forming!

Last Friday I was telling one of my Downtown Optimist Club buddies about William Gladstone, who always took a walk around four in the afternoon. He did this rain or shine. When a friend one day asked him why he was out in the pouring rain, the jurist replied: "I don't want to weaken my will by retreating from intended purpose."[28] Then my buddy responded with these lines: "Gladstone sounds like my brother. Weatherman had predicted cold and snow that day -- but he was lacing up his boots for a hike to Gregory's Bald. A neighbor asked him: 'Curtis -- you ain't going to the mountains on a day like this, are you?' My brother answered: 'Friend -- it will be a cold day in Hades before I let the weather keep me from doing what I want to do.'" Now that's determination!

Well -- here I am -- pushing 40 and I cannot remember when I was not in church on Sunday. "Neither snow nor rain nor heat nor gloom of night..." as per the lines from Herodotus.[29] But someone may question my motive by saying: "Ah! But the preacher is expected to be there!" Well -- no matter the outward appearance -- I am there:

> Not because I have to be, but because I want to be;
> Not out of duty, but out of desire;
> Not by compulsion from without, but because of the attractive
> power of the Gospel and of Christian people;
> Not because of an enforced necessity,
> but because it is a choice privilege;
> Not because I must, but because I may!

In that mood -- I would draw you all to regular, consistent participation in the life and work of the Church. Come everybody. Let's get all our ducks in a row. Let's put our good intentions into practical action. Let's put first things first. Altogether now -- next Sunday -- and for three Sundays thereafter!

Anticipating 120 days of good things at our church, I am sincerely your pastor and friend.

May 18, 1977

Dear Christian Friends:

Spent most of Monday in the Smokies with my eldest brother, J.E., and his wife Agnes. A couple hours driving the Motor Nature Trail above Gatlinburg. The mountain laurel is in bloom. The rhododendron still holding off 'til June. We were awed by the towering hemlocks. Spent a while studying the old tub mill. Strolled around the James Bales cabin and outbuildings. Hiked down to Roaring Fork. Walked the old sled trail. Relished the coolth of "the place of a thousand drips."[30]

Then over to the Sugarlands Visitors' Center. And on up to The Chimneys Picnic Area. Our table was about 8-10 steps from the edge of that torrent of pure water that tumbles over a million boulders on its way to join West Prong. For lunch: smoked ham sandwiches, cold pizza, Fritos, 7-Up, and peanut butter cookies.

Then sent J.E. and Agnes on through Newfound Gap on their way to Asheville and Washington, D.C. I reluctantly headed back for Knoxville. I had arrived in the mountains at 9:00 A.M. And I left at 1:00 P.M. Barely four hours. But four hours spent with the dearest company and in the most pleasant surroundings. I came away refreshed, invigorated, ready for work. I understand a bit more fully what the Psalmist meant:

> I will lift up mine eyes unto the hills,
>   from whence cometh my help.
> My help cometh from the Lord,
>   which made heaven and earth. (Psalms 121:1-2 KJV)

In a sense that is what Christian worship is: time spent in the dearest company in the most pleasant surroundings for the refreshment and invigoration of the human spirit. That hour on Sunday morning with the community of faith in the presence of Christ confirms the best and highest within me. Ah! What a few notes of "Joyful! Joyful!" does for the weary soul. Or an uplifting prayer at the Table. Or an insightful line for the sermon. Or a warm embrace after the service. The invitation is always open:

> Come unto me, all ye that labour and are heavy laden,
> and I will give you rest. Take my yoke upon you, and learn
> of me; for I am meek and lowly in heart: and ye shall find
> rest unto your souls. For my yoke is easy,
> and my burden is light. (Matthew 11:28-30 KJV)

Look forward with us to a soul-refreshing, spirit-invigorating experience of Christian worship on each of the next three Sundays.

Baptism Sunday -- Children will be baptized. This is a tender and touching time for them and for their families. Come rejoice with them!

All Saints Sunday -- We will remember by name all the saints of this Church who died during the past 12 months. A time of thanksgiving for them, of serious reflection upon their lives, and of more serious commitment to filling our own future years with goodness and beauty and truth.

Baccalaureate Sunday -- Our graduates will be responsible for this service of worship. This is a BIG occasion for them. Make it even BIGGER with your personal congratulations on that day.

My prayer is that you have the time -- or that you make the time -- for the refreshment and invigoration of the spirit. In the mountains, indeed! And as often as possible! And in the church sanctuary, too! And as often as possible there, too!

With fond memories of last Monday, and with high anticipations for next Sunday, I am sincerely yours.

February 21, 1979

Dear Lovers of the Mountains and Lakes and Beaches, etc.:

No! I did not feel badly about his absence. Not even if he is the Chairman of the Official Board. Not even if he missed his Sunday School class. Not even if his family pew was totally empty. Not even if he was one of the Elders scheduled to offer prayers at The Communion Table. Instead of being in church where he was supposed to be, he was up in the Smokies -- skiing. On Sunday morning! But I did not feel badly about his absence! Not at all! In fact, I felt quite "goodly" about his absence! Question: How does a minister go about feeling "goodly" about his "Number 1" member slaloming down Littlejohn Slope when he was supposed to be in Sunday School -- at worship -- presiding at The Communion Table? Answer: the fuller story which follows.

Our Chairman of the Official Board 1979 had called our Chairman of the Official Board 1978 at about 11:00 P.M. Saturday night. He must have said something like this: "Jim -- this is Bob. My family is at the Glenstone Lodge in Gatlinburg. We had a grrreattt time in the snow today. The slopes are super. The weather is perfect. We had intended to drive back to Knoxville tonight -- but we have decided to stay another day. So -- we won't be at church tomorrow. Will you stand in for me at The Communion Table?"

To make a short story shorter -- that's how it turned out. The family spent their Sabbath on the Mountainside above Gatlinburg. Jim stood in for Bob at the Communion Table. The family pew sat empty. The minister observed the absence of his First Family. He noted there was a substitute Elder at The Communion Table. And he felt "goodly" about it all. Why? Because he knew that there was at least one churchman who kept his priorities in line.

There is a yellowing newspaper clipping in my study. It's a column about John Wooden, the famed coach of the UCLA basketball team. Dated: May 18, 1973. Bylined: Tom Siler. One paragraph runs like so:

> Wooden says he is not concerned about leaving any great legacy to basketball. The veteran coach said that "Basketball is my job but it isn't first in my life. My family is first and my church is second. I know that is an improper sequence but the only one that matters will understand."[31]

Now -- there's a fellow who knows what's important in life! Family first -- church second -- job third. Thanks Coach. We needed that!

One's first responsibility is to his/her family -- spouse, children, parents, brothers and sisters. Paul, writing to his "son in the faith" Timothy, expressed that principle of healthy religion inversely:

If anyone does not provide for his relatives, and especially for his own family, he has disowned the faith and is worse than an unbeliever. (I Timothy 5:8 RSV)

One's religious obligations must not be allowed to pre-empt one's family responsibilities. One's commitment to his church or synagogue should not be so compelling that he passes up a fine opportunity to affirm his family. Jesus said, "The sabbath was made for man, not man for the sabbath." (Mark 2:27 RSV) Last Sunday, for that family to have racked up their skis and packed up their parkas in order to run back to Sunday School and worship would have been to violate the spirit of Jesus's words. "Religion was made for man, not man for religion" -- and when religion gets in the way of a fulfilling family experience -- then detour around religion. That's pushing the sense of Jesus's words to a logical extreme. Even so -- I'll buy that over its opposite which would suggest that "man was made for the sabbath, not the sabbath for man." There are altogether too many folk who -- in the name of religion -- neglect their families!

September 6, 1991

Dear Friends Everywhere and Wherever:

Beat the alarm on Monday A.M. Awoke at 4:37. That's what the clock radio showed in big, red digits: 4:37. Stumbled to the bathroom. Before stumbling back to bed I brushed my teeth, washed the sand out of my eyes, splashed on a few drops of Old Spice aftershave. I like the taste of fresh mint Crest. I like a just-soaped-and-rinsed face. I like Old Spice. So does Judie. Back in bed, I pulled the sheet over my shoulder, curved my body around Judie's, reached my right arm over her and snuggled in closer to her warmth and softness. She murmured something that wasn't quite understandable. I whispered, "I love you, too." Her second murmur was, "Ummhummh."

All was quiet except for my breathing and for the exhaust fan in the attic. But my mind was not quiet. Never is! Lying there with eyelids closed but mind in overdrive, I recalled what the preacher said the day before:

Is it too much? It is too much to suggest that five minutes in the morning -- five minutes centering our minds on God who gave us our minds -- five minutes focused on the work and the challenges God has set before us -- five minutes sensing the presence of God around us and the peace of God within us and the power of God through us -- is it too much to suggest that five minutes in the morning is enough? It is <u>not too much</u> to suggest it. And five minutes in the morning <u>is enough</u> to discover the presence and peace and power of God.

Well, right then, right there -- as snug as a weevil in a box of oatmeal -- I took the five minutes to do what the preacher had suggested to the congregation the day before:

> I mulled over the words of Jacob at Bethel: "Surely the Lord is in this place; and I did not know it... This is none other than the house of God, and this is the gate of heaven." (Genesis 28:16-17 RSV)

> Familiar faces come to me: Maw Maw and Paw Paw; Charlie who was killed in a construction accident way back in 1957; Ira whose death at 55 came suddenly by heart attack four years ago. Tears welled up under my closed eyelids.

> The faces of my brothers and sisters -- from the eldest, J.E., to the youngest, Theresa -- and all their connections (in-laws, nephews, nieces). Our daughters and their connections: Adena, Scot, Abby; Tamara, Mickey; Shana, Chris, Kelcie.

> Friends: Knoxville, Dover, Collierville, TN; Oakville, KY; Los Angeles, CA; Minneapolis, MN; New York, NY. Faces in our church family: older members who are ill; several recently bereaved; younger families struggling to get a toe-hold; students; newcomers; our little ones. Prayed, too, about "the work and the challenges" that were mine to tend to. And in the midst of it all prayed for "the presence and peace and power of God."

I was not kneeling. My head was not bowed, though my eyes were closed. I did not have my hands folded à la Albrecht Durer's sculpture of his brother's praying hands. Still, this was prayer. It took five minutes -- plus a bit. I ended my "five minutes -- plus a bit" by making Reinhold Niebuhr's prayer my own: "God, grant me the serenity to accept the things I cannot change, the courage to change the things I can change, and the wisdom to know the difference."[32] My prayers for God's presence and peace and power -- for family and friends and flock (for all who have been given to me to love and for all to whom I was given in order to be loved) -- capped off with Niebuhr's prayer for serenity -- ah! It was a good way to begin the morning.

The preacher suggested a similar five minutes in the evening: "Five minutes to note how God was at work beside us, within us, through us -- five minutes to reflect on how well we have followed the higher path -- five minutes to give thanks for good news from far away and from near -- five minutes to express gratitude for family, for friends, for church, for health, for work, for strength to do that work, for rest."

Well, my Monday ended where it began -- snuggled next to my dearest, with eyes closed, with heart full, with mind a-churning. Just five minutes in the morning. And just five minutes in the evening. Just 10 minutes altogether (plus or minus a few). That's all it takes. But what a diff it makes for all the time in between! And the difference is for good! Much good!

Prayerfully yours.

May 1, 1992

Dear Members:

They are both important. The hour of worship puts us in touch with heavenly things. That's important! The hour that consists of the half-hour before the service of worship and the half-hour immediately after keeps us in touch with earthly friends. That's important, too!

Sunday School breaks up around 10:30 A.M. Kids come bouncing down the stairs. Folk responsible for the Fellowship Half-Hour after worship are seen scrambling in the kitchen. People pull into their accustomed parking spots. They stroll past the roses and into the east doors. Mothers/fathers take their little ones to the Nursery. The choir runs through its last warmup. The Elders, Deacons, Worship Leader assemble in the Parlor. The Candlelighters slip into their robes. There is a happy chatter around the coffee pot, on the sidewalks, in the hallways. Once inside the sanctuary, things are more subdued. Some whisper. Others wave or nod their greetings. The more meditative sort sit silently with heads bowed. For all -- it is a very important half-hour.

After the Benediction and the Closing Chorus a happy buzz fills the sanctuary. The organist begins his postlude -- but the flood of greetings will not wait for the end of the postlude. The mixture of music and hugs seems right. Some folk move among the pews -- placing hymnals in their racks, collecting bulletins, checking the Friendship Pads. Several gather around the organist to thank him. Same for the soloist, the music director, the choir. Many exit through the east doors where contact is made with the minister and his wife. A lot of folk wind their way to the Community Room for coffee and cookies and conversation. For youngsters, its punch. The kids scoot around. Their grandparents look on with pride. Family groups huddle to confirm their plans for Sunday lunch. Friends who don't get to see each other as often as they'd like to linger over a cup-o-coff. On first Sundays we sing "Happy Birthday." There's lots of huggin' an' kissin' -- an' lovin' an' missin' during that Fellowship Half-Hour! It is a time to help us keep in touch.

Sandwiched between the half-hour before and the half-hour after is the full-hour of the service of worship. We gather to "Praise God from Whom All Blessings Flow."[33] Great music lifts us heavenward. Bible readings give us guidance for the pilgrimage. Prayers have a cleansing and empowering effect on us. The Lord's Supper draws us close to Jesus Christ who is, for us, the Way and the Truth and the Life. (paraphrased from John 14:6 RSV) The sermon offers the insight and inspiration of the Gospel. Altogether, it is an hour that puts us in touch with heavenly things!

The half-hour before the service of worship and the half-hour immediately after is the hour when we most sense what it is to be a fellowship of faith and hope and love. In that hour we keep in touch with our earthly friends. The full-hour of the service of worship puts us in touch with heavenly things. We need both. So! Come early! Linger late! Help make our congregation what it is at its best -- a divine fellowship of faith and hope and love!

July 16, 1993

Dear Friends:

There's lots of folk just like them -- nominal Christians who have marrying and burying privileges in the church. Nothing more. Long years before, they attended Vacation Bible School. Or maybe Aunt Zsa Zsa brought them to a revival meeting where they "got saved." Or perhaps their grandmother had them christened as infants. But nothing more! No attendance. No Bible study. No fellowship group. No committee works. No nothing! "Ye Olde Kirk in Ye Wildewood" is the congregation these folk call their own. They use the church as a convenience. First, to keep other congregations' Evangelistic Committees at bay: "No, we wouldn't be interested. Ye Olde Kirk in Ye Wildewood is our church." Second, for the "hatching-matching-dispatching" functions: christenings, weddings, funerals.

There was a family of just such wayward, non-participating members: a prodigal father and three sons made in his own image. Long years before, they had had a tentative and tenuous touch of Christianity at Ye Olde Kirk in Ye Wildewood. But now they were completely indifferent. They seemed as at ease outside the church as a sow is at home inside a hog wallow. Everything within reason had been done to draw them into the active fellowship. The Preacher had called. The Elders had visited. The Sunday School Superintendent had given it a shot. But it was all in vain.

Until one day while they were working in the south forty, a rattlesnake bit John, Jr. His foot swelled. The venom paralyzed his leg. He was rushed to the hospital. The doctor shook his head and spoke in grave tones: "This is very serious. We've done everything we can. The only thing left is prayer!" Immediately, the prodigal father, John, Sr., called for the Preacher, the Elders, the Sunday School Superintendent. The old man begged for the minister, The Reverend Doctor Dryasdust, to pray for John, Jr.'s recovery. Though that prayer was less than eloquent, it was appropriate:

O Thou Righteous and All-Wise Father in Heaven: We thank Thee that Thou hast in Thy great wisdom sent Thy messenger, the rattlesnake, to bite John, Jr., in order to bring him to his senses. He has not been inside Ye Olde Kirk in Ye Wildewood for years. And it has been a very long time since he has turned to Thee in prayer. Grant, O Lord, that this may be a valuable lesson to him. May this lead him to a change of heart and a true repentance. Cleanse his soul and put within him a new and right spirit.

And now, O Righteous Father, wilt Thou send two more rattlesnakes, one to bite Jim and one to bite Sam. And, if it please Thy great wisdom, send a big rattlesnake to bite the old man, John, Sr. Thou knowest that for years we have done everything we could to restore them, but to no avail. What all our combined efforts could not do, Thou, through Thy messenger, the rattlesnake, hast done! O Lord, Thou hast opened our eyes to see a marvelous thing, that the only thing left that will do this family any good is rattlesnakes! Even so, Lord, send us bigger and better rattlesnakes. For the good of all prodigal sons and prodigal daughters we pray -- and for our own good as well. Amen.

If you are a Prodigal Christian who deserves to be snake bitten, do something before it is too late and all that the doctor can say is, "The only thing left is prayer." Whatever, if the log fits, wear it! (last week). If it rattles, run! (this week). If it smells, get up wind! (next week).

'Nuf said again.

October 22, 1993

Dear Christian Friends:

It's a miniature wreath -- a bit more than four inches, a bit less than five inches in diameter. Made with green grapevines, then dried. Tiny rosebuds and marigolds give it a touch of color -- though faded. It was sprayed with lacquer. A sliver of a ribbon served as a loop for hanging. I retrieved it from the wastebasket. Set it gingerly on my chest-of-drawers. Want to keep it a while longer. It had fallen off its nail next to the light switch in the bathroom. For the eleventeenth time! It is pretty beat up. Actually, I am the culprit. I had knocked it off the wall when slinging my bath towel onto its rack. Done it so often it's almost a joke. Times before I would return it to its hanger. This time, I set it on Judie's vanity. She pitched it into the wastebasket.

But I retrieved it. Couldn't part with it just yet. Had to keep it a bit longer. Even if it was a dilapidated bit of twisted grapevines and faded marigolds and unraveled ribbons. Why keep it? Because of sentiment. I have strong feelings about that miniature wreath. Sara gave that piece to us long years ago. She had created it during her artsy-crafty days. Probably from vines and flowers in her yard in Grand Rapids. Every time I saw that wreath next to the light switch in our bathroom I thought of Sara. And of Stan. And of Maurice and Jane. And of their five daughters and one son. Our friendship spans about 40 years -- all the way back to 1954! We have shared life's tragedies and triumphs, its agonies and ecstasies, its miseries and glories. And every time I switched on the light in our bathroom I saw this four- or five-inch reminder of a very dear friend. Though that wreath is much worse for having been whipped with a bath towel and bounced off the carpet eleventeen times -- and though it should be replaced with a fresher, brighter piece -- still, I can't part with it. Not yet! Why? Because of sentiment -- strong feelings about the person who created it and gave it to us.

Some 15 years ago I gave my father a Swiss Army knife. A deluxe piece: about five blades, a corkscrew, a can opener, a screw-driver, etc. Expensive! Each time I'd visit Paw Paw in Lake Charles, he'd greet me by digging that knife out of his right-front pocket, hold it in his open palm, and then say, "Hi, Bobby! Good to have you home!" Well, Paw Paw misplaced that deluxe knife some eight or nine years ago. I gave him a replacement -- a smaller version, not so costly. Each time I'd visit Paw Paw, he'd dig that knife out of his right-front pocket, hold it in his open palm, say: "Hi, Bobby! Good to have you home!" Well, three -- almost four years ago, we buried Paw Paw in Prien Memorial Park. At the graveside I dug that replacement Swiss Army knife out of my right front pocket and handed it to Darren, one of the younger grandsons. I said, "Darren, this was Paw Paw's knife. You will enjoy having it." As luck would have it, while visiting Maw Maw last month before her death, the original Swiss Army knife turned up. The deluxe version! Where is that knife now? I keep it in my right-front pocket. Why? Because of my strong feelings about my father.

We all have little things that have big meanings: a miniature wreath, a knife, a handkerchief. Mementos of precious moments. Souvenirs of times with friends. Keepsakes from travels, parties, graduations, weddings. Maybe an agate used in a marble tournament 50 years ago. Or a postcard mailed from Chugwater, Wyoming. Or a ring. A belt buckle. A corsage. A snapshot. A key. A teaspoon. A coin. Each -- a small thing with a large meaning. We don't use these things. We just keep them. Why? Sentiment. These things remind us of persons and places and occasions that were -- and that still are -- significant to us!

Sundays, we gather around The Communion Table. We eat a bit of bread. We sip a taste of wine. Small things. Large meanings! That bread and wine remind us of a special person -- one whose life inspires us! Lifts us! Encourages us! We remember the stable in Bethlehem -- the synagogue in Nazareth -- the Sea of

Galilee -- the Temple in Jerusalem -- places we have visited only in the mind, but with which we are as familiar as with family. These emblems of bread and wine recall for us the Temptation of Christ, the Sermon on the Mount, the Parables of the Kingdom, the Stories of the Good Samaritan and the Prodigal Son and the Good Shepherd, the Prayer in the Garden, the Crucifixion. Sunday after Sunday after Sunday, we gather around The Table. We eat a bit of bread, we sip a taste of wine. And we remember. Little things -- very little! But BIG with meaning -- very BIG! "Do this in remembrance of me." (Luke 22:19 RSV) Come! Gather around The Table. All things are ready! Come to the feast!

April 18, 1997

Dear Christian Friends:

"I can live for two months on a good compliment!"[34] So said Mark Twain. A mere word of appreciation -- a kindly gesture -- an expression of praise -- a hand of applause -- a pat on the back -- a congratulation -- any one such piece of encouragement was enough to keep the creator of *Huckleberry Finn* and *Tom Sawyer* bubbling for 60 days! Most of us understand. We, too, can live for a month or two on a single compliment! In terms of the life of the spirit -- we can live for a week on just one service of praise and prayer and preaching. The worship hour is a time of insight and inspiration and uplift -- a refueling stop, invigorating, enthusing. And we walk away from church or synagogue or mosque with a spring in our step and a gleam in our eye. But, by the end of the week we are worn down, jaded, pooped. Then we turn again to the holy place to get a fresh supply of manna for the wilderness trek -- a second wind for the spiritual pilgrimage.

We understand what the psalmist meant when, with tired feet and thirsting heart, he exclaimed: "I was glad when they said to me: "Let us go up to the house of the Lord!'" (Psalms 122:1 KJV) Most of us can survive for seven days on one hour in the sanctuary. Two weeks is more than most of us can manage. There are those who try. They "forsake the assembly." (Hebrews 10:25 KJV, paraphrased) They attempt to maintain the life of the spirit without replenishing their supply of the spiritual bread of life. They stretch out a string of absences from the gathered fellowship. They miss the Sabbath service. They leave an empty place at the Table of the Lord.

Some try to compensate with boob-tube religion. But the electronic church is a fantasy -- a creation of some of the slickest con-artists of this generation. The spirit does not flow over the radio stations and TV channels. The only tangible things provided by the electronic hucksters are pledge cards and prayer handkerchiefs. Such pledge cards are reminiscent of John Tetzel's 15th Century indulgences.[35] And the prayer handkerchiefs are comparable to the rabbit's foot and the voodoo doll. Folk who substitute media religion for the real thing in the local congregation discover that their spiritual ardor cools, their commitment softens, their faith fails.

A coal removed from the shared heat of a heap of embers soon dies. It turns from a fiery red to a dull grey. So, too, with the life of the spirit. Christianity is a shared faith. So is Judaism. Also, Islam. We are members one of another within a community of faith. No Christian -- no Jew -- no Muslim is an island entire of itself! Each one is a piece of the continent, a part of the main, a member of the church, the synagogue, the mosque. The spirit may live for a while in solitude -- but only for a while. "Blest be the tie!" Come! Let us go up to the house of the Lord!

Your Minister and Friend.

4

🌿

Community

February 3, 1965

"Silver and gold have I none; but such as I have I give thee." (Acts 3:6 KJV) These words of the Apostle Peter aptly characterize the responses I've received from so many of our wonderfully cooperative Christians in my short four months as your pastor. Here are some of these responses:

- "I can't stand in front of a class or sing in the choir, but I can type and I'll be glad to do the bulletin."
- "I don't believe I can work with the children at church, but maybe I can call if you'll tell me who I should call on."
- "I've never done that before, but if you'll tell me how, I'll try."
- "I doubt if I could be a regular teacher, but maybe I can work out as a substitute."
- "There are some things I can't do in the church, but I'm interested in people. I like personal work."
- "Sure, I'll telephone those people for you."
- "If there's any way I can help you just holler. If I can, I will."
- "Sure, I'll bring the truck up now and haul that stuff off."
- "Can I bring refreshments for the young people tonight?"
- "I can bake bread -- and I'll bake all you want for the men's meeting."
- "Bring 'em on down. I'll put those frames around them before Sunday."

Many of you already know who these people are. And I'm not writing this just to brag on them. I'm writing in order to illustrate how it is that when everyone puts his shoulder to the wheel, the work is easier on all. The wonderful thing about the above list is that it could be extended several pages. It's been said of some churches that their members are "willing" -- half of them "willing to work," the other half of them "willing to let 'em." So far, I've met only the first half! In the church there are "varieties of gifts" and we are all "members one of another." Read 1 Corinthians 12. It's good to be in a genuinely <u>cooperative</u> church. For instance, about the middle of January, ten of our women and two men descended on our educational unit with scrubbing machines, scouring pads, dust cloths, brooms, mops, etc., and left it shining like the brass on the admiral's flagship. Now, suppose that job had been dumped on one lonely person!?

And one thing more. The word has been getting around that "our church is in the finest shape it's been in a long time." Be alert. Be interested. Contribute your ideas now -- we'll all move ahead together. Me thinks a goodly breeze blows wind in my sails!

October 11, 1972

Dear Friends:

Inspiration! What is it? Webster's defines it as the act or power or moving the intellect or emotions. For Bob Landry it is anything that stirs up that "look up and laugh and love and lift" feeling:

- like when a choir renders an exceptionally difficult anthem in an exceedingly fine way;
- like when a superlative person crosses our path and we exclaim, "Oh! That we all were like that!"
- like when a teenager devotes his entire first paycheck ever to help pay for fresh paint and new carpet for the sanctuary -- and he does it for reasons that reach to the roots of his soul;
- like when 45 college students swell the Sunday morning crowd -- all keenly interested, alert, seeking, searching;
- like when 60 friends picnicking at the local park watch nature finger-paint her way through an autumn sunset;
- like when the strains of *The Ninety and Nine* sink deeply into the consciousness as the organist leads the congregation in the quiet moments of the Lord's Supper;
- like when 600 Christians put it all together and say, "We've got a lot to live -- we've got a lot to give!"

Inspiration: "the act or power of moving the intellect or emotions." A lot of people have been "moved" recently. You can see it in their eyes. You can feel it in their hand-clasp. You can hear it in their chit-chat.

Friends -- if it's been some time since you've been "moved" -- either intellectually or emotionally -- then it's been at least that long since you've been around the Church. Everyone, including you, needs some Christian insight to lift his mind above the comic-strip level of living. Everyone, including you, needs to involve himself in his neighbor's life deeply enough to feel a tug on his heart -- and to shed a tear -- sometimes a tear of joy -- and sometimes a tear of sorrow. Come! Be "moved." Be "lifted up."

It's a great time to be alive! Get with it! You shall not pass this way again!

"My cup runneth over!"

June 20, 1973

Dear Christian Friends:

Since February 16, Judie and I and our three girls have had some 90 church members in our home to "Break Bread with the Landrys." The folk have dropped in about 6:30 P.M. on alternate Fridays carrying their cheese casseroles and lasagna and chicken and meatloaf and asparagus and chocolate cake or whatever else. After the dinner (which we always overdo!) the group of 12 to 14 sort of hang around the table until the paper plates are cleared away and the silverware is put to soaking. Then we form an intimate circle in the living room for a couple hours of friendly conversation. And what rich experiences these conversations have proven to be! We have confirmed a long-held opinion -- that the most pleasant moments in life are those spent with the home folks who feel intensely, share honestly, and care deeply. That's what the church is all about -- and these Friday evenings together have been the most!

Some folk travel thousands of miles -- searching for happiness in the glamour spots: Hollywood, Monaco, Bermuda, Acapulco, Tahiti. Some pay high prices to attend exciting events: the Indianapolis 500, the Rose Parade, the Kentucky Derby, a Presidential Inauguration. Some invest fortunes to be made comfortable: Rolls-Royce ease, penthouse luxury, Palm Springs climate. Others get their kicks from skiing, or sky-diving, or drugs, or alcohol. Often all these folk discover that their sought-after goal either eludes their grasp -- or turns sour. Meanwhile, some folk discover happiness and excitement and comfort and joy right at home -- like around the coffee table in the living room. We have -- along with 90 other members so far.

Last Thursday a handful of us scheduled another eight "Breaking Bread" dinners that will take place between now and Christmas. Names were picked from the church rolls pretty much at random. A goodly mixture of <u>new</u> as well as <u>long-time</u> members, spiced with a sprinkling of prospective members. By the time next February rolls around we will have had approximately one-third of our constituency in the parsonage. We hope <u>you</u> will have been in that one-third. But if not, please be patient. In due time you will receive a letter beginning: "Dear Friend, The Membership and the Evangelism Committees invite you to a "Breaking Bread with the Landrys" dinner on Friday, etc. Your turn will come.

Yours, for the discovery of the finer things in life right at home.

August 6, 1975

Dear Summer Friends:

We have sort of slumped into the "dawg-days" of August. The heat is unbearable. Have to stay inside to be comfortable. Seems this drought will drag on forever. Our lawn has that frizzled and kinky look of an over-done permanent wave. Bumper-to-bumper vacationers shove themselves southward to Disney World. Kids have been out of school for two months -- and are bored with the slowdown schedule. We aren't sure we will outlast them until the school board takes them off our hands in September. The 1975 baseball pennant races are dullish. And football is still six weeks off.

Things are a bit "slumpish" at church, too. We expected it. Sunday morning congregations are slim. Half-empty pews gawk up at a half-filled choir. Sunday School is coasting. Participation in extracurricular activities is normal for August -- which means it's below normal for any other month. Our last big blast was Freedom and Democracy Sunday, way back on June 29. The reverberations from Wilhousky's *Battle Hymn of the Republic* have faded over memory's horizon. And we won't have another "high, holy day" until September 14 -- our Anniversary Sunday -- our 101st -- congratulations to us all! But that's next month. Right now we are smack-dab in the middle of August -- our down, downer, downest time of the year -- which, incidentally, is equidistant from our up, upper, uppest months: April (Easter) and December (Christmas). Personally and professionally I have often wished we'd just blot August off the calendar altogether!

Yet -- there is much more going on during these "dawg-days" than shows on the surface. This seasonal break is wholesome for the jaded spirit. Everybody needs a few days or weeks to "slump"-- so why not August? Go ahead: syncopate your routine -- hike up to Gregory's Bald -- tan your hide at Myrtle Beach -- spin yourself dizzy on the tilt-a-whirl at Opryland -- hang in there with that bumper-to-bumper crowd to everywhere -- spend a few extra days with Grandpa and Grandma. "Slump-time" is not "waste time" if one returns to his work with a passion to do it well -- if one develops a greater appreciation for his home and family -- if one discovers a wider view of the world -- if one gains a clearer perspective on the things that matter -- if one finds a new delight in his "unslump" time.

August? -- Dawg-days? -- Slump time? -- Vacation season? -- Call it what you will but recognize that it can be a creative and productive part of any person's calendar.

Judie and I and Tammy and Shana are going to hit the road for 10 "off" days beginning next Monday. We will head for San Antonio where the days in August are "dawger" than any could be in Knoxville. We will shift ourselves into neutral -- stroll along beautiful Paseo del Rio -- spend half a day at The Alamo -- take in the Institute of Texan Cultures at Hemisfair Plaza -- pick up a souvenir sombrero at the Mexican Market -- endure over-long business sessions at the General Assembly of the Christian Churches -- sing-along with 8,000 fellow Disciples at the Assembly Communion Service on August 17 -- have coffee with old friends and colleagues in the ministry.

Dr. Drash, our Associate Minister, will be minding the store. It's encouraging to know that "when the cat's away the mice do <u>not</u> play." Share our good fortune in having Dr. Drash in our midst by inviting a friend to be with you in the services of worship. We'll all be back together to crank up our fall program on "Anniversary 101."

I wish for you and yours a relaxing and refreshing last month of summer.

January 7, 1976

Dear Friends:

Well! Here we are -- smack-dab into 1976 -- America's Bicentennial year! We will be doing a lot of looking to the past in these next 12 months -- and in the several years beyond. Looking back to the time of the Declaration of Independence; of the Revolutionary War: Bunker Hill, Valley Forge, Saratoga, Yorktown; of the writing and ratification of the Constitution; of the election and inauguration of our first president -- "First in war, first in peace, first in the hearts of his countrymen";[36] of the adoption of the Bill of Rights. Names will cross our minds: Thomas Paine, Samuel Adams, Ben Franklin, Patrick Henry, Nathan Hale, John Paul Jones, Thomas Jefferson, George Washington. Ah! How we look with envy onto that era 200 years ago. "Those were the days!" we exclaim. "What a great time to have lived!" We tend to see the past through rose-tinted lens -- romanticizing, idealizing, exaggerating the heroes and events of bygone eras. And this is all well and good -- especially on anniversaries such as this present national celebration.

However -- we must not so focus on the historical in all its glory that we lose sight of the contemporary with all its possibility. There are today tremendous opportunities for heroic endeavor, frightful situations that call for courage, crucial problems that demand attention, watershed decisions to be made that will reshape the world. 1976 is, too, a great time to be alive! Who of us might not cry out like the ancients before: "My God! What an age you have caused me to be born into!" And generations from now our children's children and their children will envy us in their turn, exclaiming: "Those were the days! What a great time to have lived!" We must not wait for the historians to tell us what a tremendous time ours has been!

And here in the church we are involved in some of the most crucial work being done in all the world.

In an age of terrorism -- the church struggles for
  human understanding.
In an era of immense poverty -- the church calls for
  sharing with our neighbors.
In a time when all civilization is threatened with thermonuclear
  destruction -- the church witnesses to the cohesive power
  of Christian love.
In a generation when so many are devotees of a crass materialism
  the church speaks of the spiritual dimensions of reality
  and urges us to consider ultimate values.

Friends -- I am happy to be a part of the institution which is doing more than any other to hold this old world together! And I cherish for each of you that same sense of significance and meaning and destiny which makes the adrenalin course through my arteries and causes my muscles to tense and my mind to seethe. Thanks to each of you for making my ministry in this time, in this place, possible. Thanks for the years that are past. Thanks for the year that is -- 1976. And thanks for the years that are yet to be!

December 21, 1977

Dear December Friends:

Here we are at the tail end of <u>Anno Domini</u> 1977. Only ten days left of the 365¼ days given to us last January 1. For many of us it has been a great year!

- Best year ever in business!
- Straight A's in school!
- Rediscovered romance <u>in</u> marriage!
- Moved into our dream house!
- Got two promotions at work!
- Class Reunion was super!

But for others it was otherwise:

- Almost got wiped out by a business competitor.
- Flunked Calculus, didn't do well in History, got a B in Basket Weaving.
- Marriage shipwrecked!
- Dream house was a sand castle!
- Inflation robbed me of my cost of living increase.
- Came down with the flu at our Class Reunion.

Life is an admixture of the good and of the not so good. We have <u>won</u> some. We have <u>lost</u> some. In baseball a hit every third time at bat for a 0.333 batting average is great! Anything more merits All-Star status! Life <u>is</u> an admixture!

And it is doubtful that anyone has had either a perfect year or an irretrievably disastrous one. On reflection, how does your <u>Anno Domini</u> 1977 stack up? Count your blessings and set them on one side of the scales. Then count your "un-blessings" and set them on the other side. Surely you have many causes for joy. Just as surely you have had more occasions for disappointment and tears than you wanted. On balance, what is your 1977 batting average: Dismal? Blah? O.K.? Fair? Good? Whoopee? Super? All-Star?

Life is not one-sided: total ecstasy <u>or</u> everlasting grief. Rather it is a mixture of the "good" and of the "not so good." The church is that community that is most open and sharing of life's joys and sorrows. When one member of the fellowship is happy, all rejoice. When one member hurts, all hurt together. The high privilege of being a part of such a fellowship ought not be taken lightly. "Woodbine Willie," the famous World War I chaplain, used to say that when it came his turn to stand before the Great Judgment bar, he expected God to ask him but one question. And it would be a simple one: "Well -- Willie -- what did you make of it?"[37] Now that is a big question for the Great Judgment Day. But it is also a worthwhile question as we reflect on <u>Anno Domini</u> 1977. And as we anticipate <u>Anno Domini</u> 1978. My prayers for you are two: First, that you may have the capacity, despite the awesome heap on the "not so good" side of the scales, to see the huge pile of blessings on the "good" side. Second, that you may make of the materials of the new year -- both the "good" and the "not so good" -- that you may make of those materials a tapestry of beauty and worth unexcelled in the scrapbook of your personal history! When you arrive at the tail end of <u>Anno Domini</u> 1978 and face that question: "Well -- what did you make of it?" I hope you will respond with calm and confidence: "I did the best I could with all that I had!"

May the love and joy and peace of December 25 stay with you throughout the new year.

July 12, 1979

Dear Friends:

The shoe was on the other foot! There I lay -- on sterilized linens -- in a bareback hospital gown. Every hour on the hour a nurse poked a thermometer under my tongue, felt my pulse, checked my blood pressure. Aides filled rubber surgical gloves with crushed ice and arranged these under my arms and alongside my legs. Doctors studied graphs, read lab reports, wrote instructions. An 8-foot plastic IV tube kept me short-leashed to a bottle of dextrose and antibiotics. It was attached to my left arm. Dubbed it my "armbelical cord." Like "Mary's Little Lamb," everywhere I went that IV tube and bottle followed! It dripped 30 grams of bacteria-fighting carbenicillin into my blood system every 24 hours. Dr. Leonard said I had enough of that stuff in me to kill every germ on the seventh floor of Ft. Sanders Presbyterian Hospital!

In my work I had seen dozens and dozens and dozens of people there -- on sterilized linens -- in bareback hospital sacks. Always before I had been sympathetic. That is -- standing in very healthy shoes -- I had let them know I cared about their hurt. And I had offered them a word of encouragement. And, if they asked, a prayer. In a word, I had felt _for_ them and tried to be helpful.

Someone has well-defined sympathy as "your pain in my heart." However, standing there in very healthy shoes there was a gap between what the diseased patient experienced and what the sympathetic pastor emoted. "Your pain in my heart" suggests closeness, even intimacy. But it falls short of identity. There is a stronger word in current usage: empathy. Empathy is defined as "the capacity for participating in another's feelings." Sympathy refers to feeling _for_. Empathy refers to feeling _with_. The empathizer knows, understands, has experienced the feeling himself. Empathy has an overplus of immediacy and identity which sympathy lacks.

My recent stay in the hospital taught me something. From now on I will do more than merely _sympathize_ with others there. I will _empathize_. Because I will have been where they are! I will understand! I will know! I will identify! There will be more nearly a 100% communication between the parishioner lying in the hospital bed and the pastor standing beside that bed. I will feel _with_ as well as feel _for_ that sick soul with fevered brow and aching bones and limp hands. There was a British general who spoke of "the sovereign duty of crawling under the other person's skin."[38] Doing that with the imagination is a wholesome experience. It leads to understanding and _sym_pathy (feeling _for_). Sometimes "crawling under the other person's skin" happens not merely in the imagination but in actuality! That is a very instructive experience and leads to deeper understanding and genuine _em_pathy (feeling _with_). Sympathy _and_ empathy -- we could do with much more of both.

The pastor is the minister of the congregation. His has the privilege of representing and expressing the love and care of the Christian fellowship to those of that fellowship who are under stress, experiencing disappointment, suffering illness, confined to the hospital. The pastor ministers _to_ the congregation and _on behalf_ of the congregation. But there are times, too, when the church ministers to the pastor. That's how it was two weeks ago. The shoe was on the other foot! Both for that miserable fellow sacked out in a bareback hospital gown and for that multitude of members who felt: "He is human, too. This is our time to minister to him! And we will!" My family and I are deeply grateful. Thank you! Thank you! Thank you!

Feeling _for_ and feeling _with_ you all, I am your pastor and friend.

July 17, 1979

Dear Christian Friends:

He was a visitor in church -- a young fellow -- sophomore at UT -- native of Memphis -- came to church because it was his "girlfriend's church." After the service he was discussing his first impression with his prospective grandmother-in-law:

> "I like your church!" he said with zip. "And I like your ministers. And it's the first time I've been to a church where everybody knows everybody else and where all love each other."

Maybe he was just laying it on thick for his girlfriend's sake. Maybe he had just not visited very many churches. Maybe it was just an exceptional day and he was "high." Or maybe, just maybe, he was truly impressed with what he saw, felt, experienced. Whatever, he paid the fellowship a superlative compliment!

Guests are with us every Sunday: travelers headed north or south, vacationers to or from the Smokies, students, businessmen, new residents of Knoxville and Knox County. They are the "outsiders" -- probably a bit shy, hesitant to crash into a new group in an unfamiliar setting. We are the "insiders" -- old timers, home folk, natives. It is up to us to dissolve their shyness, fling open the doors so they don't have to stand waiting. So -- let's roll out the red carpet, set them at ease, make them feel at home. All it takes is a bit of plain old hospitality: a cordial greeting, a question or two about the occasion for their being in Knoxville, an extension of the greeting to discover mutual friends, interests, experiences, an invitation to lunch. Who knows? The next stranger you greet at church may turn out to be "an angel unawares"!

Jesus painted an awesome scene of the Great Judgment Day. To the sheep on the right hand the King will say:

> "Come, O blessed of my Father, inherit the kingdom prepared for you from the foundation of the world; for
>
>> I was hungry and you gave me food,
>> I was thirsty and you gave me drink,
>> I was a stranger and you welcomed me,
>> I was naked and you clothed me,
>> I was sick and you visited me,
>> I was in prison and you came to me."
>>   (Matthew 25:34-36 RSV)

"Hungry" -- "Thirsty" -- "A Stranger" -- "Naked" -- "Sick" -- "In Prison" -- That third category catches my attention just now: "I was a stranger and you welcomed me." That is a biggie! The way we greet folk -- on the street, in the office, at school -- says much about the depth of our Christian faith and life. In terms of the Christian fellowship the way we welcome strangers before and after the service of worship says volumes to them about the quality of our life together and of our commitment to follow in the steps of him who was a friend of all -- even the least!

Every traveler, vacationer, student, businessman, new resident who shares an hour of praise and prayer and preaching with us should be helped to feel like that UT sophomore. The manner in which we greet our visitors will determine whether they exclaim: "I like your church!" or something far less complimentary. Next Sunday search out a new face -- get acquainted with a stranger -- make someone feel you are happy for their presence. Arrive at church early enough to greet a visitor. Help to set him/her at ease. Then, after the benediction, invest a few extra minutes to give and to receive the love which is so attractive a part of our life together.

July 16, 1980

Dear Vacationers:

Just back from spending my vacation with Maw Maw and Paw Paw in the Cajun Country. Pleasant? Indeed! Lazy? Of course! Hot? Very! The announcer on the radio said that the high temperatures this summer have been caused by those southwest winds blowing over Mexican jalapeno pepper plantations. Walker added that things won't cool off 'til J.R. returns to *Dallas* next September![39] J.R. could freeze Tabasco sauce!

Harvested figs for Maw Maw. First time I have had that privilege since 1958. Fresh figs -- right off the tree -- what aroma! -- what texture! -- what flavor! Maw Maw canned a dozen pints for me. I'll enjoy those preserves on wheat toast next winter. Each time I dip into a jar of Maw Maw's figs I'll remember those pleasant and lazy days I spent with my family in July. I will also remember all those other good things I enjoyed during those twelve days of vacation:

- That luscious crab meat casserole Margaret served me
- Supper with the Harts, the Keough Clan Fourth of July Pig Roast, coffee with the Webbs, all in Collierville
- The hot pear pie Aunt Della Mae baked for me
- Sharing with Shana as we drove long stretches of I-40 and I-55
- A birthday cake -- and several birthday cards
- Reading the two books Ernestine gave me last Christmas
- The services of worship:
  - with Maw Maw at the South City Church of Christ
  - with Paw Paw at Our Lady Queen of Heaven Church
  - with Lewis Rhodes's friends at the Northminster Baptist Church
- Buying a bottle of Hadacol at a country store

- A stopover at the cemetery where half of my roots are buried
- The wedding in 106° weather -- "Laissez les bon temp rouller!"
- Listening to Anne Murray while cruising the Natchez Trace

Imagine it -- I spent only three hours picking those figs! But what sweet memories are preserved along with the fruits from the tree whose leaves were first used to make aprons for Adam and Eve!

A vacation is a good thing. Provides a break when the routine becomes a rut. Restores alertness to one mentally and physically fatigued. Makes an occasion for one to dig around among the family roots. Helps one to see work, career, destiny in a broader perspective. Sends one home with a "born again" zest for life! It is good to go away for a vacation -- even if it is only as far away as the patio. It is good to take time to be idle -- even if it is only for a half hour. Whether far or near, whether long or short -- the best part of any vacation is coming home! I have been. I am back. I was happy to go. I am happier to be home!

Fall is not far down the calendar. With fall will come the end of vacations -- and the end of this jalapeno-hot summer! But -- for July and August -- most of our Church families will be taking a few days off -- spending precious hours together in station wagons -- crowding around McDonalds' hamburger counters -- hiking along mountain streams -- shelling on Atlantic or Gulf beaches -- visiting with Aunt Zsa Zsa on the homestead -- getting dizzy at "Dizzyworld" -- singing familiar hymns with unfamiliar congregations of fellow vacationers. Meanwhile -- here at this Church -- we will miss our vacationers. But we will keep their favorite pews dusted for their homecomings.

Happy to have gone -- but happier to have come home, I am, your pastor and friend.

September 11, 1992

Dear "Come Back Sunday" Christians:

She was as deaf as a post -- couldn't hear thunder! Still, every Sunday she showed up early and she stayed to be among the last to leave. She greeted folk with her bright smile and her brighter eyes. Though she had taught the Sunday School teacher 30 years before -- though she had forgotten more about the Bible than the seminary student would ever learn -- though she didn't really need any more guidance for her later years -- still -- every Sunday she showed up early and she stayed to be among the last to leave. Why?

Maybe it was because she was the village matriarch and she cherished her place in the community. Maybe it was because she was the grandmother or the great-aunt to two-thirds of the lambs in the flock. Maybe it was because she had occupied that pew with her husband for 46 years and she came to remember.

Maybe it was because she could sense the vibrations when the congregation lifted *Amazing Grace* and she could hum-along. Maybe it was because the bread and the wine which she could see and feel and taste made her stronger. Maybe it was because she felt the divine presence in that clapboard chapel with the belfry above, the cemetery on the side, the necessary out back. Maybe it was because she wanted to be with people even though she couldn't hear them when they spoke to her and they couldn't understand her when she spoke to them. She could communicate -- but only with her bright smile and her brighter eyes.

I chose to believe that every Sunday she showed up early and she stayed to be among the last to leave because it was one way -- almost the only way -- she could make a personal witness about what God and Christ and Church had meant to her. She made that witness -- and that witness made a difference. She continued to make a difference. She still makes a difference! She was a plus in my life. I remember her with gratitude!

July 30, 1993

Dear Friends:

"You cannot not teach." A family therapist once said that. It makes sense. Good sense! "You cannot not teach." This is especially true in the home. Little eyes are watching. Little ears are hearing. Little hearts are learning. Always! The father who speaks softly and cuddles his daughter gently -- that father is teaching. The father who growls at his daughter and resorts to threats to control her behavior -- that father is teaching, too. The mother who helps her son fix his bed and straighten his closet -- that mother is teaching. The mother who runs her son out of the kitchen forfeits a great opportunity to teach him the niceties of nutrition and joys of dishwashing. At the same time, she is teaching him that if he will play the part of couch potato that she will indulge him with chocolate-whatevers. "You cannot not teach!"

"You cannot not communicate." Some fill the air with words of hot air -- a tonnage of verbiage à la Styrofoam -- a monologue in overdrive. However, "they also communicate who only stand and listen." And their silence says much more than the hot air they are patiently enduring. "You cannot not communicate!"

"You cannot not make an impression." It may be the best foot forward. Or it may be the worst. Best or worst -- in either case, you will make an impression! Even when you try not to make an impression. Or, perhaps, especially when you try not to! "You cannot not make an impression!"

"You cannot not decide." For to decide not to decide is a decision. And, oh! what dreadful decisions have been made by default! Remember Pilate? Pilate tried to be neutral. He washed his hands of the whole affair. He let others decide. But what a dreadful decision Pilate made when he decided to let others decide in his stead. "You cannot <u>not</u> decide!"

"You cannot <u>not</u> make a difference." You may make a difference for good. But you may make a difference for not so good, too. You may teeter on the high wire of in-difference for a while. But only for a while. Soon or late -- you will make a difference -- either for good or for not so good. "You cannot <u>not</u> make a difference!"

At the Church we have a lot of people who are making a difference for good. Hoorah! They do their share -- plus a bit more! Hooray! You can see it in the way they look at our children. You can hear it in their voices as they ask about each other's health. You can feel it in the way they hug each other. This Church is a haven of faith and hope and love -- a home for a family of forgiveness and compassion and trust. Our church is that way because we have a lot of people who are making it that way.

But, within the church fellowship we have some folk who think they will just layout, stay on the sidelines, let others do what these folk have left undone. They think they do not make a difference. But they do! They make a difference in the negative. If only they got out of the bleachers, hustled onto the playing field, joined in with enthusiasm, did their share -- plus a bit more! What a difference for good they would make! Bonaro Overstreet summed it up for all of us:

> You say the little efforts that I make
> will do no good:
> they never will prevail
> to tip the hovering scale
> where justice hangs in balance
> I don't think
> I ever thought they would
> But I am prejudiced beyond debate
> in favor of my right to choose which side
> shall feel the stubborn ounces of my weight.[40]

We need you. You need us. We need each other! Together we can make a <u>big</u> difference for <u>good</u>!

April 8, 1994

Dear Believers:

The Golden Gate Bridge is one of the engineering wonders of the world. The Bridge spans the entrance of San Francisco Bay. Sometimes -- when the fog rolls in off the Pacific Ocean -- it settles over the two ends of the Bridge. Obscured by the fog are both The Presidio (South) and Marin County (North). Only the central span is visible. That central span is held aloft by the huge cables slung over the tall steel pillars whose foundations reach far below sea-level. The part of the Bridge that is visible seems to begin in fog and to end in clouds.

That Bridge with shrouded anchorages sometimes seems to be a picture of life -- beginning in a fog -- ending in clouds. We know nothing about what preceded life. We know nothing about what comes after life. But that is only in times of gloom and doubt. In Jesus Christ, the fogs, the clouds, the mists have been blown away. Then we see clearly. We know we have come from God! We know we are going to God!

In the beginning God created a paradise: "And God saw everything [that had been] made, and behold, it was very good." (Genesis 1:31 RSV) In the end God is preparing heaven: "Behold, the dwelling of God is with [people].... [God] will wipe away every tear from their eyes, and death shall be no more, neither shall there be mourning nor crying nor pain anymore." (Revelation 21:3-4 RSV)

Sometimes we see through a glass -- darkly. Doubt obscures our way. But sometimes, too, we see things through the eyes of Jesus. And faith grows strong and our path is clear.

> Many things about tomorrow / I don't seem to understand;
> But I know who holds tomorrow / And I know who holds my hand![41]

Jesus gives us eyes to see though the fogs and clouds and mists. And then we are confident! We know we have come from God! We know we are returning to God! And we can span the in-between -- the in-between of two eternities -- one before the beginning -- the other after the ending! "Thanks be to God, who gives us the victory through our Lord Jesus Christ! Therefore, my beloved [brothers and sisters], be steadfast, immovable, always abounding in the work of the Lord, knowing that in the Lord your labor is not in vain." (I Corinthians 15:57-58 RSV)

Your fellow believer.

July 29, 1994

Dear Loving Friends:

Here is a different definition of love: "Love is the capacity to say 'Yes!' -- to say 'Yes!' to the best in others -- to say 'Yes!' to the best in one's self." Repeat that line. Mull it over. Argue with it. Try it out. This definition of love is nonsense to a sixteen-year-old. Her heart is doing 200 pitter-patters per minute. She has a date for the Saturday night concert. Her "hunk" will drive her around town in a Mercedes! Convertible! That teenager thinks she knows what love is because of the flitter-flutters in her bosom. But she is mistaken!

More mature folk dismiss that stuff as "puppy love." They have been around the block. More than once or twice! And they understand this different definition of love: "Love is the capacity to say 'Yes!' -- to say 'Yes!' to the best in others -- to say 'Yes!' to the best in one's self." Folk who have that capacity are lovely. Folk who have it not are <u>un</u>lovely.

"Love" and "Fear" are opposites. The person who loves is affirmative, hopeful, trusting. Introduce to a friend one whose "heart's all a-bustin' with love" and immediately that loving person will discover the best in your friend. She will focus on that most beautiful aspect -- magnify it -- encourage it -- build on it. She will say "Yes!" to your friend. Suggest a worthy endeavor to one who loves and he will respond with a willing heart and a ready hand: "Why not?" -- "It can be done!" -- "It ought to be done!" -- "We should get it done!" -- "Yes! Let's give it our best!"

"Fear" has the opposite effect. The person who is all tied up in a tangle of terror is negative, hopeless, suspicious. Introduce to a friend one who is fearful and immediately that frightened person will discover the worst in your friend. She will focus on that least attractive aspect -- enlarge it -- criticize it -- let it blind her to the best in your friend. Propose a worthy project to one who fears and he will respond with a string of negatives: "Can't do much about it." -- "So, what? Let someone else tend to it." -- "We should go slow on things like this." -- "No! We'd better not!" "Love" and "Fear" are opposites! Love hopes! Fear despairs. Love trusts! Fear is suspicious. Love is creative! Fear is destructive. Love says: "Yes!" Fear says: "No!"

The writer of the Letters of John understood this distinction. He summed up the matter in these lines: "In this is love perfected with us, that we may have confidence for the day of judgment, because as he is so are we in this world! There is no fear in love, but perfect love casts out fear. For fear has to do with punishment, and he who fears is not perfected in love. We love because he first loved us." (I John 4:17-19 RSV)

Rightly understood, love is a synonym for courage -- the courage to believe the best! Love is the courage to believe the best about others and the courage to believe the best about one's self. Such is what Jesus intended when he said: "You shall love your neighbor as yourself." (Mark 12:31 RSV) A new definition? Perhaps. A different definition? Somewhat. But it makes more than pitter-patter and flitter-flutter sense. It makes <u>good</u> sense! "Love is the capacity to say 'Yes!' -- to say 'Yes!' to the best in others -- to say 'Yes!' to the best in one's self." For Christians, love is a gift: "For God so loved that God gave...." What did God give? In Christ God gave us the capacity to love. James Barrie it was who said: "To see the best is to see most clearly and that is the lover's privilege."[42] For Christians, the "lover's privilege" is a gift from heaven! "For God so loved that

God gave...." us the capacity to love -- to see the best! "We love, because he first loved us." (I John 4:19 RSV)

With a "heart all a-bustin' with love," I am, your minister and your "Yes!" man.

May 5, 1995

Dear Kind, Caring, Compassionate Friends:

Early in this century, the anthropologist, Emile Durkheim, traveled the South Sea Islands to study religion in its most primitive form. His research led him to conclude that the function of religion in early societies was not so much to put people in contact with God as it was to put individuals in touch with each other! We are uneasy with Durkheim's conclusion. Nevertheless, his conclusion underlined and highlighted what does happen when folk gather for religious ceremonies, teachings, celebrations, prayers, etc. They get in touch with each other!

Some things in life were too big to be managed in solitude. The birth of a baby was too significant an event for just one family. So, the whole community gathered to celebrate the event and to dedicate the infant. A marriage was more than just a contract between two people. So, the entire village turned out along with the priest to listen to the vows and to consecrate the man and woman as husband and wife and to pray for their marriage, their home, their family. When someone died, the whole tribe gathered to show their own grief, and to pray for the deceased on his journey through the netherworld. Religion, ceremony, priests, sacraments, prayer -- these helped people get in touch with each other and to "deal with" the big events in life that were too big to be managed in solitude. Primitive religion helped people handle life's triumphs and tragedies together!

Our fellowship of faith and hope and love logs a lot of "triumphs and tragedies." We manage these together, in company, as a community. We are in touch with each other! And in that touch, we discover the Divine. We sense God's presence. We see God's face. We touch the hem of the garment of God. We find the bread of life, the cup of salvation. It is as Jesus said it would be: "Where two or three are gathered in my name, there am I in the midst." (Matthew 18:20 RSV)

The church helps "put individuals in touch with each other." "[We] rejoice with those who rejoice. [We] weep with those who weep" (Romans 12:15 RSV) -- especially in those events that are "too big to be managed in solitude." When we are in touch with each other, we discover we are in contact with the Divine! "Blest be the tie that binds!"[43]

Your friend and pastor.

May 26, 1995

Dear Sensitive Souls:

The poet wrote of the "long, long drip of human tears."[44] With the mothers and fathers, the daughters and sons, the sisters and brothers of Oklahoma City, we, too, have sensed the pain, the sorrow, the loss, the grief. We, too, have wept for them. We -- all of us -- have not only wept <u>for</u> them. We have wept <u>with</u> them. We all are part of an intricate, reticulated web of interconnections. Touch one strand of that web and all the strands move. Sometimes the vibration is a vibration of joy! The Oklahoma City episode has been a tremor of sorrow! For all of us! We, too, know the "long, long drip of human tears."

Last Tuesday, May 23, at 8:00 A.M. the Arthur P. Murrah Federal Building was imploded. Some 360 carefully placed explosive devices were detonated in a sequential order. The bombed-out remains of that place of sorrows roiled, folded, tumbled, slumped in upon itself. About 150 pounds of dynamite is all it took. The building that had taken years to plan and many months to construct had become a rubble heap in about eight seconds! It was a sad moment that syncopated the extended grief of a great city. That scene of the implosion is already seared into our collective consciousness. Next week, that scene will be on the covers of national magazines!

Some think that this brings to an end this sadness brought on by "man's inhumanity to man." Not so! Thirty years hence -- 2025 -- mothers and fathers, daughters and sons, sisters and brothers will visit Oklahoma City cemeteries, bringing with them roses and tears. The loss of a loved one may grow distant in time. But the immensity of the loss does not lessen in the heart of the bereaved! The immensity of the loss -- if it changes at all -- grows more vast. And the intensity, too!

In August 1987, I drove my father out to Prien Park Cemetery. He struggled out of the car -- stumbled across the lane -- walked unsteadily to the head of his son's grave. He said nothing. For a long time he stood there. Tears brimmed his eyes. He sniffled. He wiped his nose, his cheeks, his eyes with a wad of Brawny towels which he always stuffed in his right front pocket. On the headstone beneath the name "Charles Landry" were the dates "January 8, 1928 – August 23, 1957." From 1957 to 1987 was 30 years. For some, thirty years is a long time. For a grieving parent, it is a vast emptiness that grows greater with every passing day. In Oklahoma City, mothers and fathers, daughters and sons, sisters and brothers will weep for a long, long time. We will, too!

May 17, 2002

Dear Fellow-Gardeners and Brown-Thumbers:

Two days! Two days from early 'til late -- from barely could see 'til couldn't see at all! Two long, hot, sweaty, grimy days. Monday he was chipping away at the hardscrabble soil -- digging out the scruffy, stunted tufts of St. Augustine mixed with a bit of ill-begotten Coastal Bermuda -- special attention to the dandelions and plantains and other less-recognizable weeds. Down on his knees, pulling/ pitching, etc. By dark-thirty he had cleared that path of once-upon-a-time-kindergartners' sandlot. Dragged himself to his pick-up. Aimed it down South Lamar toward his Barton Hills home. Shucked his shirt soaked with a long, hot, sweaty, grimy day's labor. Showered. Unlaxed with a goblet of Texas Red. Sort of like aspirin for aching muscles, sinews, bones. Lite supper. Dumped himself onto his "king-sized." Nick slept well!

Tuesday he showed up with seven-dozen sprigs of Asiatic jasmine and a pickup load of mulch. Demanded a sharp spade, a tough foot, a bunch of grunts to scoop out 84 holes in which to bed down his sprigs of Asiatic jasmine. Filled those holes with a rich compost. Set those 84 sprigs into their new homes. Took a couple more hours with a shovel and wheelbarrow to spread a layer of mulch to blanket the entire area of the former sandlot. Loaded up his hoe, rake, spade, shovel, wheelbarrow, gloves, trimmers. Ended his day by soaking each one of his 84 newly-planted sprigs with the lawn hose.

With calloused hands on his hips he surveyed the results of his two long, hot, sweaty, grimy days of hard labor. He had transformed a plot of semi-desert into a promising garden. He guess-timated: "These sprigs will take root this year -- if we keep them watered. Next year they'll begin to spread. By the third year we should have an intensely green blanket of ground cover!"

He probably felt a bit like the original Gardener:

> The earth brought forth vegetation, plants yielding seed according to their own kinds, and trees bearing fruit in which is their seed, each according to its kind. And God saw that it was good. (Genesis 1:12 RSV)

So far, so good! "He saw that it was good!?" But five days later, on Sunday morning, Nick the gardener was down on his knees again! Pulling long green shoots out of his brand-new garden. Nut grass! Nuts!

"The best laid plans o' mice and men aft gang agley."[45] The struggle to transform the Wilderness into a Paradise is not finished. Not in two days. Not in two years. Not ever! Always it is an unfinished effort, a work in process. The Gardener not only clears away the brush and trash -- not only digs the soil and enriches it with mulch and compost -- not only fertilizes and irrigates -- but also must pull out the weeds and poison the pests and fight the mold and mildew!

Thanks for a good work well-begun. Some 289 other members can help Nick pull out the nut grass!

Yours for a patch of the Garden of Eden right here "deep in the heart of...."

May 9, 2003

Dear Fellow Christians:

Some of the best things that ever happen to us happen to us in the church:

> They stand in the presence of their families and friends and exchange their vows: "...to have and to hold -- from this day forward -- for better, for worse -- for richer, for poorer -- in sickness and in health -- to love and to cherish -- 'til death us do part." They establish a marriage and a home and a family. That is one of the best that ever happens to us! And it happens in the church!

> A teenager walks to the front of the sanctuary and speaks the words: "I believe that Jesus is the Christ, the Son of the Living God, and I take him as my Lord and Savior." Those words encourage her to follow Christ in the path of love and mercy and generosity and service. That is one of the best things that ever happens to us! And it happens in the church!

> A sinner, embarrassed by his misdeeds, slumps into a pew. But he hears the Gospel promise of forgiveness -- with bowed head in prayer, he confesses his sins -- he lifts his bowed head -- he is cleansed, renewed, empowered. And he walks out into the sunlight of God's love -- a new man. That is one of the best things that ever happens to us! And it happens in the church!

> A family follows a casket down the center aisle. The minister says: "Let us lift up our hearts in thanksgiving for the gift of life to our friend..." Suddenly, the members of that family are helped to move through their feelings of grief because of a life that has ended to a sense of gratitude for a life well-ended! That is one of the best things that ever happens to us! And it happens in the church!

All this is just for starters! The list could be extended several pages! Some of the best things that ever happen to us happen in the church! Of course, the ministry of the church is not limited to what transpires within the four walls of a building. And that ministry reaches far beyond the lives of the membership of the congregation.

An alcoholic stumbles into the Salvation Army -- is given a meal -- a shower -- a clean outfit -- a warm coat -- and opportunity to dry out and get a second chance -- a third -- a fourth.

A young girl, great with child by a father who refuses to accept responsibility, is given a place of privacy -- medical attention -- security in which to make a decision for her child's future.

A family -- down on its luck -- far from home -- needing groceries, gasoline, medicine -- is given a motel room -- voucher for meals -- a tank of gasoline -- a check for medicine.

An elderly person -- without a family -- unable to fend for herself -- short on finances -- discovers a home supported by the church where she can spend her days cared for in a family atmosphere.

All this is just for starters! In terms of the ministry of the church outside its four walls and beyond its membership, many good things are made to happen for others.

Some of the best things that ever happen to us, happen to us in the church. Some of the best things that ever happen to others, happen because of the church.

5

Stewardship

August 7, 1968

The Minister's Two Minutes:

In the last newsletter, I promised an article about tithing. So here goes --!

Usually the church appeals to its membership for money in terms of its institutional needs:

> Have to pay the utilities and insurance, you know. Must not get behind in our missions giving. Building needs a new paint job…inside and out! Kids ought to go to church camp this summer. Sunday School supplies cost more…like everything else. New robes for the choir before Christmas! And the furnace is on the blink!

It's a matter of budgets and weekly needs and averages. On the average it takes about $1.77 per member to meet the "operating budget" of this Church.

But all this is the wrong place to start. The right place to start is with the Christian, the gift of life that he has received, and the responsible use of his life. Now, the word "life" is an umbrella term -- it covers a multitude of good things, such as: self-consciousness, minds to think and make plans, hands to work, natural resources such as land and water and sun, our families, the air we breathe, a pocketbook, friends, the community we live in, property. A multitude of good things -- a dictionary-full, if you please! All of life (and that's quite a bundle) is a gift from God.

Now, God doesn't just dump this multitude of good things into our laps with a jolly, "Have fun, kids!" Rather, he desires fullness of life for all his children and he asks for responsible use of life by all his children. He keeps a "prior claim" on all of life, and as his children we will be called to answer for our use of his gifts. As suggested, "life" covers everything -- "the works" so to speak. Now, tithing relates to that part of life that has to do with a person's income. God always asked of his people the best that they had:

- The spotless lamb
- The firstling of the flock
- The first fruits of the orchard
- The tithe of the income

The tithe is the cream of the income, it's that top 10%, the best part. But God asks it of us. He established the tithe from the days before Abraham as the standard by which a man expresses his gratitude for his income and indicates his responsible use of the remaining 90%. The tithe is the cream, and God desires only the very best for and the very best from his children.

Now, it's not easy to tithe. It is certainly not easy for a poor man. I'm told that it is no easier for a rich man. But, it is what God asks of every man who would be his.

Wealth is good -- very good. It is one part of God's gift of life. It is good -- but it is not good in and of itself. It is good for something. God intends wealth for the welfare of his children (wealth and welfare are from the same English root). As a child of God, use your wealth gratefully and responsibly. Now, that's the right place to start. Check it out and you will understand what the prophet Malachi meant when he wrote:

> Bring the full tithes into the storehouse, that there may be food in my house; and thereby put me to the test, says the Lord of hosts, if I will not open the windows of heaven for you and pour down for you an overflowing blessing. (Malachi 3:10 RSV)

That average of $1.77 will have a hard time measuring up to God's 10%. Do a bit of spiritual mathematics for yourself! You'll get the point.

Yours for a dime out of a dollar for God.

October 24, 1973

Dear Friends of Little Children and the Church Family:

Our little Shana will be eight years old on December 1, 1973. Last Friday she received a very important letter. "First Class!" from the church with her very own name and address showing through the cellophane window! She ripped it open -- kinda rough-like. Put the ragged envelope on her dresser. And tried to decipher what was written on the pink enclosure. At the top right was the notation: "Envelope No. 260." At the bottom was "This is the acknowledgement of your offerings for The Second Quarter." In between were 76 different numbers arranged in four wobbly columns headed, respectively: "Date, "Env. No.," "Current," and "Total."

Well -- that was a bit too much for an almost-eight-year-old third-grader. So it became her Dad's privilege to decode the hieroglyphics on that pink sheet. The bottom figure in the farthest right column was the total amount of all her giving from April 1, 1973 to September 30, 1973 -- exactly $2.54. Her smallest gift was five cents made three different times. Her largest gift was thirty-nine cents, made on "catch up Sunday." Her average was ten cents per week for the twenty-six-week period. All this was explained -- and a bit more. She studied that pink sheet over one last time, laid it gently over the ragged envelope on her dresser and hustled off for a bicycle ride with her pals.

That was indeed a very important letter. It told Shana that the church takes her seriously. It showed her that every penny she gives is carefully recorded and accounted for. It reminded her that she, too, has a finger in the church pie. Important? Very!

Shana gives a tithe of her weekly allowance to the church. Five years from now when she earns her first $1.50 for babysitting, it's a pretty safe bet that she will be putting fifteen cents of that into "Envelope No. 260." Twenty years from now -- when she is stretching her dollars to cover her tuition and fees in graduate school -- she will probably still be putting 10% of those stretched dollars into "Envelope No. 260." And 30 years from now when she is balancing the family budget -- she will make allowances for the family's usual tithe to go where it has always gone: "Envelope No. 260." And very likely -- when she draws up her last will and testament -- she will leave a very generous part of her estate to the church.

Friends -- that letter -- that ragged envelope -- that pink sheet with all kinds of figures that an eight-year-old does not easily understand -- that is a very important letter! The youth of our Church received similar letters last Friday. All "First Class!" All very important! Your child's ragged envelope and pink sheet may look a bit messy on the dresser. It isn't! Rather it is a very meaningful, a very beautiful thing. Let it hang around for a while. It will do your child's mind and heart nothing but good!

June 2, 1976

Dear Citizens of "the Greenest State in the Land of the Free":

Dick Mapes gave me eight pepper plants last Sunday: three California Wonders, three Anaheim TMRs, two bell peppers. Set them out this A.M. in Judie's mini-garden of about 40 square feet at our back gate. Four of the five tomato plants "Pop" Hamilton gave us last month are coming along real well. The fifth was a casualty of a misplaced stroke of the hoe. Several of Lulu Snyder's marigolds are struggling for their place in the sun -- intermixed with a few volunteers from last year's zinnias. At the back of that 40 square foot plot is a thick row of iris -- blooms played out around the middle of May. As I turned the soil to set Dick's pepper plants, I disturbed a bed of grub worms and angered a squiggly nightcrawler. Took a minute to jerk up a handful of grass and weed slivers that sprout everywhere without being asked. Watered my "South 40" -- washed my hands -- had my customary Raisin Bran breakfast (with a few triangles of fresh pineapple) -- and dressed for work.

Settled myself into my near antique '55 Studebaker and rolled down the driveway. The yard had that crew-cut look from yesterday's mowing. The boxwoods and hollies are a bit more attractive since being shaped up with sharpened shears. And the weeping cherry at the center of our yard no longer drags its skirt on the ground. A neat pile of unwanted trimmings lay at the street's edge. Looking back up the hill I noticed the basket of variegated ivy that a student gave Judie. It was hanging a bit ske-wum-pus at the west end of our porch -- near where I knocked down that nest of yellow jackets.

I drove up Naples Road -- feeling good about peppers and tomatoes and marigolds and zinnias and iris and grub worms and boxwood and holly and weeping cherry and ivy -- but not feeling good about yellow jackets! I utterly dislike yellow jackets! They remind me of the question once asked by a Louisiana friend: "If God made everything with a purpose -- then what is the purpose of the mosquito?"

Turned on to Gulf Park Boulevard -- my eyes taking in the lively colors and neatness of the lawns. Up the ramp to I-40 -- sped alongside the grassy median strip. The intense green of the spruces and pines at the Papermill Road exit made me glad I live in Davy Crockett country. Pulled into a parking slot on the Fifth Avenue side of the church building. Even here in the concrete and asphalt wasteland -- even here the green will not be denied! The thick turf of the lawn, the spreading crape myrtle, the huge hemlock, the ivy along the colonnade -- all bear colorful testimony of the richness of the soil, the mildness of the climate, and the adequacy of the rainfall.

Now -- what is the point of all this chit-chat about things that are green, etc.? Well, in preacherly fashion, three points:

> First -- the pepper plants and tomatoes and marigolds give us the occasion to say "Thanks!" We are immensely grateful for the privilege of living and moving and having our being in East Tennessee -- the greenest part of "the greenest state in the land of the free!" And we are deeply thankful for the opportunity to share in the joys and the sorrows, the hopes and the fears, the triumphs and the tragedies, the ecstasies and the agonies, the dreams and the dreads of the fellowship of the Church.

Second -- we rejoice with all our families, who -- with the coming of June-July-August will be spending more time together -- in the gardens, mowing lawns, trimming hedges, hiking in the Smokies, sailing on the lakes, relaxing on the seaside, traveling across the country. Be assured -- when you are not in your accustomed pew -- we will miss you. But we will be happy you are out and about -- replenishing your spirit, rediscovering the intimacy of the family, recouping your physical and mental health, opening yourselves to the wholesome influences "of Nature and of Nature's God," affirming your right to "life, liberty, and the pursuit of happiness." (Declaration of Independence)

Third -- your pastor will have his turn at a vacation in July -- a trip to Estes Park, Colorado, for Judie's 25th anniversary of her high school graduating class.

Meanwhile, I would add this single note. In all our wanderings and absences these summer months we should daily pray for our church and for those loving souls within this great fellowship. And we should especially remember and pray for our church treasurer. His is the huge task of stretching deflated receipts to cover inflated bills!

I do hope you enjoy your summer to the fullest. Life is a gift. The green, green hills of East Tennessee are gifts to us all. The Smokies, the lakes, the Bicentennial, our families, our churches, our gardens, our neighborhoods -- all gifts! Do not take any of these for granted!

> Bless the Lord, O my soul;
>   and all that is within me, bless his holy name!
> Bless the Lord, O my soul,
>   and forget not all his benefits! (Psalms 103:1-2 RSV)

Shalom!

May 3, 1978

Dear Christian Stewards:

Those days at Minnesota Bible College (1954-1957) were tough. I was 18-20 years old. Carrying 18-20 units of study. Washing dishes at the Flagg Cafe 18-20 hours per week. Earning 75¢ per hour plus the evening meal. Keeping myself solvent by the thinnest of margins. Rarely affording a black walnut ice cream cone at Bridgeman's. Somehow by the end of each quarter paying off my rent and tuition and books. Leaving barely enough money in the bank to keep my account open. Students 20 years ago didn't have it easy -- at least not financially. Many students do not have it financially easy now. Consider the note written on the back of one of last Sunday's attendance cards:

Bob Landry: Since I'm never home, I'll try to call you sometime. Subject: I'm not very good at making financial donations, but I would be very glad to spend a day now and then doing all sorts of mechanical things that a good kid with a good toolbox could take care of. Certainly you could come up with some stuff like that?

- Bye Bye! _____

He signed his name and added: "Specialist in Carpentry, Painting, Yardwork, Electrical, Mechanical, Masonry, Poetry, etc."

This UT student is enthusiastic about our church! He wants to carry his share of the load. But he can't do it with dollars and dimes because those are in short supply for him. But brains and brawn he will happily share! Our property chairman will give him ample opportunity to be a good steward of his time and energy and talent. Our secretary will set up a ledger sheet to list his special donations to the church during this fiscal year: hours, work accomplished, value in dollars and dimes. All this calls to mind one of the greatest lines in sacred scripture. Peter and John saw a cripple outside the Beautiful Gate of the Temple. The cripple asked alms of them. Peter responded: "Silver and gold have I none; but such as I have give I thee: In the name of Jesus Christ of Nazareth rise up and walk!" (Acts 3:6 KJV)

Every day throughout this year I shall remember this young student's pledge to the life and work of the church. His pledge validates a whole lot of things that are going on here!

With a lump in my throat because of personal memories -- and a thrill in my soul because of present joys, I am your Pastor and Friend.

March 21, 1979

Dear Fellow $tewards:

John D. Rockefeller, Sr., was a very rich man -- a very, very rich man! And he did much good with his wealth. For instance, in 1926 he gave one-half of the money to buy the 510,000 acres which are now known as the Great Smoky Mountains National Park. At Newfound Gap there is a bronze plaque noting that this park is a memorial to his wife, Laura Spelman Rockefeller.

John D. Rockefeller, Sr., was not only a very, very rich man. He also was a sincere Christian, a dedicated churchman, a faithful steward of his vast wealth. Once he said:

Yes, I tithe and I would like to tell you how it all came about. I had to begin work as a small boy to help support my mother. My first wages amounted to $1.50 a week. I took the $1.50 home to my mother and she held the money in her lap and explained to me that she would be happy if I would give a tenth of it to the Lord. I did, and from that week until this day I have tithed every dollar that God has entrusted to me. And I want to say if I had not tithed the first dollar made I would not have tithed the first million I made. Tell your readers to train the children to tithe and they will grow up to be faithful stewards of the Lord.[46]

Before his death, Rockefeller gave away well over 500 million dollars. Hospitals, libraries, universities, art museums, the United Nations building in New York, wildlife preserves, research centers -- all kinds of agencies and institutions for the human good have been funded by the foundations which bear the Rockefeller name. And he did it all because of the influence of his dear mother and his stewardship as a Christian.

Thirty years ago I dropped a nickel and a dime in the offering box in my home church in Lake Charles, Louisiana. It wasn't much -- but it was a tithe on my first day's wages of $1.25 as a caddy. And I felt my tithe balanced the tithe of the richest man in our congregation. Indeed, that 15¢ on one side of the scale matched the huge Rockefeller tithe on the other side of the scale! Ever since I have felt that the tithe was a great equalizer. Of course, it has never been easy -- not the first 15¢ -- not the latest $50.00. But it has always been good. And I don't regret the least penny given. Especially when I remember that it is nothing when compared to the "widow's mite." She gave all. I give only 10%.

Have you been putting off a major decision -- that of devoting a specific portion of your income and/or wealth to the Church? Now is the best time you will ever have to start. Sit down with your family. Discuss it. If the tithe seems "an impossible dream" -- then start at a lower level -- at 2% or 3% or 4% or 5%. Babies crawl before they walk. They walk before they run. With your family make a definite, regular commitment of a percentage of your income and/or wealth to the life and work of the Church. Then plan next year to jump it one notch -- say from 3% to 4. "Small strokes fell great oaks!" Within five or six years you, too, will be a tither. And like a pole vaulter who has just cleared the bar at 20 feet for the first time, you will know the joy known by every person who, like Rockefeller, could sum up his life by saying: "Yes, I am a tither and I would like to tell you how it all came about."

March 19, 1980

Dear Friends:

He excited me with his words. He wanted to know how well we were doing with our budget for 1979-80. I had to give him a "bad news -- good news" story. The bad news was that we likely will fall about $13,000 short of the budget projected for April 1, 1979 to March 31, 1980. Our Stewardship and Finance

Committee had planned a budget of $147,492. However, it appears by the end of the fiscal year contributions will have totaled only $134,492. So much for the "bad news."

The "good news" was that the Stewardship and Finance Committee has been conservative and judicious in all its expenditures over the last 11 months. Therefore, our church has been able to live within its income and will end the year in the black! That is, we will have spent no more than we will have received. That is no small achievement! Especially with inflation as it has been and with a $13,000 short fall.

After I had explained this "bad news -- good news" picture, he responded with enthusiasm. "That's great! When the members know the facts and understand how carefully the money has been spent they will rise up and meet the challenge of the new budget! My wife and I will do our fair share!"

Everything he said excited me! But those last three words really caught my ear: "our fair share." It's an attractive phrase -- clear, balanced, respectable. Made me feel good that he would use it. Most folk I know really do want to carry their part of the load. Few there are who want to "hitchhike" through life, park on somebody else's nickel, sneak by on a free ticket. Independence and self-sufficiency are etched deeply on our psyches. We do not want to be free-loaders. Most of us understand what he meant when he said "our fair share."

A "fair share" is that level of giving that helps one sense he has done something direct and specific and substantial in terms of spreading the Gospel -- at home and abroad. A "fair share" validates one's feeling of belonging to the community of faith and hope and love -- "Blest be the tie!"[47]

A "fair share" puts the ring of authenticity in the words: "I love the church. I love this church! I love the people in this church. And after I die I want this church to continue on and on and on forever! I love the church!" A "fair share" relates to one's ability to give. The "fair share" of the elderly person on Social Security is equal to the "fair share" of the 24-karat tycoon -- even though the first may be "a widow's mite" -- "two copper coins, which make a penny" (Mark 12:42 RSV) and the second a zillion dollars.

A "fair share" makes one tremble for joy as he lifts his voice with the rest of the congregation, both the rich and the poor, to sing: "Praise God from whom all blessings flow!"

Excited? Of course I was excited? I was excited he would ask a serious question and would listen for an open answer -- both "bad news" and "good news." And I was excited by his response: "That's great! When we know the facts -- how well every dollar was spent last year -- we'll rise up and meet the challenge of the new year! My wife and I will do our fair share!"

I went to bed happy last night. I slept well! Why? Among other reasons it was because my wife and I have turned in our "fair share" pledge for the April 1, 1980 - March 31, 1981 budget year. With every good wish for your personal happiness and your pleasant sleep.

June 4, 1980

Dear Fellow Insomniacs:

Got up at 3:30 A.M.! Had a nightmare -- awoke sort of trembly -- my heart beating like a hard rock drummer. My subconscious had floated some ungood notions into a dream -- and I could no longer sleep. So -- why use up good time on the horizontal? I verticalized myself -- splashed water in my face -- washed the sand out of the corners of my eyes -- brushed my teeth -- slipped into my shirt and jeans -- put on the coffee pot.

Spent an hour writing checks -- a first of the month chore I save for ungodly hours because it is such an ungodly task. Fifteen checks in all: our church pledge (June 8, 15, 22, 29), Downtown Optimist Club, Gulf, Home Federal (Mortgage), Farragut Animal Clinic, South Central Bell, Johnson's Flowers, KUB, Park National Bank, Farragut High School (for a lost book -- Shana), William E. McGhee, M.D., and Randolph-Macon College (Tammy) -- a total of $1,204.65. Enveloped each -- slapped a 15¢ stamp on the front -- and a dated Dogwood Arts Festival Seal on the back -- and laid that chore aside. Check writing is not only unpleasant -- it also consumes time. By 4:30 I was pouring myself a second cup of Kroger's Kaffee Toffee.

Took Sunday's comics in hand to relax a bit. Then read the editorials. And -- glory be! Don Whitehead is back! Judie's alarm went off. The girls started stirring. Ole Sol brightened the eastern sky over the Smokies. Shaved -- showered -- ate my soggy Raisin Bran -- and it was off to the salt mines. Tonight I shall be in bed sooner than usual.

Which brings me full circle to my 3:30 A.M. rising -- my nightmare -- that ungood dream -- the tremblies -- the drumming in my breast -- insomnia -- and a stack of checks ready to be mailed. What was it all about? Our Pastor's Cabinet met Sunday to discuss the 1980-81 Budget -- cutting it to the bare bones -- appealing to our members to do something extra to help make ends meet. We are still $29,000 short -- so we will do both -- some cutting, some appealing.

After we played "hot potato," with the 1980-81 Budget for about 75 minutes, a consensus emerged:

> Our church has a program which is vital to all our people and to all of the city -- and even beyond. It should be maintained and enlarged -- not

cut back. The budget is a realistic one, the programs are not over-funded. Our people have the resources to underwrite the budget as approved -- and they will respond when asked -- and we can have a surplus for added giving to World Outreach. We will appeal to every member to make that above and beyond effort to keep the fellowship in the black, etc., etc.

So -- let's everybody step up to the lick-log and give it a lick: If you already have pledged to the absolute maximum -- Thanks! And stay abreast with your contributions -- Sunday by Sunday. If you have pledged generously -- but still have a gap between what you have pledged and what you should pledge -- then write out a new pledge card for the higher amount. Move from 4% giving to 5%. Or from 7% to 8%. Or all the way to the tithe!

If you have not yet signed your "Statement of Intention" (pledge card) do so today! And drop it in the mail.

Our church treasurer signs checks in excess of $12,000 every month! Let's save him and ourselves any late evening nightmares and early A.M. risings. And the Church Staff and the Church Secretary and the Property Committee and the Worship Committee, etc., etc. If each one does what he/she can and should -- from a widow's mite to a rich person's thousands -- then everyone will sleep well!

Yours for a soft pillow and good dreams.

January 4, 1984

Dear Fellow Christians:

She was just a tiny thing: five years old, ski-jump nose, pig-tails. Ben, her dad, handed her 10 pennies and said, "Judie, you can use these 10 pennies for anything you want. But it would make me happy if you spent only nine of them for yourself and gave the tenth one to the Church." She did! And she has been a tither ever since!

Bobby was 13 years old, freckled, wore his older brothers' hand-me-down jeans. His first Saturday's wage was $1.25 as a caddy. The next morning, he dropped one nickel and one dime into the velvet offering box on the Communion Table. That made him a tither. And Bobby has been a tither ever since!

I have just turned in our pledge toward the 1984 Budget. It represents exactly 10% of Judie's and my combined incomes. Each Sunday there will be a check in the offering tray representing 10% of our combined incomes for the previous week. For us pledging a tithe to the Church is as normal as shutting off the alarm at 6:00 A.M. or wearing matched socks. At our home the first check written each week is the check to cover our pledge for the next Sunday's offering -- a "standard operating procedure" for us. Judie learned it at age five. I learned it at age 13.

But such a practice may not be "normal" or "standard" for you:

Your income isn't large enough yet for you to spare 10%?

If it isn't now -- it never will be!

You have too many bills: mortgage, doctors, utilities, groceries.

The older you get the more bills you will have!

Can't do it until you pay off the Chevy? By the time you get the title to this set of wheels you will need a new set -- a <u>costlier</u> set? Later you will need a truck! With a camper! Then a boat! Then a cabin in the woods! Then ….

Want to save up something for a rainy day? Fine. You ought to. Everybody ought to! But why take it out of the 10% rather than out of the 90%?

Taxes eating you up? Uncle Sam encourages all Americans to give the 10% by letting every dime of it be deducted from the adjusted gross income on IRS Form 1040. That means you may be getting back a rebate of 20% -- or 30% -- or 40% -- or even 50% of every dollar tithed to the Church!

If you gave 10% this year that means you would have to give five times as much as you gave last year? If so, shame on you for having given only 2% last year! 'Nuf said!

If you can't become an instant tither like the five year old when she gave one penny of her 10 pennies allowance to the Church -- or like the 13-year-old caddy when he dropped a dime and a nickel into the velvet offering box -- you can at least try the "Jacob's Ladder" technique for reaching the tithing level. If you gave 4% of your income to the Church last year (1983) increase your giving one percentage point to 5% this year (1984). Then, on January 1, 1985, increase your giving one more percentage point from 5% to 6%. In 1986 -- increase it from 6% to 7%. Get the picture? By 1989 you will be a full-fledged tither.

Meanwhile, keep at it. Step by step! "Every round goes higher and higher!"[48] Right now, our church needs 168 pledgers who will increase the size of their pledges to the 1984 Budget by one percentage point more than their last year's pledges: from 5% to 6%; or from 2% to 3%; or from 8% to 9%. Do your fair share.

Then we will all be able to get down to the business of being the Church without being anxious about who will pay our bills for being the Church!

October 19, 1990

Dear Fellow Receivers/Givers:

When it comes to giving -- some people stop at **nothing**. "**Nothing**" has several meanings:

- Some people give **nothing**! Period! Zip!
- Some people give -- but what they give is next to **nothing**!
- Some people give -- until they discover an objection, a trivial **nothing**, to excuse themselves from further giving. They stop at **nothing**.
- Some people give -- but in comparison to what they receive, what they give is more nearly **nothing** than it is something.
- Some people give -- and give -- and give! **Nothing** can repress their generosity.
- Some people give. They give everything! They give until there is **nothing** more to give! The poor widow who put into the temple treasury "two copper coins, which made a penny...put in everything she had." (Mark 12:42, 44 RSV) Then she stopped giving because she had **nothing** more to give. Zero!

Every person fits somewhere on this giving continuum from "zip" to "zero," from selfish to sacrificial, from "**nothing**" to "**nothing**."

Not all giving is in terms of dollars and cents -- either of the philanthropist's million dollars for a school or of the poor widow's "two copper coins, which made a penny." Those who signed the Declaration of Independence pledged "to each other our lives, our fortunes, our sacred honor." Lincoln spoke of those who died at Gettysburg as having given "the last full measure of devotion." There is giving that has to do with "time and talent" as well as with "treasure." There is giving that has to do with "blood and sweat and tears." There is giving that has to do with thoughts and prayers, deeds and cares, loves and labors, cards and calls.

So far as the giving that has to do with cash -- "dollars and cents" -- that giving can be pretty accurately characterized as tending toward one end or the other of the giving continuum from selfish to sacrificial, from greedy to generous, from giving **nothing** at all to giving until there is **nothing** more at all to give!

Philip Guedalla, who wrote a biography of the Duke of Wellington, said that one of the most revealing resources he found in his research was a stack of cancelled checks. He suggested that that stack of cancelled checks told him more about the commitments and cares of the Iron Duke than any other piece of writing over that great man's signature. Indeed! So far as giving that has to do with cash -- "dollars and cents" -- your cancelled checks speak more eloquently than the purple words of any silver-tongued orator. Your cancelled checks tally to the penny what your G.Q. (Giving Quotient) really is! "When it comes to giving -- some people stop at **nothing!**" What is "**nothing**" to you?

Your Fellow Receiver/Giver.

December 7, 1990

Dear Fellow Stewards of God's Good Gifts:

It was a new experience for me. And a delightful one! Twice delightful! Two times in the past 10 days I was asked for a pledge card. Both requests came from new members. In a conversation with the first couple in their home, the husband said, "We intend to support the church financially as well as in other ways. Of course, we have been giving for a quite a while -- ever since we started visiting. But now that we are members, we want to make a pledge to the 1991 Budget." I was delighted!

And delighted again in a chat with the second couple. It was last Sunday in the Community Room during our Fellowship Half-Hour. Cup-o-coff in one hand and cookie in the other, the wife said, "Dr. Landry, we need a pledge card. We intend to do our part in terms of money. There must be a committee or some such to manage the financial affairs of the church. Where can we get a pledge card?" Delightful! Floss Cox brought this couple to the Volunteers' Office to pick up an "Estimate of Giving Card" from our always willing treasurer. Double delightful!

When it comes to money matters, I lean over backwards not to seem forward -- seldom bring up the subject -- let the Stewardship Committee do its thing. I deal with money matters indirectly rather than head on. Some of my colleagues feel this is a mistake. Still, my approach (or non-approach) leaves the initiative with the individual Christian. It is a delightful thing when persons give out of <u>desire</u> to share in the life and ministry of the Church. Their generosity is an expression of their love for Jesus Christ and of their commitment to The Way. Example, encouragement, guidance -- that's to my liking. A gentle reminder at most -- not a two-by-four across the eyes!

My approach (non-approach) makes for some delightful surprises. It is much better than confronting folk with a demand: "Thou shalt ...! -- or else!" Browbeating, threatening, confrontation -- that kind of stuff belongs more on the football gridiron than in church. This excerpt from a recent church newsletter that crossed my desk shows coercive arm twisting that is not in keeping with wholesome and responsible Christian Stewardship:

Frankly, I am puzzled and disappointed today. Puzzled, because despite outstanding music and energetic calling by the Membership Committee, there were too many empty pews last Sunday. Disappointed, because the giving of our congregation has not kept up with the promises made. I asked the computer to summarize the giving to the church. Without revealing names, the computer told me that MOST of the church families are in fact ahead in their giving. <u>But there are some 47 families that are behind. Some members have yet to share as much as a dollar to the work of the church, even though they attend. You see, you may think that if you don't attend every Sunday, you won't be missed</u>. You ARE missed! You may think that if you miss a month's tithe, someone else will make it up. They will NOT make it up. It'll take all of our best efforts to keep the things we value most about the church alive, and to cause it to grow. I pray I can count on you!

December is the season of much giving: a tricycle for Junior and a dollhouse for Suzie, fruitcake for the mailman, cash for the maid/cook, food baskets for the poor, slippers for Grandma, gifts for close friends. Generosity is the mood of the month. My December has started on the delightful note of two new families who asked for pledge cards. They assumed the responsibility. They took the initiative. They made the first step. They went beyond merely speaking the words of the Good Confession before the gathered Congregation. They beat the Stewardship Committee to the draw. They asked for a pledge card before the Committee sent them one! Delightful! May their ilk increase! Gratefully and encouragingly, I am,

Your Fellow Steward of God's Good Gifts.

August 13, 1993

Dear Friends:

The widow who "put in two copper coins, which make a penny" (Mark 12:42 RSV) into the Temple treasury was a generous, open-handed person. It is likely that her mother taught her how to give while she was still a child -- something like this: "Suzanna, here are 10 shekels. Nine of them are for you to buy whatever you would like: a bonnet, a pair of sandals, a jar of honey. But the tenth shekel is holy. It is the tithe and it belongs to God. When we go to the synagogue next Sabbath you should drop this tenth shekel into the offering box with a prayer that it be used for the glory of God and the service of man." Many years later an elderly widow named Suzanna "put in two copper coins, which make a penny" into the Temple treasury. And Jesus applauded her gift: "Truly, I say to you, this poor widow has put in more than all those who are contributing to the treasury. For they all contributed out of their abundance; but she out of her poverty has put in everything she had, her whole living!" (Mark 12:43-44 RSV)

One may be taught "how to give." One may also be taught "how to <u>not give</u>!" It is likely that the rich young ruler had been taught "how to <u>not give</u>" while he was still a child. His money-wise father may have told him something like this: "Listen, Jonathon -- it is a hard world out there. Nobody is going to give you something for nothing. It is each man for himself and the devil take the hindmost. A dog-eat-dog world! Look at me! I didn't make my millions by giving money away!" Later, when Jesus offered that rich young man an opportunity to sign on for an exciting adventure in discipleship, the young man "went away sorrowful; for he had great possessions." (Matthew 19:22 RSV) Or rather, he did not have "great possessions" -- instead, his "great possessions" had him! His father's lessons in "how to <u>not give</u>" had been well-learned!

Oscar Hammerstein taught us about teaching and learning in a catchy tune in "South Pacific":

> You've got to be taught to hate and fear,
> You've got to be taught from year to year,
> It's got to be drummed in your dear little
>   ear --
> You've got to be carefully taught![49]

In terms of learning "how to give" and learning "how to <u>not give</u>," I'd like to revise that first line: "You've got to be taught to give, my dear." And be assured -- each of us has been taught -- carefully taught! Either we have been taught "how to give," or we have been taught "how to not give." Either we have discovered the joy of generosity, or we still snuggle in the security of selfishness. Either we have an open hand, or we have a locked purse. Either we are givers, or we are takers. Either we have learned "how to give," or we have learned "how to <u>not give</u>."

With two copper coins in one hand and a tither's check in the other, I am your minister and friend.

January 26, 1996

Dear Members and Friends:

Here are two persons. One has much. One has little. Whatever each does -- or does not do -- with what she has makes a difference. Neither can wash her hands of the consequences of what she does or of what she does not do.

Suppose the one who has much gives nothing -- or gives but little. That person's "nothing -- or but little" makes a difference. Though she has much, she grasps it close to her heart. When she gives "nothing" it is an act that says, "I don't care! It doesn't matter! Shut it down! Close it up! I'd rather have what I have for myself." When she gives "nothing," her "nothing" is a vote against the Gospel of Jesus Christ. She dims the light of God for the life of man. When she gives "nothing" she says, "I have no interest in the little children learning to lisp 'Jesus Loves Me This I Know for the Bible Tells Me So!'" When she gives "nothing" she withholds any gratitude for all she learned in Sunday School about Creation, the 23rd Psalm, the Beatitudes. When she gives "nothing" she has no share, no investment, no ownership in the kindness and care and compassion of the Church given to persons at times of bereavement. When she gives "nothing" she doesn't participate in sending teenagers to summer camp, in supporting missionaries in Africa, in helping the homeless here at home. When she gives "nothing" she doesn't even cover the cost of a bit of bread and a sip of wine at the Communion Table. Her "nothing" makes a difference. Her difference is a minus, a darkness, a midnight. She is "rich in things and poor in soul"! What a difference! One who has much, but gives nothing -- or gives but little -- makes a difference! The difference that says, "NO!"

The other person has but little. But she gives what she can. Her "little" -- whether it is "two copper coins, which make a penny" (Mark 12:42 RSV) or a bit more -- her "little" makes a difference. Her "little" is a vote for the Gospel, the light of heaven for the life on earth. Her "little" supports the children's work. Her "little" is a tangible thanksgiving for all she learned in Sunday School about Adam and Eve, The Ten Commandments, The Sermon on the Mount, John 3:16. Her "little" -- even though it is little -- buys a bit of stock in the kindness and care and compassion that flows through the Church to persons at times of bereavement. Her small gift helps send teenagers to summer camp, supports the Outreach programs that reach out to the needy. Her tiny gift makes a difference -- even if it only covers the cost of a bit of bread and a sip of wine at the Communion Table. Her "something" makes a difference. Her difference is a plus, a brightness, a noonday. She may be "poor in things" -- but she is "rich in soul"! What a difference! One who has little, but gives generously, makes a difference! The difference that says, "YES!"

One person has much, but gives nothing -- or gives but little. The other person has little, but gives as much as she is able, maybe a bit more. Each one makes a difference. One difference is dark and negative -- says, "NO!" The other difference is bright and positive -- says, "YES!"

Yet, there is a much more serious difference. This more serious difference is the difference in the heart of the one who gives -- or who does not give. Grasping -- hoarding -- keeping -- not giving -- confirms in the heart one of the seven deadly vices -- the vice of avarice. Just what is avarice? Avarice is greed. Greed that en-smallens the soul. Greed that has both feet as well as the mouth in the feeding trough. And shoves others out. Greed that makes the heart as hard as granite. Greed that imprisons oneself in a tiny castle of "I, me, my, mine!"

But opening one's purse -- sharing one's meager coins -- caring enough to say "Yes!" -- such giving engenders generosity. Generosity is one of the seven gifts of the Spirit. The heart grows. Horizons expand. Compassion circles the earth. The soul becomes more godly -- as in "For God so loved that he gave...!" (John 3:16 RSV)

"YOU Make a Difference!" Indeed! And whatever you do, the greatest difference is the difference you make inside your own heart. It is the difference between greed and generosity! "YOU Make a Difference!"

October 24, 1997

Dear Friends:

James Michener died last Friday -- full of years -- 90 plus! And they were full years! My acquaintance with Michener was from a distance. A long distance. Came through the reading of a paperback copy of *The Source* sometime during the '60s. Loved every episode in it. Then came the reading of his first book: *Tales of the South Pacific*. Michener won the Pulitzer for *Tales*. He deserved it! Rodgers and Hammerstein earned a bucket of money with their Broadway musical based on Michener's "Tales." A couple years back John Anderson gave me a copy of Michener's *The Raven and the Eagle*, a biographical piece of special interest to Texans. Had alternating chapters about *The Raven* (Sam Houston) *and the Eagle* (Santa Anna). About a year ago I read most of *The Legacy*. Only four books out of his fifty-plus. So little done! So much to do! If had the time I'd read the other 46. If I had...!

I live with a lady who has read several of the other 46, including: *Centennial, Poland, Texas, Alaska, Hawaii, Caravans* (about Afghanistan), and most recently, *Recessional*. Hers is a much broader and deeper acquaintance with Michener. And as an English teacher she has better tools with which to critique Michener's life-work.

My more serious interest in Michener at the moment has little to do with his books. Rather, my interest has to do with Michener's generosity and with his self-discipline. His *Tales* won for him the Pulitzer and earned for him substantial royalties. Many of Michener's books were bestsellers! Several were blockbusters! His royalties were immense -- in the millions of dollars! Some say over $100 million! These royalties will continue to accrue far into the 21st century! But Michener did not hoard his wealth. Early on, he and his wife learned to share their wealth. They gave! And gave! And gave! After she died, he continued to give! And give! And give! And he gave it all away before he died! Michener probably felt a bit like Andrew Carnegie who said, "It is not wrong for a man to get rich; but it is wrong for a man to die rich!"[50] Michener and his wife were gentle and generous souls. They enriched and enhanced and enlarged our community through their gentle spirits and their generous gifts. We are grateful!

As appreciative as I am for his books and as grateful as I am for his generosity, I hold Michener in even higher regard because of his self-discipline. Started his day early, at his work before others had stirred, dedicated to careful research in the setting/history/personalities about which he wrote, focused, steady, in control of his destiny. And the last act of his life was characteristic of all of his life. Rather than to stretch out his existence by artificial means, Michener chose to have his kidney dialysis machine removed. Gradually, the toxemia built up in his body. After five days he breathed his last. Michener died -- full of years -- 90 plus! And they were full years! Respected because of his immense productivity! Appreciated because of his gentle and generous spirit! Held in highest esteem because of his example of courage in the face of the ultimate enemy! We were acquainted with him from a distance. A <u>long</u> distance! And though he is now gone, our respect and appreciation and esteem will continue to grow! Four down and forty-six to go! If I had the time I'd read the other 46. If I had the time....

November 6, 1998

Dear Friends:

John Q. Christian was in the woods hunting. A thundercloud stormed over. It began raining. A real gully-washer! A frog-strangler! John Q. searched for shelter. There was none! But he discovered a hollow log and crawled into it. Like hand in glove, he in the log fit snugly. The downpour continued for a while. The water soaked the log. The log swelled which turned John Q.'s snug fit into a tight squeeze. The thunderstorm slacked off, but John Q. was trapped. He couldn't get out of the log. He knew that if he could not free himself he would starve to death! Like a drowning man going under for the third time, John Q.'s whole life flashed before him -- especially his mistakes! Among which was that he had not been very generous. Especially toward the church! This made him feel so small that the tight squeeze became a snug fit again and he was able to crawl out of the log. Guess what John Q. delivered to the Church Treasurer the next morning!

We chuckle at that story! Particularly if we are not hunters. But that story has a point for all of us: hunters, fisherman, travelers, balloon-enthusiasts, stamp-collectors, beachcombers, couch potatoes. A lot of "John Q. Christians" would benefit from that waterlogged hunter's experience! And the Church would, too, once each crawled out of her "tight squeeze" and then dropped by the Church Treasurer's home the next morning with a generous check to redeem past mistakes. Our prayer might well be:

> O Lord, Whose chariots of wrath the deep thunderclouds form, And dark is Thy path on the wings of the storm -- Send a rainstorm upon all stingy hunters and fisherman and travelers and balloon-enthusiasts, etc. Make

it a gullywasher! A frog-strangler! And grant, O Lord, that each one may discover a hollow log in which to snuggle during the downpour! And may those logs swell and trap them tightly inside! Then, O Lord, open their eyes that they may see how small they really are! Small enough to crawl out again. Finally, O Great Teacher of Generosity, when they get unstuck, teach them to move their hands to sign long overdue checks that will be "showers of blessing" to others. Amen! Hallelujah!

'Nuf said.

August 13, 1999

Dear Givers:

"Deep pockets, but short arms!" Don't remember when or where I first heard that line. Whenever and wherever, it made instant sense. Many of us have much! More than enough! "Deep pockets!" But we have little desire to give. We lack the motivation: "Short arms!" We have the capacity to give. But we are short on the ability to give. "Deep pockets, but short arms!" On occasion that line rises like cream to the top of my consciousness. Like last Sunday.

Stood in the pulpit. New threads. "Botany 500." Navy blue with a narrow gray stripe. Cuffed at the bottom as in the "Lands' End" catalogue. Stylish. Gift from my wife. She opined that my "Sunday-Go-to-Meetin' Suit" had shrunk. Or something. Whatever, "Men's Wearhouse" lightened her purse by several "C" bills. Sunday A.M. Miz L. clipped the thread that kept the back flap from flapping. (A small detail the "Men's Wearhouse" should have included in the alteration and cuffs charges for zip!)

Whatever, standing in the pulpit I tried to slip my hands into my jacket's pockets. No luck. The flaps over my pockets would flap, but the pockets were still sewed shut. Tight as they had been when the suit was shipped from the garment factory. No way to get into those pockets without first scissoring them open! That's the moment the notion about "Deep pockets, but short arms!" came to mind. My new threads had deep pockets. Large pockets! Roomy pockets! Enough space for a wallet, a check book, a money clip. And I had long arms to reach way down into those deep pockets. But those deep pockets were sewed shut! Closed! Tighter than the bark on a hickory tree!

"Deep pockets, but short arms!" Many of us have enough! And then some! More than enough! We have deep pockets. Yet, many of us have short arms. Too short to reach down into the deep pockets where our gold is stashed! Or just too weak to slice open the slot below the flap that leads into the deep pockets?

Giving has two prerequisites: (1) Enough stuff to give; (2) Enough desire to give. Many of us have "enough stuff"! Not so many of us have "enough desire"! Most of us have deep pockets. What we most need is long arms!

6

Role of the Minister

June 27, 1963

How Free Is the Pulpit?

I was fully aware last Sunday that what I had to say regarding the images and idols of American religion cut right across the grain of the feelings of most of our church's membership. Supporting the recent decision of the Supreme Court of our land is not a popular endeavor. Moreover, to show that Paul himself might have preached a like sermon (Acts 17) doesn't make the pill any easier to swallow. But I preached this sermon anyway -- in spite of the fact that I knew almost everyone was on the opposite side of the plow furrow from me. Why? Because I believe in the freedom of the pulpit! The man who occupies the pulpit is not commissioned to reflect the general opinion of the majority of his church members -- to please itching ears -- to pat soft backs. He is commissioned to preach the word of God -- the Gospel of Jesus Christ as he best understands it. If he hesitates in this task, he is unworthy of his office -- indeed he is <u>not free</u> and neither is his pulpit and neither <u>is the word which he preaches</u>.

Reactions to last Sunday's sermon as received at the door were various -- from outright rebuttals to glib comments about the weather and the wheat harvest (some do sleep!) to warm approval (some were on this side the furrow, to my joyful surprise). Whether in agreement or not, I do feel that all were aware that the pulpit is free -- the Word is "unfettered." And there is not one member who would not fight to keep it so! It is a pleasure to serve a congregation that is awake and that defends the freedom of its pulpit even though the sermons bounced from its sounding board often grind on the ears and hearts of the hearers.

God bless you all, and then some.

September 19, 1973

Dear Christian Friends:

If you see the pastor only on Sunday mornings you may conclude that he is an incurable, unsinkable, indefatigable optimist. I am not! Admittedly I am inclined to look through a problem to its possibilities. I tend to view difficulties from the perspective of hope. I prefer to say "Yes!" than to groan "No!" Even so -- my optimism is balanced with a healthy dose of realism. Your pastor carries more than a pasteboard smile into the pulpit!

For instance, this morning I am rather blue, depressed. My sister, Ena, just called to tell me that Daddy is in The Methodist Hospital, Houston, Texas. Tests seem to confirm the judgment that he will not get much better. The diagnosticians and surgeons have not given up -- but they do not encourage us to expect much. With this kind of news you may be sure I am not riding on an optimistic Cloud 9.

People facing death can sometimes be quite courageous, honest, forthright. Last month Daddy told me: "Yep! This freeway will be finished within another year. And me -- I am going to be buried within another year." Daddy may have beat the physicians in Houston to a diagnosis! My hope trembles before those very realistic lab reports. It seems that I may not have the privilege of introducing the greatest man in my life to the congregation that I love and to the community where I will spend the bulk of my ministerial career. Dad's days are numbered -- and I am not so pollyanna as to believe that one of those numbered days has Knoxville marked on it. So -- today I am blue, I am depressed.

Well -- why share all this personal stuff with you? Because I, too, need encouragement; I, too, cannot go it alone.

Moreover, <u>my</u> hurt, <u>my</u> agony makes me more sensitive to <u>your</u> hurt, <u>your</u> agony. For, many of you have lost your parents. Many others of you have lost your husbands, your wives, your children. Others of you are stumbling along under immense burdens -- like the camel loaded down with all but the very last straw. Yes, friend, I too, know what you are going through.

"Lift up your hearts. We lift them up unto the Lord." What sacred words those are with which to begin any service of Christian worship! Know this -- <u>all</u> our hearts need to be lifted up -- including that of the minister in the sometimes too, too lonely pulpit.

With love for you all and with every good wish to you all, I am your pastor with a "feel for things."

July 6, 1978

Dear Friends:

Was up real late last night! Or was it real early this A.M.? Either is correct. Take your pick. Why was I unable to sleep soundly?

Maybe it was the family -- both sets of our daughters' grandparents were with us.

Or could it have been the weather? Our air conditioner has been running 24 hours a day -- struggling like the "Little Engine That Could" -- but not, as yet, winning its battle against July temperatures.

Perhaps it was the excitement about tomorrow -- next week -- next month. And the remembered joys of yesterday -- last week -- last month.

Or guilt about "things we ought not to have done"…or about "things left undone that we ought to have done."

Could have been anxieties about bills, birthdays, correspondence, taxes, school, politics, dandelions in the lawn, next Sunday's sermon, this article.

Shucks! It may merely have been just "one too many" of Daddy's brew of the special brand of coffee he brought with him from Louisiana! One sip is enough to keep a truck driver popeyed on a 500-mile run!

Whatever the reason -- I didn't sleep well!

Friends who have been this way before tell me that they, too, have such nights. Insomnia is more widespread than we suspect. Millions of us can't turn off the engine in the evening without the help of a pill: Sleep-Eze, Nytol, Valium, Triavil, Librium, Placidyl. We are a "hyped" generation: Too many stimuli bombard us! Too fast! We try to respond too often! And end up a bundle of quivering nerves on an uneasy pillow! Much of our problem stems from an inability to be selective in focusing our attention and energy and resources. We try to do everything at once -- neglecting nothing. Like Sherwin-Williams: "Covering the Whole World."

Well, the minister wrestles with this problem every day -- and every night! He loses more often than he wins! Every unforgiving minute is filled -- but sometimes with more chaff than wheat.

In three or four weeks Judie and I are going to load up the old station wagon and ride off like Stephen Leacock's famous horseman who "flung himself upon his mount and rode madly off in all directions."[51] Well, not really. We intend to have a couple weeks of "early to bed and <u>late</u> to rise" with a lot of snoring in between. We will see a new part of the old U.S. of A., polish off some unfinished novels, renew friendships, hike some leisurely Smoky Mountains trails, ignore a lot of external stimuli, rediscover ourselves from inside out. We want to accomplish what Thoreau did over 100 years ago. Some of the last lines in his *Walden* read:

> I went to the woods because I wished to live deliberately, to front only the essential facts of life, and see if I could learn what it had to teach, and not, when I came to die, discover that I had not lived.[52]

During the next several weeks I hope something like that happens to each of us -- and to all of us.

With every good wish, I am your pastor and friend.

August 1, 1979

Dear Fellow Workaholics:

Some folk have the capacity to relax. They shift themselves into neutral. Their muscles detensify. Their heartbeat slows down. Their fevered world of consciousness cools. A quietness settles upon them. They are still -- very, very still. A brainwave machine measuring their intellectual and emotional activity would show a smooth line at the bottom of the oscilloscope -- "flatline." Complete relaxation is much like death.

Millions crave such a state of non-awareness. They would blot out the harsh realities of life in the raw. They would float in a netherworld where neither pain nor delight reached them. All would be grey, middlish, tepid.

Gurus from the East merchandise techniques whereby Westerners can achieve momentary escape from reality. Muzak cushions the discordant sounds of human activity with a shield of soft harmonies piped from hidden speakers in dentists' reception rooms, shopping malls, elevators. Doctors prescribe and pharmacists dispense pink pills and yellow capsules to anesthetize persons against pain -- either physical or psychic. Many turn to the brewer and/or the bartender: a shot or two -- a cocktail and more -- and things do not appear so rough as before. Preachers have capitalized on this craving for relaxation. They ride the radio and TV wavelengths, peddling a "peace of mind" gospel. "Snake-oil salesmen" they are. They do very well at it.

I have never developed the capacity to relax -- and I certainly refuse to use any external means to get what is not a part of my internal makeup. It is rare for me to be totally at ease. Even when I rest, I work at it! My mind is never turned off. Not even in sleep. I am too conscious of the swift passage of my hours to let any of them slip unfilled into the void. It grieves me to do nothing, to feel nothing, to see nothing -- to leave any minute unfilled with "60 seconds worth of distance run." My head, my heart, my hands are always in gear -- cruising along at the speed limit -- often in overdrive. Keats felt that sense of urgency with which I live 24 hours a day:

> When I have fears that I may cease to be
> Before my pen has glean'd my teeming brain...[53]

Maybe it's just one of the hazards of the profession. Comes with the territory. Ministers must be involved. They swim in a whirlpool of activity. They spin in a tornado of demands. Ministers hear, feel, see, experience more sorrow and more joy than most others. Consequently, there are few moments left for leisure. Ministers labor for the Master who called them into the vineyard with the words: "Work for the night is coming!"[54]

The "peace of mind" of the minister cannot be learned at the footstool of an Eastern guru, or absorbed by an open ear filled with Muzak's harmonies, or picked up at the drug store, or carried in a brown bag, or sipped à la condensed milk gospel broadcast over radio and TV. Peace of mind for the minister -- and for all Christians -- can never be an escape from reality. Rather peace of mind will come coincidentally with an advance into reality. The Christian's faith is not a retreat from the world. Rather -- it is a faith that overcomes the world! Jesus offered these encouraging words:

> Peace I leave with you; my peace
> I give to you.... Let not your hearts
> be troubled, neither let them be afraid. (John 14:27 RSV)
> I have said this to you, that in me you may have peace.
> In the world you have tribulation; but be of good cheer, I have
> overcome the world. (John 16:33 RSV)

Unrelaxed and harried though I may be, I am happy that this Church grants me the privilege of being a minister in its midst. There will come a time for rest. That time comes too soon.

February 27, 1987

Dear Christian Friends:

Ash Wednesday 'minds me of my mortality. Our young people burn the palm fronds from last year's Palm Sunday worship service. With her index finger a fellow mortal stirs the ashes of those palm fronds. Then, with her ash-darkened fingertip she marks a cross on my forehead and speaks those solemn words: "Remember man that thou art dust and to dust thou shalt return." (based on Genesis 3:19). It is a shivery moment -- raises goosebumps on my arms -- makes a lump form in my throat.

Death and I are no strangers. Being a minister, it just comes with the territory. I deal with death quite often -- but it is always other people's death. I visit folk who have heard the word "cancer" -- and who know they are terminally ill. I sit with families in the ICU/CCU lounge -- families who know that the end is near for their loved one. I precede the casket down the church aisle intoning the opening words of the funeral service: "'I am the resurrection and the life,' [saith the Lord.] 'He who believes in me, though he die, yet shall he live.'" (John 11:25 RSV) I stand at the head of the grave and speak the somber phrases: "Earth to earth -- ashes to ashes -- dust to dust." Death and I are no strangers. But we are not friends, either. We are enemies. And will be enemies to the end.

Though I am well-acquainted with death, still it is seldom that I consider my own mortality. A colleague in the ministry may suffer a fatal heart attack, but not me. My dad is beyond the "three score and ten, or even by reason of strength, fourscore." He doesn't have much longer before he will answer the "Sunset and evening star, And one clear call for me!"[55] But that time is far away for me. My neighbor may be diagnosed as inoperable and terminal, but not me! Death is for others -- not for me!

Until Ash Wednesday, and a friend dips her finger in ashes, marks a cross on my forehead and speaks the words: "Remember man that thou art dust and to dust thou shalt return." Somberness floods my soul. The atmosphere becomes grey. The conversation loses it lightness. Then death -- my own death -- becomes real to me. Each person at our Ash Wednesday ceremony will be 'minded of her mortality in a tangible, visible fashion. That ceremony may not change your way of looking at death. But it will change your way of looking at life! Come!

September 30, 1988

Dear Christian Friends:

Paw Paw Landry had a cornea implant three months ago. The surgeon had hoped to save the eye, and, if possible, restore its vision. The surgery seemed to be successful at first. But an infection set in, grew worse, the eye had to be removed. Well, that eye saw him through 83 years of life: flowers, check-writing, hunting, foods, holidays, sunrises, graduations, neighbors, driving, fishing, grandchildren, funerals, gardens. The list is over 80 years long! His regret on the failure of his surgery was expressed to me briefly, "Bobby, I sure hate it that I lost my eye."

For the rest of his life Paw Paw will have to do with only one eye -- that eye is over 80 also! Still, with that one eye he can enjoy TV sports. And he can see, as well as hear, the news and weather. Of course, the best things he ever sees are the faces of his family: wife, children, grandchildren. That one eye will stand him in good stead for the latter years: flowers, check-writing, sunrises, gardens, etc. If and when he loses that eye he won't be getting a seeing-eye dog. Paw Paw has a seeing-eye wife! Together, they will celebrate their 63rd Wedding Anniversary December 26! She will show him around. And when she can't show him around any longer, they have five seeing-eye sons and three seeing-eye daughters! And ten seeing-eye sons and daughters-in-law!

The story goes that when General William Booth became blind he asked his son, Bramwell, "Is that so?" His son answered, "Yes, Father, you are blind." Then General Booth said, "You mean that I shall never again be able to see your face!" His son, Bramwell, answered, "Father, I am afraid that you shall never again be able to see my face." Then it was that the founder of the Salvation Army showed the stuff of which he was made, "God knows best. I have done what I could for God and the people with my eyes. Now I must do what I can for God and the people without my eyes."[56] And so, he did! On the Great Judgment Day, General William Booth will lead a host of his fellows right through the gates of pearl -- without his eyes! Booth died blind and still by faith he trod, eyes still dazzled by the ways of God.

Vision is a precious gift. With it we see the clouds on the horizon -- the ski-jump nose on an infant's face -- the dew-pearled rose -- the traffic signal -- the morning headlines -- the Communion cup -- the voting ballot. The eye is the door through which the universe of history and novels and friends and letters and seasons and places enters the heart. A precious gift -- yes! And we are grateful! Last week I took a couple of days off to go to Lake Charles to see my family: father, mother, brothers, sisters. My vision has improved.

April 28, 1989

Dear Friends of Children and Youth:

The highlight of my teenage summers was a week at the Acadian Christian Service Camp in Lake Arthur, Louisiana. Great things happened there. Our days started with a bell calling us to "Morning Watch" where we put on our most pious faces, read prescribed passages of scripture, devoted ourselves to prayer. After breakfast we cleaned up our bunks for inspection. Then we had an hour of "Old Testament" followed by an hour of "The Four-Fold Gospel." After chapel there was a class about Christian living in the 20th Century. Lunch. Rest period (but not much rest). Recreation (Softball, Swimming, Music). Cleanup for supper. Vesper hour. Canteen. Friendship Circle. Bedtime was signaled by the same bell that had awakened us. These weeks were enriched by talent nights, Bible drills, stunt nights, devotionals, concerts, visits with missionaries, etc. We serenaded the girls with "Tell Me Why?" Joined in pillow fights (before foam rubber pillows!). Paired-off with new friends. Memorized the books of the Bible. Exchanged addresses. Wept when we broke camp on Saturday!

But camp didn't end when we broke camp. We took "camp" home with us. We were different. On arriving home after my first week at Acadian Christian Service Camp, I ran to my father, threw my arms around him, kissed him. He was so surprised he held me by the shoulders and exclaimed: "Hey! My little Bobby went off for a week of camp and came home and kissed his Daddy!" That was different! We both were surprised because such a spontaneous show of joy and affection was unusual in our family. "Camp" continued its good influence on us for the remainder of the summer. We were more responsible in our work around the house. Our language was less coarse. When we were back in school, we were more serious about our studies. We were better persons. We stayed in touch with our camp friends at youth rallies and revival meetings. We wrote letters. Looked forward to the next summer when we would again gather under the screened-in pavilion with the sawdust floor and join with 150 other teenagers to lift the Gospel favorites: *Amazing Grace -- When the Roll Is Called up Yonder -- Revive Us Again -- I Come to the Garden Alone.*

My faith has grown in the 35-40 years since. I see Christianity in a much broader frame of reference. I take the Bible more seriously -- but less literally. My church connections are different. Still, it all started way back there in summer camp on Lake Arthur. I am so grateful for the good influence of those dear and gentle people who gave up a week of hard-earned vacation -- endured six hot, humid days on the lakeside -- put up with our foibles and shenanigans -- in order to share with us the faith and hope and love of Christ. And I shall never forget my older brother who paid my registration fees so I could benefit from a church program that had not even existed when he was a teenager.

This summer we will have many campers and youth attending camps and conferences. The Church will automatically cover one-half of their registration fees. Most of our kids are able to pay the other half. Some cannot. If you want to help, your gift will make a big difference in a young person's life.

June 21, 1991

Dear Christian Friends:

I lost last Thursday, June 13. Don't know where it is. Can't remember how I spent it. My daily journal for that 24-hour period is missing! In that journal I keep a record of my activities: conferences, correspondence, phone calls, hospital visits, more significant items (worship services, funerals, weddings, pastoral letters, sermons, etc.) Even note some lesser matters: errands, chores, personal items. But last Thursday, June 13, I was whirling in such a tornado of calls and chores and writings and committees that I had no time to jot down notes of what was going on. Now, there is a blank space in the record of my past -- even though that day was really quite unblank! And I am bothered by this. I like to know where I have been. Keeping my daily journal is a discipline that drives me to attempt putting 62 seconds worth of distance run into every unforgiving minute. Can't be done -- but I keep trying. Paradoxically, having no record of Thursday, June 13, is mute testimony that I was doing so much I had no time to keep a record of what I was doing! And I am uneasy about that! Why? Because I may have been very busy with trivialities, stuffing each unforgiving minute with empty motion, shadow-boxing my way through the day, filling that space of time with 24 hours of Styrofoam! But I doubt that!

I not only like to keep a record of where I have been, whom I have seen, what I have done -- I also like to anticipate where I am headed, who I must see, what I am going to do. Yes, I generally keep a journal of what happened yesterday and a plan-book for what I intend for tomorrow: hospital visits, phone calls, letters, committee meetings, sermons, etc. My daily list of "to-do's" runs from 12 to 16 items. Seldom get them all done. But it feels good each time I check off one of these dozen or so items -- such as finishing a Sunday School lesson or spending an hour with a bereaved family. It takes only about five minutes to jot down my daily list of "to-do's." That list helps me put first things first, tend to significant matters, postpone the small stuff 'til later. Both Erma Bombeck and I have been into this list business for years -- a long time before the Irvings came out with their best sellers of Lists! But neither Erma nor I have turned our lists into commercial ventures.

Knowing where we have been -- anticipating where we are headed -- these help us to fill to the brim the time in between! I like to think of Paul's triad in this light: "Now abide faith, hope, and love." Faith is trust based on yesterday experiences. Because of this faith/trust we lean into the future with confidence. That's hope! God has not failed us in the past. God will not forsake us in the future. God's steadfast, sure love is from everlasting to everlasting. Meanwhile, our faith (memory of yesterday) and our hope (anticipation about tomorrow) issues in energetic, confident, compassionate action today! That's love! "So faith, hope, love abide, these three; but the greatest of these is love!" (I Corinthians 13:13 RSV)

Where we have been is not so significant as where we are headed. And both "where we have been" and "where we are headed" -- both together are not near so important as what we do in between these two times -- that razor's edge that slices through the millisecond between past and future. Paul Tillich called it "The Eternal Now." My own record of last Thursday, June 13, is lost -- both the daily journal of what I did, as well as the list of "to-dos" I intended. No matter! The intentions and memories of that day are written on the mind of God -- indelibly. Even if that day held nothing greater (or lesser) than a cup of cold water for a thirsty soul. And on the Great Judgment Day the angel bookkeeper will hand me both the daily journal and the list of "to-do's." That angel's smile will reassure me that what I lost last Thursday was found and treasured in heaven. Jesus came that we might have life and have it abundantly.

Now! Today! This moment. "Behold, now is the accepted time; behold, now is the day of salvation!" (II Corinthians 6:2 RSV) Remembering yesterday is important. Planning tomorrow is important, too. But filling today is most important. Whoever fills "The Eternal Now" to the brim will hear the kind judgment, "Well done!"

Whether you keep "lists of to-do's" and "daily journals" or not -- still -- I am confident that your life, too, is abundant and full and rich. Together let us all give thanks for God's good gifts to us of life and energy and desire and health and family and friends and faith and hope and love!

June 25, 1993

Dear Fellow Christians:

In a pitching frame of mind. Had to come to this sooner or later. And "sooner" is better than "later." Otherwise my stacks of stuff would shove me out of the house! Was up early Tuesday. Shuffling through stacks in the living room: books -- notes -- letters -- newspaper clippings -- greeting cards. File this. Pitch that! Keep this. Pitch that! Save this. Pitch that! Two hours added up to two Hefty bags of tossings! All stuff I should not have kept in the first place. Off with the trash. The living room looks a lot less trashy!

Same story -- second verse on Thursday night. Cleared things off the dining table and chairs. Stacks of stuff had multiplied in this most hallowed place where once we shared family meals: magazines -- paid bills -- IRS files -- articles by Mike Kelley, John Kelso, Billy Porterfield -- travel maps/pamphlets -- letters to re-read. Two hours -- one more Hefty. And we were able to clean, dust, re-set things for our Father's Day dinner.

Friday, my file drawer for back issues of church newsletters had reached its capacity -- plus! Something had to go if I was to squeeze in our May and June back issues. Dragged out two overstuffed file folders: The first was marked: "General Assembly -- Louisville -- 1971." The second: "General Assembly -- Cincinnati -- 1973." Contents? Voting badges -- Assembly Business Dockets -- programs -- flyers for various church agencies -- reports -- hotel receipts -- maps of Louisville and Cincinnati. By actual weight (USPS scales) exactly 3-pounds-4-and-one-half ounces! Needless stuff that has taken up needed space in my files for over 20 years! From it all I salvaged two program booklets with favorite hymns, mimeographed copies of five Bible studies by Fred Craddock, four addresses delivered at the Cincinnati Assembly. The rest I pitched! Tossed! Disposed of! Now my back issues of the May and June are snugged in that space.

For years I have been a collector. Clutter gets rid of wasted space! Tables were loaded down with books. Chairs received stacks of unread newspapers. Our wall-to-wall carpet was covered with wall-to-wall stuff. Judie is teaching me about pitching! Tossing! Disposing of! And it feels good. Our living room has been neat-ified. Our dining room was the setting for a great dinner last Sunday. Last night I got a start on my office. And there's lots more! Tables in my "Upper Room" need to be unloaded à la "two hours -- two Hefties." Our bedroom. Garage. Oldsmobile trunk. Collecting and keeping all this stuff -- 20-25-30 years -- has become a burden. Feels good to get shed of it. Won't be a distraction to me anymore. I'll be able to focus more on the more significant part of my ministry. I am trading off a lot of trash so I can concentrate on a few treasures!

Fosdick once told the story of the famous Bargello portrait of Dante. It had been lost for years. Art enthusiasts knew there was such a portrait. It was listed in all of Bargello's inventories. But, they didn't know where it was. Then a student started his search with the room where tradition had located it. That room was a storehouse for wastage: straw and lumber littered the floor; whitewash covered the walls. The rubbish was carted out. The whitewash was removed. Old lines long obscured began to appear. Colors long hidden became visible. At last, the grave, lofty face of the great poet was recovered for the world. Nobody had destroyed the Bargello portrait of Dante. But somebody had littered it up. Straw and lumber and whitewash had seemed to somebody more important than that portrait! That student carted out the trash. And he uncovered the treasure!

Well, I'm into my last decade of work as a minister. Next month I'll turn 57! Eight years is not enough time to finish all I had intended. But I'll do better in those eight years if I pitch away a lot of trash and concentrate on the treasure! No more stuff made of Styrofoam and straw. From here to the end it's all sterling and 24 carat!

August 19, 1994

Dear Christian Friends:

Some years ago a Scottish minister was given a well-earned, though honorary, doctor's degree by his alma mater. The dean of the seminary suggested the minister submit a book of his own to the seminary on the occasion of receiving his doctoral robe and hood. He did. The book the minister submitted was his "Appointments Book and Daily Journal" for the previous year! A very original piece! Weddings -- funerals -- baptisms -- worship services -- Sunday School classes -- board meetings -- camps and retreats -- civic affairs -- committees -- sermons -- letters -- counseling -- appointments -- church dinners -- hospital visits -- financial campaigns -- Advent and Christmas and Lenten schedules -- staff meetings -- the 365 pages of his book were well-filled, foot-noted, dog-eared! Not much good for reading - except by the writer. Never would make a best-seller. Destined to be tossed aside by grandchildren as they rummaged through his library decades later. Still, his "Appointments Book and Daily

Journal" was the book the minister handed to the seminary dean on the occasion when he was robed in black and hooded in red and purple.

My own doctoral robe with three chevrons on each sleeve and my own doctoral hood trimmed with black and gold (our school colors) and red (for divinity) were set on my shoulders by The Reverend Doctor John R. Killinger, Jr. The date was May 30, 1972 -- over 22 years ago! The place was Vanderbilt Divinity School, Nashville, Tennessee. (To outsiders, Nashville is "Music City, U.S.A." To insiders, Nashville is "the Athens of the South.") For the occasion I had submitted a "book"-- a dissertation on the life and ministry of Harry Emerson Fosdick. That "book" had been three years in the making: research, writing, rewriting. It was a substantial piece of scholarly work then. It remains today a basic item in the bibliography of any subsequent scholar writing a dissertation on the life and ministry of Harry Emerson Fosdick.

Since 1972 I have written 22 more "books" -- "Appointments Books and Daily Journals." Each of these has been filled with notes relating to 365 days in the life and ministry of Fabaus Landry! None of these makes for much good reading -- except by the writer. None of them will ever be turned into a best-seller. All of them will be disposed of decades from now by grandchildren rummaging through my undusted library. But, for the present, those "books" are very significant to the present writer! The current "Appointments Book and Daily Journal" is very significant! The first eight months of the year have been brimming with good things. "My cup runneth over!" And already, the latter four months: September-October-November-December are filling up -- a great four months! It certainly appears so in prospect. Let's do everything we can -- together! -- to make it so in retrospect! As great as are the problems before us -- the possibilities for good are greater!

March 27, 1998

Dear Friends Far and Near--Then and Now--Yesterday and Tomorrow:

"It is so constantly there!" Dr. Jessie Fletcher was describing his pastor/preacher role at the First Baptist Church (FBC). Dr. Fletcher had come to FBC hoping to gear down from his speedy career in the fast lane as the Executive Director of the Foreign Missions Board of the Southern Baptist Convention. Before FBC, he had been throughout this world! Much of his time and energy had been devoted to studying resumes and interviewing candidates. Much of his time and energy had been spent reviewing standards, making evaluations, gathering resources, assessing needs. Much in supervising a considerable office staff. Much in visiting Southern Baptist seminaries. Much in convincing congregations to dig a little deeper. Much in inspecting mission stations, schools, hospitals, chapels, etc. -- from Mexico to Madagascar, from Alaska to Zaire. Much in praying for all sorts and conditions of missionaries: some energetic and resourceful, others lethargic and inefficient -- some youthful and hopeful, others wrinkled and worn -- some successes who were camouflaged failures and others failures who were camouflaged successes. Much too much of his time and energy had been dissipated rushing from airport to airport to airport trying to cover the world. It was impossible!

Shifting out of his fast-lane administrative career, Dr. Fletcher thought he would steer into the slow-lane pastor/preacher thing. In Knoxville he intended to schedule a weekly game of golf. Maybe two! Mondays would be a day off. He would fish, paint, garden, hike, shop. He would block off a day or two a month for his grandchildren in Asheville. Morning hours would be protected for uninterrupted reading, study, reflection. Followed by leisurely lunches. His long postponed missionary novel would be finished. He and his wife would build a cabin retreat near the Smoky Mountains National Park. Enjoy breezes and blossoms and beasties. No phone. No TV. No mailbox.

Surprise! Surprise! Surprise! The Shangri-La leisure Dr. Fletcher had envisioned remained a vision. After 36 months at FBC, he confessed that his pastor/preacher role had consumed him, his time, his energy, his family, his everything! "It is so constantly there!" Saturday nights without the sermon laid by. Hospital visits put off 'til later. Fellowship dinners that pre-empted evenings with his lovely wife. Phone calls that went unanswered. Funerals and all that came before them and more that followed after them. Civic luncheons with mashed potatoes, green beans, rubber chicken. Weddings! Many of which he had to finesse to his associate. Refereeing battles between the Deacons and the Trustees. Letters. Difficulties in the Sunday School. Patching together a ballooning budget with smaller patches. Roof leaks! Turf struggles between staff members. "It is so constantly there!"

After only three years as pastor/preacher at the Baptist church, Dr. Fletcher was convinced his time and energy would be better managed as President of Hardin-Simmons University in Abilene, Texas. A third generation Texan, he pulled on his boots and returned to his roots. Surprise! Surprise! Surprise! Within three months, he discovered that button-holing West Texas ranchers for millions to build libraries and to endow chairs and to underwrite scholarships, recruiting faculty, revising budgets, presiding at ceremonies, dealing with alumni, and much, much more would consume all his time and energy. And then some! Being a college president was a lot like being a mission board executive or being a pastor/preacher. As Yogi Berra said, "It was deja vu all over again!"[57] "It is so constantly there!"

Dr. Fletcher's confession rang true twenty years ago! It rings true now! "It is so constantly there!" Does it ever go away? Such as when we bed down and slumber off into the benevolent armistice of sleep? Hardly! Though our bodies are motionless and our eyes are closed, still, the delights and the disappointments of yesterday are like an unfinished symphony in our subconscious. And the desires and the demands of tomorrow awaken us early. "It is so constantly there!" Dr. Fletcher "hung it up" six years ago. Golfing -- fishing -- painting -- gardening -- grandchildren -- leisurely lunches with his lovely wife -- mountain retreat -- maybe. But maybe not, too! My friend is probably having a kind of "fast-lane retirement." In a changing world that in many ways is unchanging, he still confesses, "It is so constantly there!" So it goes! So it comes! But there is something worse. Much worse: "It is so constantly not there!"

Your friend and pastor/preacher.

May 1, 1998

Dear Christian Friends:

Sumtimes, Ah is up! Sumtimes, Ah is down! Oh, yes! Lord! Sumtimes, Ah feels Ah'm upside-down! Oh, yes! Lord! Right on! Life is not on a level. Rather, there are highs and there are lows. Peaks and valleys. Sunshine and shadow. Good times and not so good times. And whoever pretends otherwise is but a pretender.

The bright optimist with the perma-pressed smile may fool others who see only the surface. But she cannot fool herself. Her happy facade may camouflage a load of loneliness, disappointment, fear, sorrow, grief.

The dark pessimist who covers his world with gloomy notions and sad sighs of "Woe is me! Woe is me!" sees a grey cloud within every silver lining! But surely, there must be more than depression and despair and doom in any person's life. He may complain about the weeds in his garden. But it is a garden!

The pastor/preacher's life is like a seesaw, too. Sumtimes Ah is up! Sumtimes Ah is down! Oh, yes! Lord! Sumtimes Ah is up! -- elated, as on Easter Sunday when the pews are packed, the music is magnificent, the lilies testify to new life in Christ! Sumtimes Ah is down! -- deflated, as on the low Sundays after Easter when the congregation has thinned down, the music is ordinary, and our routine returns with the "same old same old."

Welcoming new infants into the church family -- that's a high! Leading a bride and a groom in speaking their marriage vows -- that's a high! Giving thanks for a successful surgery -- that's a high! Sumtimes Ah is up! Oh, yes! Lord! Following a hearse to the cemetery -- that's a low! Failing in an attempt to help patch together a failed marriage -- that's a low! Finding folk who have so much for which to be thankful, yet have so little gratitude -- that's a low! Sumtimes Ah is down! Oh, yes! Lord! Sumtimes Ah is up! Sumtimes Ah is down! Oh, yes! Lord! We all enjoy moments when we can sing: "Surely goodness and mercy shall follow me all the days of my life; and I shall dwell in the house of the

Lord for ever!" (Psalms 23:6 RSV) But there are times, too, when with a heart as heavy as lead we must "walk through the valley of the shadow of death." (Psalms 23:4 KJV) Our life swings like a pendulum between the brightness of heaven and the darkness of hell. Up! Down! -- High! Low! -- Peak! Valley! -- Sunshine! Shadow! -- Good times! Not so good times! "Sumtimes Ah is up! Sumtimes Ah is down! Oh, yes! Lord! Sumtimes Ah feels Ah'm upside-down! Oh, yes! Lord!" Leslie Weatherhead, the reverend pastor/preacher of London's City Temple, encouraged all of us -- both smilers and frowners -- with these hopeful and helpful lines: "I can only write down this simple testimony. Like all men, I love and prefer the sunny uplands of experience when health, happiness and success abound.... There are such things as the treasures of darkness. The darkness, thank God, passes, but what one learns in the darkness, one possesses forever!"[58]

7

Social/Political

December 9, 1963

Of National Import:

The dark cloud of tragedy and death hung over our Thanksgiving Season -- and continues to over-shadow our days as we approach Christmas. The shock and sorrow over our President's death has left us momentarily helpless. What can we do? Erect a memorial of stone and steel? Send a note of consolation to the President's widow? Take our vengeance out on the assassin? Blame the radicals? Write an article expressing admiration for the fallen martyr of "The American Way"? Preach a sermon interpreting his life in terms of "Faith and Destiny"? Or preach another sermon on the "Hope" that was his for America and for all men everywhere? Editorialize his work for peace? Memorialize his name by engraving it on the steel spans that bridge the Ohio between Louisville and New Albany?

Yes -- these and many other things have been and will be done -- despite our helplessness. But how pitifully mean and small are these things in contrast to Lyndon Johnson's suggestion in his address to Congress: "...no memorial, oration, or eulogy could more eloquently honor President Kennedy's memory than the earliest possible passage of the civil rights bill for which he fought."[59]

You can share in this living memorial by writing a brief note to Mr. Johnson endorsing his stand on civil rights, or to your Congressman (House Office Building, Washington, D.C.) or your Senators (Senate Office Building, Washington, D.C.) to urge them to pass the bill that had top priority on Kennedy's list.

In behalf of brotherhood, I am, faithfully, your pastor.

July 3, 1964

Should Logan County Remain Dry?

First of all -- Logan County is not dry! It is "legally dry" -- but actually it is as wet as is Hopkinsville or Bowling Green. For instance, Todd County is "legally dry," too. But two weeks ago a tragic accident occurred on the road between Elkton and Guthrie, taking 3 lives. It was rumored, and it was a mighty strong rumor, that the cause of the accident was liquor. Where did the young man driving from Elkton get his liquor? As for our own county, our jailor spends most of his weekends sobering up yokels who have taken on too much moonshine. Where do they get their liquor?

One of our citizens of Berea, KY, tells of testifying on behalf of an acquaintance who was in court for drunk driving and for having caused an accident. When asked if he had seen the man before the accident, he said, "Yes, I talked with him on the way to town. And he wasn't drunk. And he came to town and he had an accident in Russellville. How could he have been drunk? He couldn't get any liquor in Russellville." To which the courtroom roared with laughter. Unbeknownst to him, anyone could get all the liquor be wanted in Russellville! And he didn't have to be 21, either.

If we are going to allow the bootleggers to operate we just might as well be "legally wet." In fact, it would be better if we were wet. Then perhaps we could control the sale and use of alcohol. Then perhaps our political situation would clear up a bit. Then perhaps we could allow a person the liberty of his own conscience instead of attempting to legislate his morals for him.

There is a real moral and religious issue involved. We can't dodge it by theoretically "tee-totalling" our whole county on election day. Bootleggers and preachers, crooked politicians and the W.C.T.U. (Women's Christian Temperance Union) are all against legalized liquor. They make strange bedfellows, indeed! This preacher will not be around when and if this matter is again placed on the ballot. But if he were, there is no doubt as to how he would encourage his parishioners to vote.

November 19, 1964

Dear Friends in Christ,

Next Sunday, November 22, is the anniversary of the tragic death of President Kennedy. A year ago our words of Thanksgiving turned to ashes, our hymns of praise brought forth tears, our national anthem sounded as a funeral dirge, the land was draped in black, the flags flew at half-mast -- and so did our hearts. Sunday will mark the end of one year of national mourning for the young man who lifted up our hearts and hands and gave us a hope for peace. The mood of sadness still lingers in our hearts despite the passage of 365 days. And the sense of emptiness that must still be his widow's and his children's is shared by all Americans. John Fitzgerald Kennedy has left a void that has in no way been filled -- even by a landslide election.

Your minister, for a time a student of history and of political science, had a fine appreciation for the man from Hyannis, who was himself a keen historian and political scientist. Mr. Kennedy was known and loved; he was disagreed with but respected; he shared himself with his people -- but his task made him a lonely man. He had a sense of history and destiny unmatched by any president since Woodrow Wilson. He wrote *Profiles in Courage*, but he himself was a profile in courage. And his wife wrote her profile in courage in those tragic four days when we all sat glued to our T.V. sets -- a nation bearing a great loss -- with none to comfort her.

It will not at all be inappropriate in our worship next Sunday to remember this national tragedy -- and also to look to the future with faith and hope -- a faith and hope that was shared by JFK. Our service will include the hymns *God of Our Fathers, Dear Lord and Father of Mankind*, and *O Beautiful For Spacious Skies*. The sermon is entitled "Land -- Man -- Hope: Gifts of God" and is based on Deuteronomy 8. You will do well to read the entire chapter before coming to worship. May all praise and thanks be given to God.

Faithfully, your pastor.

October 17, 1973

Dear Friends on the Right and Friends on the Left:

I am a conservative sort of fellow. Never did feel comfortable in this season's outfit -- always ran a year or two behind in fashions: shoes, shirts, suits, ties. Likewise in church I generally prefer the traditional, the accepted, the familiar, the accustomed, the usual. What about change? It's O.K. I don't resent it or impede it -- but I rather like to go at it moderate-like, less than break-neck speed. In an era of sweeping revolutions when the rules of the game seem to change in process I do have a hankering for the tried and proven, for the stable, steadfast techniques of the past. Though I am not a moss back, a diehard, a reactionary, I am, nonetheless, a conservative sort of fellow.

But there is another side of me, too. The side that is not yet satisfied with things as they are. The side that believes things can be made better. The side that is impatient with rigidity, obstinacy, inflexibility, stagnation. I am not content merely to retrace our fathers' ruts, beating the same well-worn path, doing it all "the way we have always done it." This side of me takes exception to that line we sing every Sunday: "...as it was in the beginning, is now and ever shall be...."[60] This side of me wants to experiment, venture out a bit, live dangerously, risk, try something new. This side of me is unwilling to believe that "our fathers were wiser than we."

A dear friend put it in these words: "the most successful business man is the man who holds onto the old just as long as it is good and grabs the new just as soon as it is better." That's how it should be within the church -- a tentative balance between old stability and new creativity, an equilibrium between conservative and liberal attitudes. Order amidst change -- change amidst order. Sometimes we move a bit to the right (conservative). Then sometimes we tend a bit to the left (liberal). But always we move ahead!

What is your temperament? Do you wish to conserve the values hammered out in generations past? We need that! Or do you want to design and create new values for 1973 and beyond? We need that too!

The church provides a broad umbrella for all kinds of people -- some rich, some poor; some old, some young; some sophisticated, some simple; some "citified," some "country-fied," some conservative, some liberal. And a whole lot of room, too, for a whole lot of people who are rather in between the extremes. What a salmagundi[61] it is that we have within this happy fellowship! "Variety is the spice of life." Variety of thought, diversity of opinion, intermixture of ideas: these add "something extra" to our church life! I am delighted we were not all made by the same cookie cutter! And so are you!

With "a friend on the right and a friend on the left," I am, your friend and pastor.

November 7, 1973

Dear Autumn and Armistice Day Friends:

The sugar maple outside our kitchen window is about 35% of the way from a vivid green to an angry red. It is "a thing of beauty." And the blue jay that plays in its branches and the fluffy cat that sleeps in the "Snoopy" house at its roots make that tree more so "a thing of beauty."

This morning I was rinsing the soggy Raisin Bran and Grape-Nuts Flakes out of the breakfast dishes, cleaning the mustard off two knives (why does it take an 8 year old two knives to spread mustard on one sandwich?), delighting in that mixed-up sugar maple -- then came the tune and words of "Little Green Apples" over our $25.95 radio. What a pleasant, what a magnificent way to begin the day -- soapsuds and all!

Out front the Great Smoky Mountains cut a jagged outline against the eastern horizon -- a silent reminder of strength and of eternity. Took a minute to run out and scrape the ice off the old Ford's windshield so that Judie could drive to school. Should have had more than a T-shirt on! Brrrr!

Then back to the kitchen -- to the reds and greens of the sugar maple -- to the soggy Raisin Bran -- to the mustard-covered knives -- to the radio with its bad news about the fuel shortage this winter. Drudgery? Some folk may think so. But I refuse to believe it! To live and to move and to have my being in East Tennessee in November 1973 -- this is an immense privilege -- soapsuds and all! "This is the day which the Lord hath made; [I will] rejoice and be glad in it!" (Psalms 118:24 RSV)

Yet -- I sense not only the immense privilege of it all. I feel also the <u>immense responsibility</u> involved. That's a big word -- <u>responsibility</u>. I feel that all the time. But I feel it much more at 10:50 A.M. Sunday than at 8:00 A.M. Tuesday. At 10:50 A.M. Sunday -- that's when I stand in the pulpit! Privilege! Of course, it is! Responsibility? Amen! In what proportions? About an ounce of privilege for a pound of responsibility!

As I look out over a congregation as variegated as the leaves in Cade's Cove -- as I see people who drudge their way through soggy Raisin Bran and mustardy knives -- as I remember folk who have lost the gleam in the eye and the spring in the step -- as I reflect on men and women, on boys and girls who are botching it all up -- Gosh! My shoes at that moment are not filled with privilege, good friend. It's that other word -- <u>responsibility</u>!

This will be especially true next Sunday, November 11, which is the 55th anniversary of Armistice Day.[62] My responsibility will be to offer a Christian perspective on the most crucial issue of this 20th century -- the issue of war and peace. I hope to lift several of you above the level of "doing-nothing-about-it-ness." Ideas already are churning around in my head. An undelivered sermon is a bothersome thing. Sometimes a delivered sermon is a bothersome thing, too! My prayer is that next Sunday's sermon will bother you into a sense of responsibility -- and that you will be moved to do something about it!

With a gleam in my eye and a spring in my step -- and with a sense of immense responsibility in my heart, I am your pastor and friend.

March 5, 1981

EXCERPT FROM A SERMON BY DR. FABAUS LANDRY -- March 1, 1981

The issue being discussed at Heska Amuna Synagogue was unfair religious pressure exerted on minor children 11 and 12 years of age <u>on school grounds during school hours</u>. These children were Jewish. They were being harassed to change from the religion of their homes and synagogues to the faith of the representatives of YOKE (Youth of Knoxville Evangelism). My own children have felt similar pressures from similar organizations <u>on school grounds during school hours</u>. The pressure for the conversion of any minor child under such conditions is clearly unacceptable. That holds whether it be pressure for a conversion from Christianity to Judaism or pressure for a conversion from Judaism to Christianity. This also holds true with reference to pressure for a conversion from one Christian denomination to another, such as, from Methodist to Presbyterian, or from Christian Church (Disciples of Christ) to Baptist.

Since I desire no such pressures on my children -- I will place no such pressures on the children of my Jewish brothers and sisters -- or on anybody else's children. Within this framework the two sentences reported out of context now make good and wholesome sense: "I don't want anyone pressuring my children to become Baptists. I would almost as soon they became Jewish." In either case the conversion of my minor child yielding to unfair pressures on school grounds during school hours is highly unacceptable to me. One such conversion of my child to be Baptist -- is only slightly less unacceptable than the other -- to be a Jew. The only difference in degree being that a conversion of my child to the Baptist faith would leave her still under the Christian umbrella -- whereas a conversion to Judaism would place her under an umbrella with which I am much less familiar. In either case, I would prefer no conversion whatever.

My friends know me to be a man of gentleness and peace whose religious sympathies are broad enough to include not only Christians of a different stripe or polka dot than my own -- but also broad enough to embrace persons of other religions as well: Jews, Muslims, Hindus, Buddhists. "The love of God is broader than the measure of the [man's] mind!"[63]

Though in classical Christian terminology some may be outside the pall of "salvation in Christ" -- I still believe that God's love extends to all mankind -- whether "in Christ" or out. God's affections are more extensive than the borders of the church. I believe that all are children of the Creator God and that ultimately we shall be joined in one loving family where social justice and personal liberty and individual fulfillment and community compassion and universal peace are the characteristics of our life together. "Thy kingdom come, Thy will be done in earth, as it is in heaven!" (Matthew 6:10 KJV)

I am sorry that some were offended by what appeared to be remarks unbecoming a minister. Compassion and forgiveness are at the heart of the Judeo-Christian tradition -- whether expressed in Orthodox or Protestant or Catholic or Jewish terms. My sin was surely not of the heart. Rather, it was in ad-libbing several words which could be so easily misconstrued when excerpted and reproduced in black and white -- totally apart from the wholesome setting and tone of voice and the contextual statement in which they were first uttered. The issue is a serious one. If I did sin I am happy to have sinned in the process of addressing a concern of major consequence to the spiritual life and the religious freedom of our community than to have sinned by my silence.

November 29, 1985

Dear Fellow Citizens of the World:

It was something big! And we are grateful for it. President Reagan and First Secretary Gorbachev talked with each other last week. We do not know what they said in their private conversations. A bit of small talk: family, weather, pets, tastes, friends. A lot of big talk: disarmament. Reagan and Gorbachev talked <u>with</u> each other. That was so much better than talking <u>about</u> each other. What a difference!

Harry Emerson Fosdick preached the sermon "The Constructive Use of Fear" during World War II. A paragraph from that sermon might well have been written about the Reagan/Gorbachev dialogue in Geneva last week:

> One of Aesop's fables describes a lion and a goat quarreling at a water-hole as to which should drink first. There was plenty of room for them to drink together. Nonetheless, they quarreled about precedence and were preparing to fight it out when, looking up, they saw the vultures wheeling low above them, waiting for the battle and its aftermath. So, says the fable, they decided to drink together. Certainly the vultures are flying low over the world today; they have picked the bones of previous generations that fought it out, and they may pick ours yet. Only a fool feels no fear.[64]

Much was at stake at that summit conference in Geneva. <u>Everything</u> was at stake! And still is! The nuclear madness that has held our world hostage for the last two decades must be dealt with. Not should be. <u>Must</u> be! The insanity of Mutually Assured Destruction is the "vulture flying low over the world today." It is time for us to quit "quarreling about precedence and preparing to fight it out." We must begin talking <u>with</u> each other. We must down-scale our hostilities. We must de-escalate our belligerence. We must begin a dialogue toward disarmament. We must deal with our fears. We must develop understanding and trust. It all starts with talk. Geneva was a beginning. A small beginning. And we are grateful.

The anecdote with which John F. Kennedy closed so many speeches in the 1960 campaign concerned a certain Col. Davenport, the Speaker of the Connecticut House of Representatives, and a day in 1789 when the sky of Hartford darkened and religious men feared the end was at hand. Quelling a clamor for immediate adjournment, Davenport rose to his feet, rapped his gavel, and said, "Gentlemen! The Day of Judgment is either approaching or it is not. If it is not, there is no cause for adjournment. If it is, I choose to be found doing my duty. Therefore, I wish that candles be brought."[65]

Last week, in Geneva, a candle was lighted. Ever so small a candle, ever so flickering a flame. But it was lighted! And we have hope. Reagan and Gorbachev will talk again next year. And again in 1987. By the time of their third conversation that flickering flame may have been fanned into a torch to brighten these latter years of the 20th century with understanding and trust and human dignity and hope and world peace! Our prayer, as we leave the Thanksgiving season behind and look toward Christmas Day, was sung by angels long ago: "Glory to God in the highest, and on earth peace, good will toward men!" (Luke 2:14 KJV)

With hope in my heart and a candle in my hand, I am, your minister and friend.

October 10, 1986

Dear Members of the Christian Community of Saints and Sinners!

It was a new experience for me, too! There were six kinds of bread on the Communion tray. I broke a corner off a dark, flat piece with sesame seeds. It had a strong, spicy flavor -- tasty. And it had a heavy consistency. I liked it. At the same time I regretted not being free to savor the other five kinds of bread. Overheard a number of remarks after the benediction -- all of them favorable. One young man took a whole chunk of bread off the Communion tray. This posed no great problem as he was on the last pew to be served. But it did take him a while to wash it down with that thimbleful of fruit of the vine.

Our Worship Committee Chair drew up a list of the "kinds of bread" used in our 1986 World Communion Day Service.

> Dark Bagels (Pumpernickel)
> Light Bagels (with sesame seeds)
> Paraguayan Cornbread (with Cayenne pepper)
> Arabian something-or-other (flat with dark spices & sesame seeds)
> Scones (with raisins)
> Flaxseed Buns

This is a tangible and tasty way to heighten our awareness that the Christian fellowship circles the globe. Brown-skinned Samoans, Japanese in kimonos, the "more English than the English" in New Zealand, new converts in Indonesia, Aborigines down under, former Hindus in Malaysia, members of the Church of South India, Baptists behind the Iron Curtain, congregations of the Masai in Africa, Catholics and Protestants in North Ireland, officers and enlisted men in Quonset huts wherever, charismatics in storefront churches -- all gathered around the Lord's Table last Sunday. This was a visible expression of our unity in Christ. That unity in Christ transcends national boundaries, erases language differences, spans geographical barriers, and ends racial distinctions. Within the Christian community, "There is neither Jew nor Greek, there is neither slave nor free, there is neither male nor female; for you are all one in Christ Jesus." (Galatians 3:28 RSV)

Last Sunday as I chewed a bit of dark bread flavored with spices and sesame seeds, I was reminded -- tastily so -- that:

> In Christ there is no East or West,
> In him no South or North;
> But one great fellowship of love
> Throughout the whole wide earth.[66]

On the first Sunday in October more Christians break bread together than on any Sunday of the year. This act, of itself, nurtures understanding, regard, identity, communication. That last word, communication, looks a lot like communion and community. According to the dictionary communion and community and communication not only look alike -- they are closely related. And we need lots of all three -- especially next week in Reykjavik, Iceland.[67]

One final note worth noting: World Communion Sunday was conceived, promoted, encouraged, and organized by one man, Jesse Bader. The Reverend Bader was a minister for the Christian Church (Disciples of Christ). His ministry made a difference -- a big difference. "He died, but through his faith he is still speaking." (Hebrews 11:4 RSV)

Every Sunday is World Communion Sunday at our Church. On Christ's behalf we extend the gracious invitation: "All things are ready. Come to the feast!"[68] Come! Come! Come!

August 28, 1987

Dear Friends:

The dawg days of August are dragging our summer to its end. It has been hot -- very! It has been dry -- very! It has been brown -- very! The 31 days of August are an ordeal. But we Texans endure. And we prevail! It is a bit like the youngster hitting his thumb with a toy hammer. An oldster asked him, "Junior, doesn't that hurt?" The kid answered, "Yep." The oldster asked again, "If it hurts, why do you do it?" The youngster hit his thumb again, grimaced and said, "Ouch!" -- then continued, "The reason I hit my thumb with the hammer is because it feels so good when I stop!" Somewhat like that, we Texans endure the dawg days of August because it feels so good when they are over!

Then we enjoy some of the most pleasant weather in the universe for the next ten months. Ten months! Ten months is a large chunk -- a bit more than most of us can manage at one time. So -- instead of speaking of ten months, let's speak of one month. When the 31st day of August slips off the calendar we will have a fresh new month to manage: "30 days hath September." What shall we do with those 30 days? It is a choice gift of 720 hours. In terms of minutes -- 43,200 small gifts. It will take some doing to fill every unforgiving minute with 60 seconds worth of distance run -- (2,592,000 seconds!) Here's a few things with which you may fill this coming month:

1. <u>A sense of gratitude</u>. When you first awaken, go to the bathroom, splash some cold water on your face, wash the grit out of your eyes, brush your teeth. Then snuggle back in bed for five minutes to set your gratitude attitude for the day. That picture near the door -- a gift from a friend of 40 years -- give thanks for that picture and for that friend! Touch that book on the reading table -- give thanks! Whisper the name of your sweetheart, spouse, grandparent, sister -- give thanks! Others: the mailman, the doctor, the Sunday School teacher -- give thanks! Health -- thanks! Friends -- thanks! Three squares a day -- thanks!

2. <u>A measure of generosity</u>. Once you are up and at 'em, focus your thoughts on one person who needs what you can offer: a letter, a trip to the mall, a visit over coffee, a sack of groceries, a word of sympathy, a vase of roses. There's bunches of such folk in your world. But if you think of what you can do for all of them at the same time, you will never get around to doing anything for any of them. Make your generosity specific. It may only be a cheery phone call. Well, pick up the phone. Do it now. Later, there will be 29 gestures of generosity for 29 other needs for the rest of September -- one per day!

3. <u>A touch of self-improvement</u>. The biggest room in all the world is the room for improvement! So to it! See that gal in the mirror? Talk to her a minute: Hey! Hey! Good-lookin' -- Whatcha got cookin'? How's about cookin' som'thin' up with me?[69] That's a perky piece to start with. Follow it with a reminder that you are a child of God -- created in God's image -- a chip off the divine block! Shoulders back -- chin up -- sing it out: "I'm a child of the King." Repeat Tennyson's ascription to the Queen: "O [be] loyal to the royal in thyself!"[70] Divinity is in your heart. Smile at that figure in the mirror. You are God's son -- God's daughter. Be who you are!

4. <u>A concern for peace</u>. Every day you are reminded that our world teeters on the brink of economic and military disaster. Anyone who reads the headlines or watches the evening news or thumbs through *TIME* and *Newsweek* knows that! Our world is so intricately interconnected that what happens in the Persian Gulf affects the real estate market in Austin; the weather conditions in Siberia change the price of wheat in Nebraska. At the peak of this heap of happenings and conditions there is a conference table where the greatest difference of all can be made. It is the table where President Ronald Reagan and Secretary Mikhail Gorbachev will sit down to talk to each other. They will talk earnestly and honestly about what they can do to transfer our investments in the machinery of war

(for Mutually Assured Destruction) into the tools of peace (for Mutually Assured Benefits). "And they shall beat their swords into ploughshares, and their spears into pruning hooks; nation shall not lift up sword against nation, neither shall they learn war any more!" (Isaiah 2:4 RSV) Each of the 30 days in September offer a prayer for peace! And for Ronald Reagan! And for Mikhail Gorbachev!

The dawg days of August -- hot, dry, brown -- are about gone. September will be a better month: if not cool, at least less hot; if not a monsoon season, at least a few "showers of blessing"; if not green, at least a lighter shade of brown. There's bunches of good things with which to fill these more pleasant days of September: gratitude; generosity; self-improvement; peace! Fill every one of those unforgiving 30 days with 24 hours' worth of distance run.

June 29, 1990

Instead of riding the buses from the Custis-Lee Mansion back to the parking lot of the Arlington National Cemetery, Tammy and I chose to walk. We followed a curving road under great maples and oaks. We took a shortcut through that silent city of the heroes of our nation's Armed Forces. Generals are buried there. So are Buck-Privates. Able-bodied Seamen and Admirals, too. Rough-riders who had rushed up San Juan Hill and Marines who had fallen at Guadalcanal. Tammy and I stopped at one gravestone. My heartbeat became syncopated. I felt a lump in my throat. My eyes glistened. Goosebumps covered my arms.

We lingered there a while -- a long while. It was the gravestone of Mark A. Whiteheart. He died in 1970. Nothing more was noted about his branch of service or about his rank or about his medals. But there was an inscription on that gravestone that made me pull out my notepad and very carefully copy each word. "For those who fought for it -- Freedom is a taste -- The protected will never know."

Tammy and I lingered there a while -- a long while. She was a youngster of 13 years. I was her 38-year-old father. I do not know what Tammy was thinking. But I well remember my own most compelling thoughts: "I am one of the 'protected.'"

There are so many things to see at Arlington National Cemetery:

The Custis-Lee Mansion where Robert E. Lee spent his youth.

The Tomb of the Unknown Soldier of World War I -- and the tombs of his compatriots from each of the wars in which America has been involved since.

The Eternal Flame above the grave of John Fitzgerald Kennedy -- and the picket fence around Bobby Kennedy's grave.

The Flagstaff from the *Battleship Maine.*

The United States Marine Monument -- those courageous men raising the Stars and Stripes atop Mt. Suribachi on Iwo Jima.

There are so many things to see and by which to be inspired in Arlington National Cemetery. But of all the things we saw and by which we were inspired -- above all else these lines on a modest tombstone have stayed with me: "For those who fought for it -- Freedom is a taste -- The protected will never know."

With gratitude for the sacrifices of others on my behalf, I am, sincerely yours.

January 18, 1991
"The Dreams and the Dreads of 1991"
(Excerpts from a New Year's Sermon -- January 6, 1991)

Remember those perplexing words by Charles Dickens -- the prologue to *A Tale of Two Cities:*

> It was the best of times, it was the worst of times,
> it was the age of wisdom, it was the age of foolishness,
> it was the epoch of belief, it was the epoch of incredulity,
> it was the season of Light, it was the season of Darkness,
> it was the spring of hope, it was the winter of despair,
> we had everything before us, we had nothing before us,
> we were all going direct to Heaven, we were all going direct the other
> way -- in short, the period was so far like the present period, that some
> of its noisiest authorities insisted on its being received, for good or evil,
> in the superlative degree for comparison only![71]

These lines were Dickens's attempt to set the mood for his story about the French Revolution. Hopes and fears were bundled together in one package of history: "...best of times -- worst of times...age of wisdom -- age of foolishness...epoch of belief -- epoch of incredulity...etc." Hopes and fears, dreams and dreads were bundled together in one package of history. The mixed mood of that moment in time -- 1791 -- is not unlike the mixed mood of this moment in time -- 1991.

We feel the confusion, the ambiguity, the tension of living in a moment in time that offers the promise of paradise on the one hand -- and on the other hand, threatens the peril of perdition. For us, this one moment is both "the best of times and the worst of times"! We are on the verge of a new world order of communication and cooperation and compassion. At the same time we are on the brink of a new world <u>dis</u>order of disintegration and disaster and despair. The visionary pearly gates may turn out to be the gates of hell.

It is as though we were standing on a diving platform. At the signal -- we bounce -- bounce -- bounce -- we spring high up into the air -- we stretch our bodies to full length -- we glide upward, outward, downward -- we curve downward in the form of a swan dive. But we do not yet know whether that into which we are plunging is a pool of cool, clear, clean water that refreshes and invigorates us -- or is a lake of fire and brimstone that burns and destroys us. We do not really know how things will turn out in this New Year that is heavy with both dreams and dreads!

Our President believes that we are on the verge of establishing a new world order of understanding and cooperation -- of adequacy for all and of protection for the weak. At the same time that this high hope is held before us, our President has warned that we tread the dangerous edge of Armageddon. He says that if we do not make the great sacrifice needed at this moment, we will be forced to make a greater sacrifice later. We may be plunging into a pool of cool, clear, clean water that brings life -- or we may be diving into a lake of fire and brimstone that delivers death. It was so just before the French Revolution -- 1791. It is just so in our own generation -- 1991. Only those persons among us who were adults before the beginning of World War II, fifty years ago, can remember such a moment in time when our brightest hopes and our darkest fears were so tangled in one magnificent mess! "The best of times! The worst of times!"

This New Year is a mixed bag. It holds for us tantalizing promises of great and good things: a new world order of communication and cooperation and compassion. At the same time, this New Year holds for us dreadful threats of utter chaos: disintegration and disaster and despair. Best of times? Worst of times? This New Year may be our brightest and best. This New Year may be our darkest and worst. And we are trapped in the tension between hope and despair -- between courage and cowardice -- between heaven and hell.

Come what may -- we shall not lose our trust in God. As Robert Louis Stevenson put it: "I believe in the ultimate decency of things! Aye! And if I awoke in hell, I still would believe it."[72] In brightness or in gloom -- in fair weather or in foul -- in triumph or in tragedy we shall hold our rudder true, we shall trust in the Polar Star, we shall keep the faith: "Be strong and of good courage, do not fear or be in dread of them: for it is the Lord your God who goes with you; he will not fail you or forsake you." (Deuteronomy 31:6 RSV)

February 8, 1991

Dear Friends:

Aimed Ole Blue (our '57 Pontiac Star Chief) down Jollyville Road. Turned south on Business Park Drive, dog-legged around the Holiday Inn and the Hawthorne Suites. Left on Tallwood, right on Amelia, headed toward a church member's home on Hyridge. Then that pleasant moment. There it was -- on my left -- a magnificent American flag billowing from a staff anchored to the door frame of a residence. Pleasant! Pleasant! Pleasant! My heart leaps up when I behold Old Glory -- the red-white-and-blue. That flag represents the best we know of America! And there it was, too -- a magnificent yellow bow tied around the leafless pin oak tree in the lawn of that residence. My heart leaps up when I behold a yellow bow tied around a tree, a fence post, a gate, a mailbox. It is a sign telling all who see it, "Welcome home!" The feelings stirred within me by that red-white-and-blue flag and by that yellow bow were not new feelings.

The Friday before, Judie and I had been at the local school district to have a document notarized. The superintendent walked into the personnel office as we were leaving. On his lapel was a red-white-and-blue ribbon. Lining the back of that ribbon was a similar-sized strip of yellow ribbon placed so the combination of two ribbons appeared to be one: red-white-blue-and-yellow. My heart leapt up twice in the same instant! Like the flag on the door frame and the bow on the pin oak, that four-colored ribbon said: We support our sons and daughters in the Mid-East -- And we want them home! If it were available I'd buy a mile of red-white-blue and yellow ribbon. I'd cut it in strips for folk to pin on their lapels, to tie on their antennae, to hang from door knockers, to use as bookmarks, to enclose in letters. The superintendent explained that the four-colored ribbon was his wife's idea. His explanation confirmed for us the modern version of that old adage: "Behind every great man is a great woman with great ideas!"

TV has shown us more of the gung-ho flag-wavers than we care again to see. They are too quick to let our sons and daughters be turned into cannon fodder for dubious reasons. Likewise for the peacenik types who would purchase tranquility even at the price of injustice and oppression. The word for such is cowardice -- and the color of cowardice is yellow. Either group -- either the gung-ho flag-wavers or the lily-livered peaceniks -- either group proposes a simple solution to a very complex problem. As some would put it, "Every complex problem has a simple solution that usually is wrong!" Some pro-war demonstrators have urged the Pentagon generals to "Bomb 'em back into the Stone Age." That is a simple solution to a complex problem! Some anti-war demonstrators have urged our leaders to "Bring our sons and daughters home and let's let the Arabs settle their own family squabbles." That is another simple solution to a complex problem! Both super-patriotic flag-wavers and yellow-streaked peaceniks are extremists. The Middle-East muddle in which we are mired will not be resolved by extremists.

Most Americans are seriously patriotic. Most Americans deeply regret placing our fellow citizens in harm's way. Most Americans support our sons and daughters. At the same time, most Americans are peacemakers, not warmongers. Most Americans care about human rights and justice and freedom for all nations. Most Americans want our sons and daughters home -- sound and safe! Just so -- most Americans are not extremists -- neither of the flag-waver sort, nor of the peacenik type. There is much to be said <u>for</u> either extreme. But, there is much more to be said <u>against</u> either extreme. The more sane and balanced stance was symbolized for me by the flag billowing from a staff anchored to the door frame of a residence that also had a yellow bow tied around the pin oak tree in the lawn. That combination of red-white-and-blue flag and yellow bow stirred up strong feelings for me. So did the red-white-blue-and-yellow ribbon on the superintendent's lapel.

It is too tardy now to second-guess our President and his advisors. Three weeks into this misbegotten and disastrous and probably fruitless war we see there is enough blame to go around to everyone. For misunderstandings, for ill-considered moves, for resolutions in need of revision, for blusterings and threats, for distortions and lies, for miscalculations, for ultimatums, we all share the blame. For the remainder of this war, the high ground will not be held by extremists, either gung-ho warmakers or naive peacemongers. Rather, the high ground will be held by those who think and feel and act like that greatest of all Americans, Abraham Lincoln. In his Second Inaugural Address he said:

> With malice toward none; with charity for all; with firmness in the right, as God gives us to see the right, let us strive on to finish the work we are in; to bind up the nation's wounds; to care for him who shall have borne the battle, and for his widow and his orphan -- to do all which may achieve and cherish a just and lasting peace among ourselves, and with all nations.

October 25, 1991

Dear Christian Friends:

<u>Two</u> votes in the House -- <u>one</u> vote in the Senate -- those were the margins when the Texas Legislature voted to submit a referendum to the citizens of the state to authorize or to reject a proposed lottery. On Tuesday, November 5, I will vote an emphatic "No!" Let me explain.

I get a kick out of parking on somebody else's quarter. Time is still there on the meter -- fifteen minutes or so. Why not back in and park Ole Blue for free? That's what I do. Sometimes, too, I leave time on the meter and someone else comes along and parks on my quarter. All I had needed was a dime's worth, but the meter took quarters only. So I had to pay for fifteen minutes meter-time that I did not need. Why shouldn't someone else back in and park on my quarter? That's just how things are in a city where we finance street repairs and traffic lights and police patrols with revenue from parking meters that take quarters only!

Likewise with our airports. Landing fees are charged to airlines for using the gates at the municipal airport. The airlines add these charges to the passengers' tickets. These charges are called "head taxes." These "head taxes" on the folk who fly in and out of the airport pay for the air traffic controllers, the security guards, the concourses, the restrooms, etc. One difference is that no time meters are involved so we don't get to use the airport facilities on somebody else's quarter.

So it goes: Parking meter fees -- Airport "head taxes" -- Gasoline taxes -- Tobacco taxes -- Franchise taxes -- Property taxes -- Sales taxes -- Income taxes. We do not really like any of these, but we know that taxes are necessary for street repairs and traffic lights and police patrols and air traffic controllers and security guards and schools and parks and health clinics, etc. Taxes help us pay for things none of us could afford alone. It's a heavy burden, but we get what we pay for.

Some 33 states and the District of Columbia run lotteries in order to ease their tax burden. But the easing of the tax burden by lotteries is an illusion. Statistics show that lotteries promise much but deliver little in terms of actual revenue that trickles down into the state treasury. The most extravagant estimated income from the proposed Texas State Lottery would not fund public education alone for even 30 days! The much larger share of the lottery is divided up for:

1. Administration (Executives) and Promotion (Advertising)
2. Sales Commissions, Printing, Clerks, etc.
3. Winners -- often only one-in-a-million!

Most of the money used to buy lottery tickets would come from folk who have little money to spare! Those poor people take a very long shot on striking it rich. A few hit the jackpot. Millions end up with ticket stubs and disappointed hopes. The money spent to buy lottery stubs would have been better spent on groceries and clothes and furniture. The bottom line: Lotteries soak money from folk who are already at the bottom. This system of trying to ease the tax burden is self-defeating. The tax burden is shifted to those least able to bear it!

One thing particularly odious about the lottery system to be voted on this coming November 5 is that the bill would create an autonomous state division. This autonomous (independent!) state division would have more power to set policies and establish procedures than other governmental units. Moreover, it would have no external budget reviews. Furthermore, the salary schedule for the administrative agency of the lottery would be exempt from the schedule for all other state officials! Conceivably, the salary of the Executive Director of the proposed Texas State Lottery could be double that of the governor! The notion of soaking the poor to ease the tax load of all is an insult to every responsible taxpayer. And it adds injury to insult to pay the head of state gambling twice what we pay the head of the state.

I have only one vote. My one vote will be cast against the referendum to establish a Texas State Lottery. It probably will be a vote on the losing side of the issue. Still, I will vote "No!" Emphatically! And I will continue to vote "No!" by refusing to buy even the first lottery ticket. I'd rather pay money out in quarters for parking meters that offer me more meter-time than I need at the moment. At least I will have the satisfaction of knowing my quarter was being used to repair streets and traffic lights and to pay policemen!

May 28, 1993

Dear Concerned Christians:

"It is not hard to do the right thing. It is hard to know what is the right thing to do!"[73] Recognize those lines? Used often by our fellow Disciple, Lyndon Baines Johnson! We suppose he was taught those lines by his mother, Rebecca Baines Johnson. She probably also had her son memorize the Biblical quotation he used so often in the Senate: "Come now, and let us reason together." (Isaiah 1:18 KJV) Despite what Robert Caro has done to uncover Johnson's clay feet, LBJ still comes off as an American who very much wanted "to do the right thing." His difficulty was "to know what is the right thing to do." Members of his cabinet, Congressional leaders, generals from the Pentagon, close friends offered him contradictory advice and conflicting counsel. From this tangle of distortion and misinformation LBJ had to sort out the trash and grasp the treasure. Then, in lonely isolation, he had to decide "what is the right thing to do." That was the hard part. After that, it was not hard "to do the right thing." Most often, the advice and counsel given him were on target. Sometimes the advice and counsel given him were faulty. A few times, the consequences were dreadful! Both his successes and his failures were shared successes and shared failures. His mistakes were of the head, not of the heart. "It is not hard to do the right thing. It is hard to know what is the right thing to do."

As one of 250,000,000 -- citizens and only one -- I have generally been sympathetic with, hesitant to be critical of our national presidents. This goes all the way back to Harry Truman. And it runs all the way forward to George Bush. Theirs -- each one -- has been a very difficult task. Each one has wanted "to do the right thing." Each one found it hard "to know what is the right thing to do." Truman -- Eisenhower -- Kennedy -- Johnson -- Nixon -- Ford -- Carter -- Reagan -- Bush -- each one knew it was "harder to know what was the right thing to do" than it was "to do the right thing."

Our present president has quickly discovered that things are not so black and white as he painted them in last year's campaign. He faces a number of issues -- each one of which is very complicated -- none of which will be resolved without compromises. One great moral issue he faces has to do with the impossible situation in Bosnia-Herzegovina. Bill Clinton wants "to do the right thing." The question is: Does he know "what is the right thing to do"? Clinton will decide on the basis of the advice and counsel offered him -- by members of his cabinet, Congressional leaders, generals from the Pentagon, close friends. We pray every day for our national leaders. Our prayers include President Bill Clinton. Whether he chooses "to just stand by" as was done in the '30s or "to risk American arms and lives" we cannot tell. But one thing we do believe: we believe he wants "to do the right thing." And one thing we pray for: we pray he will know "what is the right thing to do."

8

🌿

Time

August 1, 1973

Dear Friends:

"So little done -- so much to do!" That is the frustrating footnote that is scratched at the bottom of so many of the pages of our daily journals. And that line will be graved deep on our consciousness toward the sunset of all our days: "So little done -- so much to do!"

There are more books to read than ever we will lay a hand on -- or even note the titles. There are more mountains to climb that ever we will set a foot upon. There are more letters to write than ever we will compose. More telephone calls to make than AT&T can handle. More flowers to enjoy than ever we will see. More personal visits to make than the time allows. More songs to sing, more foods to taste, more places to go, more sermons to deliver -- and on and on and on!

Given 1,000 years to live -- we still would not accomplish 3% of all those things we would like! "Our reach exceeds our grasp -- else what's a heaven for?!"[74] There is so much to do -- but our time and energy and resources are limited. Only 24 hours every day. Only 365¼ days every year. And an indefinite number of years in each life.

The years of our life are threescore and ten, or even by reason of strength, fourscore; but they are soon gone, and we fly away. (Based on Psalms 90:10 RSV)

Some "threescore and ten" -- some "fourscore" -- but for so many so much less! (Parenthetically, your pastor marked his 37th birthday back on July 8. Insurance actuaries figure that I have already passed high noon and am heading toward the sunset!)

"So little done -- so much to do!" That is the melancholic mood of the moment as your minister speeds toward the end of his first year in Knoxville. "So little done -- so much to do!" Wish there were two of me -- or three or even more. It's that "wish" that makes a lot of people believe in reincarnation. They've "got a lot to live" -- but they can't live it all the first time around. Indeed -- no one can! So up springs the reincarnation "wish" -- and it's a pleasant thought: that we might have a second chance.

A pleasant thought, yes. But not at all realistic. As for me and my house we will cast our lot with Joshua who said: "You have not passed this way before" (Joshua 3:4 RSV) (and by implication: "You shall not pass this way again"). Likewise, we would throw in with Jesus: "We must work the works of him who sent me, while it is day; night comes, when no one can work." (John 9:4 RSV) Those words put a compelling awareness of a deadline into our consciousness. "Awake thou that sleepest!" (Ephesians 5:14 KJV) That line shall never be said of us!

"So little done -- so much to do!" Friends -- as we close our first year with you we are deeply grateful for the privilege of doing our two-bits worth in this time, in this place. As for those things that we must leave <u>undone</u> -- it was not because we did not have the desire but because the clock and the calendar ran out and the steam ran low. That "So much" which shall forever remain unaccomplished -- that we will leave in the hands of The Eternal. That "So little" that we have done -- <u>that</u> is our gift to the Church and to the Christ whose call to the ministry we have heard and to which we have responded: "Yes!"

With mixed feelings: "So little done -- so much to do!"

I am, your friend and pastor.

May 6, 1981

Dear Christian Friends:

Time speeds! Only yesterday it was New Year's. January-February-March-April have flipped past! Soon it will be summer and vacation. Then Labor Day -- followed by Thanksgiving. Finally, "the most wonderful time of the year" -- Christmas! How the calendar zips by on its way to a rendezvous with "the last syllable of recorded time"![75] Time speeds! Indeed! As Job put it: "[Our] days are swifter than a weaver's shuttle!" (Job 7:6 RSV)

So many things we intended to do have gotten only "a lick and a promise." And many other things not even that! It is a stingy calendar -- this thing of only 12 months per year -- of only 30 days or so per month -- of only seven days per week. To do a thing or two -- one must leave undone three things or four! Why? Because of the limitations of time. There is not enough of it! Moreover, our reserve of energy does not match our desire to do. Our physical stamina is not inexhaustible. Reluctantly we adjust to that fact of life -- with the unhaste of a teenager dragging to bed while the party is still on.

Our intentions and our endeavors to do, to visit, to see, to write, to work, to travel, to read, to phone, to learn, to entertain, to be -- even our best intentions and our finest endeavors are frustrated by short months and shorter days -- and by a personal energy crisis. It is a universal problem -- faced alike by child and by grandparent, by fool and by philosopher. Should we live to be 90 as did Humboldt -- we will probably make his lines our own: "O that I had another century to live. I have just begun to learn!"[76]

No! We do not have unlimited amounts of time or of energy. So we must compress both to accomplish Kipling's stern challenge to "fill the unforgiving minute with sixty seconds worth of distance run"![77] Many of us try! Not so many of us succeed!

Do you find yourself a bit over-scheduled? Pushed for time? Pounding a treadmill? Dealing with a "stingy calendar"? Struggling with a "personal energy crisis"? If so -- then two hours a week at Sunday School and Worship will do you much good. In a relaxed, unhurried setting you will catch your second wind -- sort out your priorities -- replenish your exhausted spirit. A faith to undergird a hope to allure upward -- a profound resource of strength can be yours through Christian study and fellowship and worship.

Friends -- don't short-change yourselves! The Gospel can give you the handles with which to get hold of yourselves -- and your over-spent calendars -- and of your thinned-out energies. Come! Grasp those handles before your soul is shredded and your nerves are a shambles. All things are ready! Come to the feast!

April 28, 1982

Dear Friends:

I am at ease just now. But wasn't 15 minutes ago. Was all astir: rushing to get this newsletter together -- a stack of phone calls to return -- three people in the hospital to visit -- papers from the Regional Assembly to sort out -- commitments to "The Church's Presence" to fulfill -- letters to answer -- Next Sunday's sermon crying for attention -- errands for the family -- yard work neglected -- etc., etc.! Get the picture. Old Landry was pulled in two dozen directions. By matters that each claimed #1 priority! What a hairy, hurried, harried schedule! Just setting me up for a Type A coronary!

But I am at ease just now. I laid down my pencil -- shoved aside my papers -- lifted the receiver off the hook -- leaned back in my swivel chair. Closed my mind to all these claims on my time. And closed my eyes. Breathed deeply. Centered my thoughts on things that really matter: persons, love, community, justice, health, peace. My merry-go-round world slowed down. The dizziness outside me was replaced by a calm inside me. The disordered pieces of my schedule rearranged themselves into a manageable pattern. And I am at ease just now!

Do you sometimes feel like I felt 15 minutes ago? Rushed? Pushed? Bushed? Do you need a pause that <u>really</u> refreshes? If so -- take a three-minute retreat from the tornado outside to the peace inside. And listen for the "still small voice" within. (I Kings 19:12 RSV) You will be amazed at the difference it will make! Both for you -- and for all those around you! Both for the world outside you -- and for the universe inside you!

Sincerely and <u>prayer</u>fully yours.

February 22, 1985

Dear Fellow Frozen Friends:

We moved to the Sunbelt thinking we were getting away from harsh winters. But in the last 45 days here deep in the heart of Texas we have been deep into the white stuff -- snow! Three snow-and-ice storms in one season! That's more than any of our old timers remembers. Blizzards in Minneapolis are O.K. Their homes are built for such weather. And their road crews have the equipment with which to keep the highways clear. But a blizzard in San Antonio!

But all things are relative. By comparison to winters elsewhere, ours has been mild. Europe is shoveling its way out from under the worst ice and snow drifts in its history. In the Midwest, Kansas/Nebraska wheat fields have had 10-12-foot snow drifts! Our East Tennessee friends have suffered the lowest temperatures since the 18th century. Our friends in Grand Rapids, Michigan, are still hip-deep in the white stuff! It will be several weeks before Siberia thaws for the spring plowing. Wherever -- throughout the Northern Hemisphere -- the winter of '84 -'85 has been terrific! It will be remembered well into the 21st century.

But there have been worse winters. Such as the winter of 55-56. Now that was a real winter -- in capitals: WINTER! Folk were "cabin'd" by the plunging temperatures. Most for days on end. Some for weeks! Travel was stopped -- altogether. One fellow was stuck for three months. Couldn't go anywhere! Not much to do except wait for the spring thaw. But he occupied his "closed-in" time well. He put pen to papyrus and scratched out a letter to his friends in faraway Rome. Here, 1,900 years later, we have come to know that letter as Paul's "Epistle to the Romans." It is a classic. For Christian theology that letter has proved to be the most germinal piece of correspondence ever written. The winter of 55-56 forced Paul off the highways of the Empire -- trapped him in a garret opposite a writing desk. What a wonderfully good consequence to flow from a woefully <u>un</u>-good circumstance!

Parallels flash readily before us:

John Bunyan, in Bedford Prison, scratched out *The Pilgrim's Progress.*

Robert Louis Stevenson, confined by tuberculosis to his bed, penned *Treasure Island* and *Kidnapped*!

George Washington Carver, limited to the primitive research laboratory at Tuskegee Institute, focused on the peanut and developed from the lowly plant nearly 300 products.

John Fitzgerald Kennedy, in the hospital for eight weeks for back surgery, researched and dictated his inspiring *Profiles in Courage*.

Bad circumstances can issue in good consequences! How is it with you? Have you had a hard winter of '84-'85? Weatherwise or otherwise? Have you been shut in by frigid temperatures -- frosted either by north winds or by cold people? Have you had to adjust your schedule, routine, travels? Delayed? Forced to take a detour? Your best laid plans have "gang awry"? Barred from your best intentions? Circumstances frozen you out of your ambitions? Dreams dead-ended? Stuck in a cul-de-sac? Spinning your wheels? Psychologically, emotionally, professionally snowed-in? "Cabin'd, cribb'd, confin'd"?[78] If so -- then the remainder of the winter of '84-'85 may become your greatest opportunity! A philosopher-psychologist long ago applauded a person's ability to transform a "minus" into a "plus"! Give it a fling! This winter of your discontent may thaw into your spring of bluebonnets and azaleas! You can do something good -- not merely in spite of your limitations -- but precisely because of your limitations. Glenn Cunningham[79] became the greatest runner of his day -- not in spite of his burned, crippled feet and legs -- but because of his burned, crippled feet and legs. Franklin Roosevelt became the President of the United States -- not in spite of his polio -- but because of his polio. Airplanes rise up in flight -- not in spite of the opposing wind -- but, in part, because of the opposing wind!

My prayer is that this winter of '84-'85 will be a great one for us all -- if not in process -- then surely in retrospect. Looking forward to a warm and flowery April so I can look back on a cold and frustrating January.

March 20, 1992

Dear Friends in the Fast Lane:

We'd like to live in the leisurely lane. Cruising about the slowth of *Driving Miss Daisy*. Time enough to stroll, to sit and sip a second cup-o-coff, to linger. Like in the good ole days when folk weren't in such a rush. That's a pleasant thought. Sort of dreamy. Before sliced bread and TV dinners and fax machines, folk had more time. Spent lazy evenings on the porch swing. Enjoyed writing letters. They did? Did they? Maybe? Or, maybe that's all a "pleasant thought" -- "sort of dreamy." The good old days had exactly 24 hours in each -- just like the 24 hours in each of the not so good new days. In the good ole days, Daddy and

Mama had to invest many more hours and much more energy to bring home the bacon, to cover the bills, to keep the jeans patched and washed.

Life in the leisurely lane -- Cruising about the slowth of *Driving Miss Daisy*. Time enough to stroll, to sit and sip a second cup-o-coff, to linger. Like in the good ole days when folk weren't in such a rush -- all that is an illusion, a figment of a Norman Rockwell imagination, a remembrance of things that never were.

Our fast and not so good new days have exactly 24 hours in each -- just like the 24 hours in each of the good ole days. In our fast and not so good new days, it takes far fewer hours and much less energy "to bring home the bacon, to cover the bills, to keep the jeans patched and washed." If that is so (and it is so!) -- then why fret and worry, run and scurry in a rat race endeavor to shove sixty seconds worth of distance run into every unforgiving minute? We have more discretionary hours and greater reserves of energy than our fathers and mothers ever had. If that is so (and it is so!) -- then why not slow down and share both time and energy with our brothers and sisters. They would cherish a half-hour visit, relish an encouraging word, appreciate a shoulder to lean on. Whether it's "life in the leisurely lane" or "pushing it to the limit in a high-speed environment" -- all of us would do well to invest a bit of time in prayer and praise. Such as one hour of our time on Sundays. Such as a half-hour in the fellowship hall after worship. Our brothers and sisters will return a strong handclasp and will offer us a supporting shoulder in our time of need. There are many less worthy ways to invest that time and energy, both of which we have so much more than our fathers and mothers had back yonder in the good ole days. Come! We need you!

You need us! COME!

April 15, 1994

Dear Christian Friends:

Can it be that already 30% of our "1994 Year of Celebrations" is behind us? Time speeds! Hardly yesterday we were doing Thanksgiving things, humming Christmas carols, making plans for the New Year, A.D. 1994. And already one-third of that year is history -- water under the bridge. It has been a fullish four months: Jan/Feb/Mar/Apr 1994. Our first "Celebration" was the installation of newly elected officers on January 9. Our "Celebration of Ministry" on our tenth anniversary as Pastor-Congregation on March 6-7-8 was a BIGTIME PLUS. And on April 3 -- Easter! Our heart-strings are still vibrating from the Good News: "Thanks be to God, who gives us the victory through our Lord Jesus Christ!" (I Corinthians 15:57 RSV)

And we are anticipating eight more months brimming with good things. Our next Celebration is "Christian Family Day" on May 8. This is Mother's Day.

Every lady-over-eighty will be honored with a red rose! In June we will have a service of "Re-Affirmation of Marriage Vows." July 3 will bring us a "Red-White-Blue Sunday." So on down the calendar to the last Sunday of 1994 -- Christmas! The calendar pages do flash past!

Life is a smorgasbord of all kinds of good things. How we wish we had enough time and energy to take in all the options. But we don't. Even if we had a thousand years in which to do it all -- we would not get even one-tenth of it all done! What we do have is some "three score and ten years" -- sometimes a bit more, sometimes a bit less. Since our time is not unlimited, we would do well to choose carefully which things we will let claim our attention -- take our interest -- consume our hours -- drain our energies. We would do well to choose the best over the good, the substantial over the flimsy, the permanent over the temporary, the gold over the gilded. So, too, in the life of the church. Though we are oft tempted to follow fads, to chase after bandwagons, to flirt with the flashy, still, we stick to matters that really matter: worship, prayer, study, outreach, service, fellowship.

You may feel as though time is fleeting -- that your days are distracted -- that you are depleted from much going and coming -- that your priorities are jumbled. If so, then you would do well to draw aside for a few moments in the sanctuary -- to synchronize your time with God's time -- to give an hour in praise that will prepare you for all your other hours: "For a day in thy courts, [O Lord,] is better than a thousand [elsewhere]." (Psalms 84:10 KJV) It takes time to make time! Time spent in the presence of the divine is refreshing, invigorating.

Time speeds! Already one-third of A.D. 1994 is gone -- only a memory now, soon to be ancient history. The bluebonnets are fading. Summer in the offing. Shortly summer, too, will slide past. Before long we will be humming *Silent Night, Holy Night*. And the time of changing calendars will again be upon us. Take time to make time! Such as one hour this Sunday. That one hour on Sunday will brighten up all the rest of your hours next week!

September 6, 1996

Dear Family and Friends:

Each year is a marathon -- a long, demanding, exhausting race! We begin each year at the stroke of midnight that splits December 31 from January 1. Before us is a calendar of 12 months -- of 52 weeks -- of 365 days. Hopes and Fears -- Possibilities and Problems -- Dreams and Nightmares are all bundled up in that calendar. A marathon of both Delight and Dread.

We end each year at the stroke of midnight that splits December 31 from January 1. Behind us is a record of 12 months -- of 52 weeks -- of 365 days. Achievements and Disappointments -- Thanksgivings and Regrets -- Dreams that were delayed and Nightmares that were not as dreadful as first thought. When we stand before the great judgment bar of God we will be asked but one question: "Well, what did you make of it?"

In terms of 1996, we have eight months <u>behind us</u>. So far, so good! We have more gratitudes than griefs! And we still have four months <u>before us</u>. Our Hopes, Possibilities, Dreams are greater than our Fears, Problems, Nightmares. At the stroke of midnight that will separate December 31, 1996, from January 1, 1997, each one of us will face the question: Well, what did you make of it? And all of us, altogether, will also face that question: "Well, what did you make of it?" So far, so good! But, there is more to come.

Each year is a marathon. Each month is a marathon, too. From the first of the month to the 31st, we shove as much onto each page of the calendar as we are able. And then some! Likewise, each week is a marathon -- from Sunday through Saturday! The months, the weeks, overlap into each other! Each day is a marathon, too! From the moment we blink open our eyes in the morning to the unspoken prayer as our eyelids droop in the evening. From sunup to sundown -- from sundown to sunup -- our work is never done. The race goes on. An unending marathon:

At the end of each year: At the end of each month: At the end of each week: At the end of each day:

At the end of each year:	"Well, what did you make of it?"
At the end of each month:	"Well, what did you make of it?"
At the end of each week:	"Well, what did you make of it?"
At the end of each day:	"Well, what did you make of it?"

Not until "the fever of life is over and our work on earth is done"[80] will we be free to say: "I have fought the good fight, I have finished the race, I have kept the faith!" (II Timothy 4:7-8 RSV)

And God bless us all!

Your Pastor and Friend.

September 8, 2000

Dear Fellow Workaholics:

Our days begin quite early. Our days end quite late. In between "early" and "late" our days are quite full! A bit like the farmer/rancher/dairyman who worked "from barely can see by the morning light in the eastern sky 'til can't see none-at-all past dark-thirty." Thomas Edison made it possible for us to stretch our days from before sunrise 'til long after sunset. Many of us have swallowed an overdose of the Protestant work ethic. So, we go at it early. We stay with it late. And we sweat a lot in between!

In the creation story, God said, "Let us make man in our image, after our likeness." (Genesis 1:26 KJV) At that point in the Biblical narrative, the image, the likeness of God, is that of a Creator: bringing order out of chaos -- separating the waters from the waters, making dry land to appear -- setting the sun and moon and stars in the skies -- shaping mountains and valleys -- planting forests and orchards -- evolving beasts of the field, birds of the air, fish of the sea. Then, sweaty from the hard labor of the first five days, the Creator knelt beside a creek, scooped up clay, molded it into man/woman, breathed into its nostrils the breath of life, gave the instructions: "Be fruitful and multiply, and fill the earth and subdue it." (Genesis 1:28 RSV)

To be in the image and likeness of the Creator is to be a worker: bringing order out of chaos -- lighting a candle in the midst of darkness -- producing food and fiber for the family -- landscaping the world with evergreens and flowers -- conserving the natural resources of soil and water and air -- caring for our companions on earth: furred, feathered, finned -- embellishing our living spaces with architecture and art -- enriching our days and our nights with music and poetry -- creating a friendly home for young and for old and for all in between! And we have done all this and much more on a daily basis for a long, long time!

For myself, my day begins with two cups of flavored coffee sweetened with brown sugar and lightened with a splash of 2%. Drip! Drip! Stir! Stir! Sip! Sip! Sitting at our breakfast table in the pre-dawn darkness brightened by Edison's incandescent bulb, I draw up lists of tasks to tend to -- persons to visit -- phone calls to return -- errands to run. The unshaped day ahead comes into focus on a sheet of paper -- often two sheets of paper -- sometimes three: sermons, pastoral prayers, letters -- worship bulletins, newsletters, flyers -- committees, appointments, hospital calls -- weddings, funerals, youth activities -- names, addresses, phone numbers -- errands of all kinds. My intent is to fill every unforgiving hour with 61 minutes worth of distance run. I don't succeed. But I try. Yesterday's unfinished lists give me a head start on tomorrow's plans. "Ah, but a man's reach should exceed his grasp, Or what's a heaven for?"[81] It all makes for a full day! Quite full!

After dinner Judie and I visit with *Jim Lehrer and the News Hour* on TV. A couple hours later it is past time to shower and to drag a limp corpse to bed. As I slumber off into the nether world of dreams and visions I review the day behind me and I begin an inventory of work for the day before me. Even while sleeping I work at it!

A best-seller for this Third Millennium might well be entitled: *Twelve Steps for the Recovering Workaholic.* Such a book could not compete with J. K. Rowling's

Harry Potter series, but it sure might help a lot of us who worship at the altar of the God of Work. At least one of those 12 steps would be about playing. Such as in the lines: "So God blessed the seventh day and hallowed it, because in it God rested from all his work which he had done in creation." (Genesis 2:3 RSV) I need a bit of Sabbath rest before I "shuffle off this mortal coil."[82] Else, my epitaph may well read: "He sweated too much! He danced too little!"

Good Shabbas to you all! Shalom, too! And Salaam!

May 2, 2003

Dear Pilgrim Friends:

We are future-oriented. Our posture inclines toward tomorrow -- next week -- a month from now. The bright possibilities of the time that is yet to be -- those possibilities lure us ahead. Beethoven's cadences and van Dyke's poetry and our feelings meld into an inspiring musical moment: "Ever singing, march we onward, Victors in the midst of strife, Joyful music leads us sunward, In the triumph song of life!"[83] Enthusiastically, we march onward, forward, upward!

At the same time we carry with us much of the past. Memory keeps alive for us the great events of that part of our pilgrimage that is behind us: our first day in the first grade, the time Daddy showed us how to bait a hook, the summer at Aunt Zsa Zsa's ranch, the evening we received our high school diploma, the night we got engaged, the day Junior totaled the new Olds, etc. Lighting the briquets to barbeque, setting out a handful of pecans for the squirrels, arguing with the blue jay in the tree yonder -- reminiscing -- that is one of life's pleasures! We do carry with us much of the past.

This business of living between yesterday and tomorrow is well-expressed in Kyle Haselden's interpretation of Giovanni Bernini's marble sculpture of *The Flight of Aeneas from Burning Troy*. On his bent back Aeneas carries his old, frail father, Anchises, and by the hand leads his toddling son, Ascanius. In this piece Bernini portrayed not a man, but <u>man</u>. Arrest the movement of the human race at any moment and this is the essence of the moment: fleeing and seeking man, man in transition, man between peril and uncertainty, carries on his back the blessings and the burdens of the past, while at his feet trot the infant promises and threats of the future. As we move from one day to the next we carry on our backs the inherited themes of human tragedy and triumph, all the struggles with their gains and losses, the lessons learned and remembered and forgotten, the knowledge cherished and lost, the wisdom obtained and spurned. And the timorous child, the unproved future, clings to our free hand. Past and future, memory, and hope -- both precious, both burdensome. All that we really have is the Now, the moment, the margin of time in which the near side of the future touches the receding past. How does Aeneas decide where to go and what to do? Does he listen to the aged and weary lore riding on his back or does he trust the innocence and spontaneity tugging at his hand?

We live neither in the future, nor in the past. Rather, we live on that razor's edge that slices through that millisecond just after the split-second past and just before the split-second future. All the memories of yesterday and all the hopes of tomorrow are packed into that slender moment of the Eternal Now. Both the past and the future are important. But the present is more so! The light by which we walk towards tomorrow shines on us and ahead of us from yesterday. We do not live in the past, but we live <u>out of</u> the past. We do not live in the future, but we live <u>into</u> the future. So we pray:

> Eternal God, the Source of our life, the Companion of our way, the Destiny of our pilgrimage:
>
> > Make us aware of the past -- lest we become superficial;
> > Make us conscious of the present -- lest we become irrelevant;
> > Make us committed to the future -- lest we lose hope.
>
> We pray this in the name of Jesus Christ, who is, for us, the Way, the Truth, the Life. Amen.

Gratefully and hopefully and sincerely, I am your fellow "now and here" pilgrim on the way from the Garden of Eden to the Kingdom of Heaven!

9

Lent and Easter

March 4, 1965

Dear Friends:

Received a bit of "feedback" about a couple of the sermons last month, for which I say "Hurrah!" This preacher believes that a negative response is a good indicator that the message is getting through. A critical word is more to be desired than applause…even much fine applause. He that kicketh hath been pricked.

Saw a tear or two at our "Service of Thanksgiving and Blessing for Little Children." We all have a very soft spot for babies. I'm not one for ceremony, but William Blake's blessing, "Little Lamb, God Bless Thee" may become an annual tradition with your minister.

Looking back, I now realize that we might better have received our Week of Compassion offering <u>after</u> the February 21 sermon rather than <u>before</u>. But everyone was gratified by the additional $100 given on February 28.

Now that the mass is being read in English we have the interesting situation that the average Roman Catholic will hear more scripture in his own language than will the average Protestant on any given Sunday. Now who are the people of the Book? A real switch! Should have happened 1,000 years ago. But rather than talk about "should have" let's ask, "What are we going to do about it? How will we catch up!?"

Lent is upon us. And who is "Lent"? It's not a "who"! It's a what! It is the period of 40 days prior to Easter when the Church concentrates on the last weeks of the ministry of Jesus. "Lent" is an old Anglo-Saxon word akin to our "lengthen" and has reference to the lengthening of days of sunlight during the early spring. The 40 days of Lent from Ash Wednesday to Easter, exclusive of Sundays, recalls the 40 days Jesus spent in the wilderness following his baptism. Traditionally it has been a time for considering the temptations and conflicts which confront every Christian in life, and confronting the realization that the Christian choice, and this alone, leads to meaningful living. The hymns, the scripture selections, the sermons, the prayers, everything in the life of our church will be directed toward a deepening of our understanding of the Christian faith and life.

I do hope that during this season every Christian will try to live a more disciplined life. I suggest a more careful use of our devotional materials. Perhaps the reading of one of the books from our church library will help deepen your Christian faith. Through worship each Lord's Day you will find a closer identification with "the man of sorrows"[84] who suffered for us. It is in such fellowship that we too can learn to suffer for others. Pray for God's guidance and strength in these days.

March 5, 1975

Dear March Friends:

Out at 7205 Sheffield some 390 jonquils have pushed their heads up through the frosty crust of a late-winter night's dream. But this morning's near freeze will punish them for their early rising. Their sleepier neighbors -- some 75 tulips -- will shortly be yawning and stretching themselves awake in a world called to new life by spring's warmth. And then the dogwoods and redbuds and azaleas and so on! Soon we will be driving through Holston Hills and Fountain City and Sequoyah and Lakemoor and Cades Cove drinking in April's gift to East Tennessee. What happy anticipations! Meantime -- we will be living with frostbitten buttercups and bare-boned sycamores. And, of course, tending the store, keeping house, catching up on our knitting, etc.

Here at the church, there are a few extras on the agenda: an old church year to be closed out, new elders and deacons and deacons-in-training to be oriented into their work, committee assignments to be made for the year beginning April 1 and plans to be developed for the ensuring twelve months, music to be arranged for Palm Sunday and Easter, a record budget to be raised, youth activities to be expanded -- and 1000 individual and personal ministries to be extended. To some it may seem like so much "tending the store, keeping hours, catching up on our knitting, etc." -- rather "business-as-usual-ish." But for those who have eyes to see -- things are blossoming. Folk are discovering a new sense of freedom and well-being. Young people are finding that life can be beautiful. Our more mature members are rejoicing in the goodness and mercy which has followed them all the days of their lives. Persons in their middle years are affirming for themselves and for their families a higher, a finer, a more Christian life. Individuals are achieving a deeper faith and a stronger commitment. It's quite a sight to see! And it is my daily prayer that you -- and those near and dear to you -- are sharing in this re-awakening of the faith and hope and love of Easter.

Easter? Did someone say, "Easter!"? Yes! And with an exclamation point, like so: "EASTER!" Comes early this year -- March 30. And it will be a BIG day for us all! Come blossom with us!

With high hopes because of buttercups and dogwoods and redbuds and azaleas and Easter lilies, I am, your pastor and friend.

April 8, 1981

Dear Christian Friends:

The dogwoods are ready to burst open -- a bit like popcorn. First, there will be a few scattered blossoms. Then -- as things warm up -- a thousand blossoms all at once! East Tennessee is a Garden of Eden in April! What a joy it is to live and move and have our being in this paradise of green hills and delicate flowers. "My heart leaps up when I behold"[85] the dogwoods and redbuds and azaleas in their spring splendor.

> This is my Father's world; Oh, let me ne'er forget
> That though the wrong seems oft so strong,
> God is the ruler yet!
> This is my Father's world; why should my heart be sad?
> The Lord is King; let the heavens sing.
> God reigns; let the earth be glad![86]

> Indeed! Spring is sprung! "Let the earth...be glad!" (Psalms 97:1 RSV)

There are a thousand other reasons for our joy! For instance, we rejoice with persons who have heard good news from their doctors: "Your reports are all clear. You are well!" Yes! Let the earth be glad!

But there are those for whom the news is dreadful. For them the "valley of the shadow" is around the next bend. "The wrong seems oft so strong!"

We rejoice with the families of the hostages recently returned from Iran. What reunions of warmth! Embraces! Happy hugs! Glistening eyes! Pounding hearts! "Let the earth be glad!"

But there are the families of those who died at Desert One. Those eight young men paid the "last full measure of devotion."[87] Their deaths have left a great emptiness at home. "The wrong seems oft so strong!"

We rejoice with little children who sing and dance their way to school. There they discover the amazing complexity of a tulip bulb or a butterfly wing. And there they master the basics of the alphabet -- the foundation upon which they will build careers in accounting or in medicine or in journalism or in engineering. "Let the earth be glad!"

But there are thousands of little children of very poor families. These children have not so much been born into the world as rather they have been damned into the world. Their prospects for the abundant life are two: slim and very slim! "The wrong seems oft so strong!"

We rejoice with the coming of Easter -- that greatest day of the Christian calendar -- that celebration of the soul's invincible surmise -- the occasion that reassures us that love is stronger than hate, that light overpowers darkness, that life is conqueror of death -- the moment when we will lift that crescendo of faith's highest affirmation: "The Hallelujah Chorus"! "Let the earth be very glad!"

But -- there are many who count out their dull and dark days in gloomy cynicism and despair. Their unfaith is a cloud that obscures the light of the candle of life. "The wrong seems oft so strong!"

The dogwoods and redbuds and azaleas are painting the hillsides and lawns white and pink and lipstick red. But -- the dandelions and the thorn-bushes and chick-weed are coming into their own, too! "Our Father's world" needs gardeners -- who will cut away the underbrush, root out disease and hostility and poverty and unfaith. Let us be realistic enough to see the wild onions and crabgrass of life. But let us also be optimistic enough to believe that the ultimate reality is reflected not in the weeds and thorns -- but in the Easter lilies of spring and the roses of summer.

With faith and hope and love, I am, your pastor and friend.

April 7, 1982

Dear Spring Friends:

Is there a finer month in the year than April? Hardly! The frigid winter is past. The hot summer is future. Just now we have 30 days of gentle breezes and refreshing rains and moderate temperatures. And throughout this month a parade of beauty: pink buds, plum blossoms, weeping cherries, tulips, dogwoods, azaleas. The Creator smiled on April -- dressed it more lavishly than any other two months combined!

Easter -- the greatest day on the Christian calendar -- often falls in this month. The coincidence is a fortunate one. The natural world around us is flowering into new beauty. The spiritual world within us is being resurrected to new life in Christ. After winter comes spring. After Crucifixion comes the Resurrection. After the tragedy of Good Friday comes the triumph of Easter Sunday. The essential message of the season was encompassed by George Matheson's lines:

O Cross that liftest up my head,
I dare not ask to fly from thee;
I lay in dust life's glory dead,
And from the ground there blossoms red
Life that shall endless be.[88]

That's the Gospel in poetry. Next Sunday hear that same Gospel in music from the choir and in preaching from the pulpit. Come!

Yours, in the hope that springs eternal.

April 1, 1988

Dear Easter Friends:

Tears, tears. Balzac summarized that he knew tears -- just a little phosphorus and water. In terms of chemistry, Balzac was right: "...just a little phosphorus and water"![89] For the cynic that is enough. But the lens of chemistry is not the only lens through which we see tears:

A bride and a groom meet at the wedding altar. Their eyes are blurred. She dabs a hanky to her cheek. He represses his instinctual move to do the same. Men don't cry. But he does anyway. Together, they are looking toward tomorrow with hope -- through tears of joy, commitment, expectation. Much more than "...just a little phosphorus and water"!

She watches her teenager as the lead actor in the senior play. Every scene --- every line -- every gesture seems to the mother to be her own. Her ambitions for herself have been transferred to her daughter. The curtain closes. The audience rises in unanimous and enthusiastic and extended applause. Mother and daughter embrace. They look at each other through tears. Tears of identity, pride, encouragement. Much more than "...just a little phosphorus and water"!

The members of the honor guard set the casket over the grave. The chaplain intones the words: "...earth to earth, ashes to ashes, dust to dust." Six riflemen present arms, fire a *salute,* step back to one side. The bugler sounds "Taps." The officer hands the triangle of white stars on a field of blue to the next-of-kin. Tears flow -- tears of sacrifice, grief, patriotism. Much more than "...just a little phosphorus and water."

Lilies -- their white trumpets facing the East -- crowd the chancel area. The candles on the Communion Table flutter. The choir assembles at the head of the aisle. The organist finishes the prelude. The chimes sound. The congregation lifts the Easter hymn: "Christ the Lord is risen today!

Alleluia!"[90] Tears! Every Christian in the house weeps tears -- tears that speak eloquently of the power of light over darkness, of the triumph of courage over despair, of the victory of life over death! Much more than "...just a little phosphorus and water"!

The worship service on Easter Sunday is the Mt. Everest of the Christian year. Our faith and hope and love are bundled in one climactic hour of praise and prayer and preaching. Our spirits are lifted! Our souls are strengthened! Our hearts are warmed! Come early this Sunday. Be in your pew for the prelude. During the service weep tears of triumph and joy with your fellow Christians. Stay afterward for the Fellowship Half-Hour. Leave with the resurrection message echoing in your consciousness: "The strife is o'er, the battle done; The victory of life is won; The song of triumph has begun: Alleluia!"[91]

March 2, 1990

Dear Advent/Christmas and Lent/Easter Friends:

Included in the grand essentials of the good life are "Someone to love, something to do, something to hope for."[92] Whoever first said that was on target -- especially about the third grand essential: "Something to hope for." Life is better when you have something to look forward to:

> The assembly-line worker whistles while he repeats the same task a thousand times during an eight-hour shift -- and he watches the clock. After quittin' time he hustles home to his wife, his children, a happy supper, an evening of TV, a night of rest. He whistles while he works because he has something to look forward to. And life is better!

> The gardener, leaning on his hoe, is happy. Hidden below the surface of the neat rows of fresh soil are seeds. Before long there will be sprigs of green. Soon after there with be carrots, beets, radishes, cucumbers, okra. The gardener looks forward to showing off the first ripe tomato of the season. And life is better!

> The couple painting the nursery, hanging new curtains, collecting baby things -- that couple has something to look forward to! "A child more than all other gifts which earth offers to man in his declining years brings hope with it and forward-looking thoughts."[93] And life is better!

Something to look forward to -- "something to hope for" -- makes church life better, too. Right now we are looking forward to Easter -- Resurrection Sunday -- April 15, 1990. We will lift up the lines: "Christ the Lord is risen today! Alleluia!"[94] In music, in scripture, in poetry, in sermon, in communion we will rejoice in Christ's victory over death: "The strife is o'er, the battle done; The victory of life is won; The song of triumph has begun: Alleluia!"[95]

But Easter is six weeks down the calendar! We are looking forward to that great day -- April 15. But for the time being we are retracing the footsteps of Jesus: from Galilee to Jerusalem; from Mount Horeb (the Temptation) to Mount Calvary (the Crucifixion); and in the last week, from the triumph of Palm Sunday to the tragedy of Good Friday. Then comes the brightness of the Easter dawn: "The Lord is risen!" The six weeks of the Lenten season demand disciplined commitment before we can know the joy of the resurrection. But we are like the Israelites. They wanted to reach the Promised Land without struggling through the Wilderness. We Christians crave the brightness of Easter. But we dread the darkness that precedes it! So we must be reminded: No Pain -- No Gain! No Wilderness -- No Promised Land! No Cross -- No Crown!

For the next six weeks join the rest of your Christian friends in a Lenten season of self-discipline:

- Brighten someone else's world. Each day invest a bit of time and energy in someone who will benefit from the care you offer -- by phone, by note, by visit.
- Give up reading the lightweight stuff: Erma Bombeck, John Kelso, Billy Porterfield. Take on the heavyweights, the Gospels: Matthew, Mark, Luke, John.
- Control your appetites: mental, emotional, physical. Cultivate your best self: integrity, compassion, health. Leave the low road. Take the high way!

The six weeks of Lent need not be gloomy -- dark with negatives -- heavy with obligations. Rather, six weeks of focused thought and caring deeds and disciplined behavior can lead from a desolate wilderness into an oasis of joy. Following Christ from the mountain of temptation to the mountain of sacrifice can be the gestation for a new birth of faith and hope and love. That is a kind of personal Easter! That's something to look forward to! And life is better!

March 15, 1991

Dear Friends:

We have followed many a casket -- out of the sanctuary -- into the hearse -- to the cemetery -- to the grave. We have read the opening lines of Psalm 23: "The Lord is my shepherd; I shall not want" and continued on to the last affirmation: "...and I [shall] dwell in the house of the Lord forever." (Psalms 23:1, 6 KJV) Then the committal:

> Forasmuch as Almighty God has received unto himself our sister we therefore do now commit her body to the ground -- earth to earth, ashes to ashes, dust to dust -- in sure and certain hope of the resurrection -- trusting that as she has lived and moved and had her being within God's

loving care -- that she rests now in the loving embrace of the everlasting arms of God and that she shall dwell in the house of the Lord forever.

A prayer of benediction. A whispered word to the next-of-kin. The pallbearers follow in turn -- then hugs from friends. It is a bittersweet moment. There is grief because one has died. There is gratitude that one has lived. We leave the cemetery with hearts that are heavy -- yet hopeful.

What does it all mean: eulogy -- casket -- pallbearers -- hearse -- cemetery -- flowers -- Psalm 23 -- committal -- benediction -- hugs and tears -- the bittersweet mix of grief and gratitude? How do we maintain the tension between those two phrases in the committal: "earth to earth, ashes to ashes, dust to dust" and "in sure and certain hope of the Resurrection"?[96] We do believe that even death cannot separate us from the love of God in Christ Jesus. The mixture of grief and gratitude does have a bittersweet aftertaste. Which is dominant: the bitter? or the sweet? Why? Sadness and joy -- despair and hope -- regret and thanksgiving -- fear and courage -- defeat and victory -- these follow each other to the cemetery -- and back -- to the empty house, empty chair, empty shoes, empty schedule, empty future. What about the future?

Sometimes we find it difficult to be clear, absolute, definite. Things are relative. Maybe yes -- maybe no. Perhaps -- perhaps not. We think -- but we are not certain. Black and white won't do -- there are many shades of grey. On the one hand -- on the other hand. Often we limp between two opinions. But not at Easter time. This is the time we offer a clear, definite, affirmative, enthusiastic word! On Sunday, March 31, we will celebrate Christ's triumph over the grave and proclaim our own "sure and certain hope of the resurrection." COME!

With faith and hope and love, I am, your minister and friend.

March 29, 1991

Dear Fellow Believers:

"The heart has its reasons which reason cannot know."[97] Emotion has a logic beyond logic. Feelings cannot be reduced to precisely balanced formulae. The sensitive soul decides, chooses, acts out of a spiritual calculus that cannot be rationally computed. "We walk by faith, not by sight." (II Corinthians 5:7 RSV) We all know what Paul meant. Even our strictest scientists know: our physicists, our chemists, our mathematicians. "We all walk by faith, not by sight." The scientists' most certain knowledge is still uncertain, indefinite, not sure. For what is the most famous scientist/mathematician of this century most famous? The theory of relativity! In his theory of relativity Einstein expressed the notion that even our most exact measurements are inexact! Our second-grade teacher taught us the equation: 2 plus 2 equals 4. Yet, some mathematicians are not so sure about that equation. Under most circumstances, 2 plus 2 equals 4. But those who really know numbers know that there are circumstances in which 2 plus 2 does not equal 4!

For the most part we are rational persons. We tend to trust what we can see and hear and feel and smell and taste. We absorb most of our information, knowledge, wisdom through the five senses -- so we say, "Things have to make sense to me." Yet, there are many things that we do not grasp with the rational senses. But we feel them with the <u>sensitive</u> soul! There are many things that are beyond reason, logic, formula, equations, rationality -- things beyond our understanding that are grasped by the heart, not by the head. "'What no eye has seen, nor ear heard, nor the heart of man conceived, what God has prepared for those who love him,' God has revealed to us through the Spirit." (I Corinthians 2:9-10 RSV)

See that tear on the cheek. Maybe you saw it at a birthday party -- or in a cemetery -- or during a wedding. A tear. Just a tear. Balzac would say, "Tears? Tears? I know tears -- a *little* water and phosphorus!"[98] But the sensitive soul knows that tears are much more than "a little phosphorus and water." "The heart has its reasons which reason cannot know." Dismantle an Easter lily into its several parts: root -- stem -- leaf -- sepal -- petal -- stamen -- pistil. Lay those parts neatly on a counter in a botany lab. Those are the parts of an Easter lily. But the sensitive soul feels that an Easter lily is so much more than the sum of all its parts! "The heart has its reasons which reason cannot know." A rainbow -- a pair of bronzed infant's shoes -- a kiss -- a packet of letters -- a yellow ribbon -- a ring -- a last will and testament -- each has a measure of meaning beyond measure! "The heart has its reasons which reason cannot know."

It is so with religious truths. God slips through the net of logic, but God is grasped by the trusting child of God: "The Lord is my shepherd; I shall not want!" (Psalms 23:1 KJV) Likewise with Christ. The high priest condemned Jesus; a squad of soldiers crucified him; the seal of Rome was set on his tomb. That was almost 2000 years ago. Yet, we still sing:

> He lives! He lives! Christ Jesus lives today!
> He lives! He lives! Salvation to impart!
> You ask me how I know he lives?
> He lives within my heart![99]

So too the net of reason is of too large a mesh to net the notion of Spirit. But the believer understands. "The Spirit...intercedes for us with sighs too deep for words." (Romans 8:26 RSV) Or, "with sighs too deep for" logic -- or rationality -- or equations -- or dictionaries! Creation -- Sin and Forgiveness -- Sacrifice -- Atonement -- Reconciliation -- Conversion -- Kingdom of God -- Baptism -- Heaven -- Salvation -- Resurrection -- like God and Christ and Spirit, these are religious terms. They cannot be reduced to precise definitions understood by the head. Rather, they are seen, heard, felt by an intuition beyond logic. "The heart has its reasons which reason cannot know."

To paraphrase Harriet Martineau, "We do not believe the resurrection because we have proved it; rather, we eternally try to prove the resurrection because we believe it!"[100] "Proving" the resurrection is not needed for those who already believe. "Proving" the resurrection will not convince those who do not believe. "A man convinced against his will is of the same opinion still."[101] This Sunday, the minister will not prove the resurrection. Won't even try. But he will bear witness to the presence and power and peace of the risen Christ in our world. Come! Whether you need it or not -- COME!

March 19, 1993

Dear Christian Friends:

In an Easter frame of mind! Already! Even though Resurrection Sunday is still four Sundays down the calendar. Started feeling this way on February 14 -- Valentine's Day. That's when Deena and Jeff Long seeded the west hillside on San Antonio Street with a Texas Wildflower "Confetti Mix." Soon that hillside will be an Impressionist's pallet: indefinite blues -- soft pinks -- splotches of red -- bright yellow. Easter Lilies on Resurrection Sunday speak of new life. Purple Cornflowers and Black-Eyed Susans do, too!

My Easter frame of mind was reinforced by a similar good deed by Roland Kinney. Our AAA favorite rosarian has cleared out some of our non-productive rose bushes, freshened up our rosebeds, and is in the process of transplanting 15 hybrids: "Perfume Delight -- Tiffany -- Touch of Class -- Mr. Lincoln -- etc." Soon we will have some 40 blossoming rose bushes around our buildings. We will enjoy these on Resurrection Sunday, April 11. And throughout 1993! Easter Lilies speak of new Life! So do Scarlet Flax and Indian Paintbrushes! And the Peace Rose and Crimson Glory Rose do, too!

My Easter frame of mind was reinforced this week by the Flaming Azaleas in the flower bed at the base of the bell-tower. These were planted two years ago by Gilbert Escovedo and Stan Perry and C.B. Teel. They were a gift by Mary Lee Philippi -- offered as a memorial to her husband, Olaf. This week the Philippi Azaleas are a fiery fuchsia! 'Minds us of the burning bush that was not consumed.

> Moses...led his flock to the west side of the wilderness, and came to Horeb, the mountain of God. And the angel of the Lord appeared to him in a flame of fire out of the midst of a bush; and he looked, and lo, the bush was burning, yet it was not consumed. And Moses said, "I will turn aside and see this great sight, why the bush is not burnt." When the

Lord saw that he turned aside to see, God called to him out of the bush, "Moses, Moses!" And he said, "Here am I." Then he said, "Do not come near, put off your shoes from your feet, for the place on which you are standing is holy ground." (Exodus 3:1-5 RSV)

That is a great message to each of us -- whoever we are -- wherever we are standing: "The place on which you are standing is holy ground"! This Sunday as you make your way from the Community Room to the Sanctuary for worship -- or as you leave the Sanctuary after worship to share in the Fellowship Half-Hour over a cup-o-coff -- pause a moment near the Philippi Azaleas. These are our own "burning bush that was not consumed"! And whisper to yourself: "The place on which you are standing is holy ground"! It is! Easter Lilies speak of new life. So do Rocket Larkspurs and Texas Bluebells! And so do Elmhurst Roses and Tropicanas! And Flaming Azaleas do, too!

March 3, 1995

Dear Resurrection Friends:

Easter is still seven Sundays down the calendar. But these seven Sundays will slip past so fast! Soon we will hear the lines: "The Lord is risen! He is risen, indeed!"[102] And we will stand with the congregation singing "Christ the Lord is risen today! Alleluia!"[103] What a thrilling tune -- what inspiring words -- with which to begin a service of worship: "Alleluia!" Some seventy Easter lilies will transform the sanctuary into a garden. The pews will be crowded. The hymns, the scriptures, the prayers, the sermon will focus on the theme: "I am the resurrection and the life; he who believes in me, though he die, yet shall he live, and whoever lives and believes in me shall never die!" (John 11:25-26 RSV) The service of worship will close with Handel's *Hallelujah!* After that, greetings and embraces and love for everyone. Plenty!

Meanwhile! And that's such a significant word: "Meanwhile." Meanwhile, we have some six Sundays before the seventh -- the six weeks of Lent -- 40 days (not counting Sundays) between Ash Wednesday and Resurrection Sunday. A season for self-discipline -- controlling physical appetites -- nurturing spiritual hungers! A month-and-a-half for quietness and introspection! A time of turning from the low road and of turning onto the high way! A retreat from the distractions that disturb us into the closet for prayer that empowers us! A toning down of the noise and clangor of the moment in order to tune in on the music of eternity. All this and more -- that's what the 40-days' Lenten pilgrimage is all about!

Some folk (many!) try to cash in on the joy of Easter without investing in the seriousness of Lent. Their spring celebration is one of bonnets and blossoms, of parades and parties. Such things are a part of -- but only a part of -- the happiest of days on the Christian calendar. One does not sense the ecstasy of Easter until one shares the agony that precedes it. The Children of Israel did not make it to the Promised Land without first enduring the Wilderness. Crucifixion Friday precedes Resurrection Sunday! No pain -- no gain! No cross -- no crown!

Our 40-days' Lenten journey of self-discipline, of introspection, of sacrifice, of prayer has begun. Soon these six weeks will slip past. And then, on the seventh Sunday, all together we will lift the lines:

> Christ the Lord is risen today, Alleluia!
> Sons of men and angels say, Alleluia!
> Raise your joys and triumphs high, Alleluia!
> Sing, ye heavens, and earth reply, Alleluia! [104]

March 17, 1995

Dear Resurrection Friends:

Easter is only five Sundays down the calendar -- all five soon to be gone! On the fifth Sunday we will sing: "Christ the Lord is risen today! Alleluia!"[105] Inspiring music! Seventy Easter lilies! Hymns, scriptures, prayers, sermon focused on the theme: "I am the resurrection and the life!" And at the end of the service a "sing-a-long" as the congregation joins the choir to lift Handel's "Hallelujah!"

Meanwhile! And that's such a significant word: "Meanwhile." Meanwhile, the browns of winter are becoming the greens of spring. Soon, all Central Texas will be a wildflower paradise: bluebonnets, Indian paintbrushes, primroses, azaleas, Easter lilies. I saw my first bluebonnet blossom of 1995 last Sunday A.M. It smiled at me from the hillside above San Antonio Street as I wheeled my old Olds into the parking lot. 'Twas such a happy greeting. Then, as I waltzed through the breezeway, my eyes gathered in a host of azaleas in the Olaf and Mary Lee Philippi corner. Blushing pink and kissy red, they, too, smiled at me. 'Twas such a happy greeting!

Smiling bluebonnets! Smiling azaleas! But those colorful smiles were no match for the watermelon-slice smile of Taylor Gaines as he stumbled through the gate from the parking lot. He had not done that for two months! That long? Yes! Taylor took a 2-months' detour around the Valley of the Shadow! A happier soul than Taylor Gaines can hardly be found in all of Central Texas. A brush with death sensitizes us so we never again take things for granted! Even tiny things. After a detour around the Valley of the Shadow, a single bluebonnet has a beauty we had not seen before. A blushing azalea, too! A crust of bread, a dab of jam, a sip of coff -- become a banquet! A familiar shoe is ecstasy! The privilege of sitting in a long empty pew is a privilege! An Easter lily moves us to tears of appreciation and delight!

"Meanwhile!" Meanwhile, the 1995 Lenten season of 40 days has shortened to less than 30. Soon comes Palm Sunday -- April 9. Then comes Maundy Thursday -- April 13. Finally, Resurrection Sunday -- April 16. Soon! So soon we will stand with the congregation singing Handel's "Hallelujah Chorus":

> Hallelujah!
> For the Lord God Omnipotent reigneth
> Hallelujah!
> The kingdom of this world
> Is become
> The Kingdom of our Lord,
> And of His Christ
> And He shall reign forever and ever
> King of Kings
> And Lord of Lords
> Forever and ever.
> Hallelujah![106]

Taylor isn't much of a singer. But he is a foot-patter! And a whistler! And a hummer! He'll do all three on Resurrection Sunday. "Hallelujah! Amen!"

I am, your friend and pastor -- in winter and in spring -- in dark times and in bright.

April 2, 1999

Dear Resurrection Friends:

For most of us it is a matter of "no pain -- no gain"! That's where we are at this moment on the Christian calendar. We are entering the darkness of Good Friday when the worst of hell destroyed the best of heaven. But we must pass through the midnight of the soul before we can open our eyes to the dawn of Easter Sunday! Without the tragedy of the crucifixion we cannot grasp the triumph of the resurrection. "No cross -- No crown!"

Some have interpreted the death of Jesus of Nazareth as a transaction by which the sins of many were cleansed by the sacrifice of one. The notion has been reinforced by a number of our hymns:

> Alas! And did my Savior bleed, and did my Sovereign die?
> Would he devote that sacred head for such a worm as I?
> What can wash away my sin? Nothing but the blood of Jesus!
> What can make one whole again? Nothing but the blood of Jesus!
> There is a fountain filled with the blood drawn from Immanuel's veins,
> And sinners, plunged beneath that flood, lose all their guilty stains.

> Just as I am, without one plea but that thy blood was shed for me,
> And that thou bid'st me come to thee, O Lamb of God, I come! I
>   come![107]

Was the crucifixion of Jesus the vicarious atonement by which the demands of God's justice were satisfied by the death of God's son? "Well might the sun in darkness hide and shut its glories in, when Christ, the mighty Maker, died for his own creature's sin."[108] That equation balanced in ancient days. But this convoluted doctrine obscures a more valid interpretation about the ministry and death and resurrection of Jesus.

This more attractive notion is that Jesus's teaching that God is love, his commitment to truth, his compassion for the weak, his capacity to forgive -- all these lift us above the ordinary level of humanity onto the extraordinary plane of divinity. By looking at Jesus we become like Jesus! Way back in the second century, Irenaeus expressed it this way: "God became man so that man might become God." [Irenaeus also said: "The glory of God is a man (person) fully alive."][109] Paul expressed this transformation like so: "And we all, with unveiled face, beholding the glory of the Lord, are being changed into his likeness from one degree of glory to another." (II Corinthians 3:18 RSV)

Looking back from this side of Easter to the tragedy of Good Friday, we Christians see -- not the defeat of the human spirit -- but the victory of the human spirit. We learn that faith is more powerful than fear. We discover that hope triumphs over despair. We believe that love is stronger than hate. We trust that forgiveness wins over vengeance. No matter what was destroyed by crucifixion on Good Friday, faith and hope and love and forgiveness blossomed into new life in the hearts of the disciples on Easter Sunday! The spirit of Christ -- his teaching that God is love, his commitment to truth, his compassion for the weak, his capacity to forgive -- these could *not* be sealed in a tomb. "Truth, crushed to earth, shall rise again!"[110]

> He lives! He lives! Christ Jesus lives today! He walks with me and
>   talks with me along life's narrow way!
> He lives! He lives! Salvation to impart! You ask me how I know he
>   lives? He lives within my heart![111]

Resurrection Sunday is upon us! We will begin at 10:55 A.M. by lifting the Easter hymn: "Christ the Lord is risen today! Alleluia!" We will end at high noon with "He Lives! He Lives!" Then we all will leave -- lifted, inspired, strengthened, encouraged to follow in the footsteps of the risen Christ whom we confess as Lord and Savior!

10

Thanksgiving

November 14, 1973

Dear Friends Old and New and Otherwise:

Some things grow old real quickly: like this morning's pancakes, like yesterday's headlines, like last year's auto models. Some things are new every morning: like the ivy beside the porch steps, like the light in a child's eyes, like the secretary's smile. Some things get better with age: like a chunk of Roquefort cheese, like a fine wine, like a treasured heirloom. Some things are ageless: like Rome-The Eternal City, like Michelangelo's *David* or Shakespeare's *Hamlet,* like *The Gettysburg Address*, or The 23rd Psalm or The Sermon on the Mount.

Last Sunday we heard Handel's *Messiah* for the umpteenth time. Rendered by the 71-voice Maryville College and Community Choir and a 52-piece orchestra including tympani and harpsichord -- it was "a thing of beauty -- a joy forever!"[112] Ah! -- Friends Old and New and Otherwise -- Handel's *Messiah,* like Abe Lincoln, "...belongs to the ages!"

For the umpteenth time I was stirred to the depth -- only more so than ever before. Next year for the umpteenther time it will be more so again. Our almost-8-year-old Shana heard Handel's masterpiece for the first time last Sunday. When she is 88 years young this timeless piece will still be to her a source of joy and of high inspiration.

As a church family, it will be ours in a smaller way to share in Handel's gift to mankind on Sunday, December 16. Our Chancel Choir will present excerpts from the *Messiah* at our service of worship on that day at 10:50 A.M. -- sans tympani, sans harpsichord -- but with organ and stringed quartet accompaniment. All you lovers of things good and beautiful and true will be there -- as well as a lot of your friends. For the umpteenth time your hearts will be stirred and thrilled and lifted.

Something that never grows old is our Children's Christmas Program. Even Handel has to take a back seat for that. On Sunday, December 23, our children will present *Lo! A Star!* at the 10:50 A.M. service. Ah! What a very special occasion that will be. And it will be climaxed by a baptismal service for 10 of our children who will be graduating from The Pastor's Class. That will make for a very exciting hour for a whole lot of people.

Finally, "Thanksgiving" has an eternal quality about it. From Adam in the Garden of Eden savoring the first ripe fig of the summer season to the Psalmist singing out: "The Lord is my shepherd, I shall not want" (Psalms 23:1 KJV) all the way to the nuclear physicist overawed by the order and splendor revealed by his electron microscope -- from Adam to Einstein -- man has within himself the urge to say "Thanks!"

No! "Thanksgiving" is never out of date! Jamais!

Next Sunday at 10:50 A.M. our church family will lift grateful hearts and enthusiastic voices, singing "God of Our Fathers" and "Now Thank We All Our God!" Friends Old and New and Otherwise -- join your hearts and voices with us. And then bend your ear to take in the pastor's somewhat old, somewhat new, somewhat otherwise perspectives on the gratitude attitude entitled "A Second Look at the First Thanksgiving."

With a song in my heart and a sermon in my head, I am, Thanksgivingly yours.

November 6, 1974

Dear November Friends:

Spent a couple of hours this morning sanding and varnishing a walnut cabinet of drawers for Adena's bedroom. Two years ago I had brought it back from Grandpa Schiller's in Joplin, Missouri, in a U-Haul trailer. It's an old piece -- mid-19th century. A hand-tooled thing put together with glue and pegs. A wedding gift made especially for Adena's great-great-grandmother. Carries its age well -- has a lot of character: chipped corners, scarred surfaces, drawers several times repaired, water and oil stains on top. But it is serviceable -- and has a lot of sentiment attached to it. Adena will enjoy it for the next half century -- then she will pass it on to a granddaughter of her own -- say about the year 2024.

Left home at 9:30. Dropped by the Cedar Bluff Middle School to exercise my inalienable right to cancel Judie's vote. Then drove leisurely up I-40. The skies were unusually clean, fresh -- having been scrubbed and shampooed by last night's welcome rain. The sharp outline of the Smokies sort-of framed things on the right of the highway. Cruised past the Alcoa Exit -- and then I saw it! That huge, bright new flag waving in front of the administration offices at Rohm and Haas. Wordsworth it was who said:

"My heart leaps up when I behold
A rainbow in the sky."[113]

That rainbow of red, white, and blue that we call "Old Glory" did that for me this morning! My heart leapt up! Friends, it is an immense privilege to live and move and have one's being in America in 1974! To linger lovingly over an old piece of furniture that will still be around after I am gone -- to flip a lever in the privacy of a voting booth -- to salute the flag -- to see the reshaping of Knoxville's skyline (the steel for the top story of the TVA building is going in place this week) -- to hear the hum of industry and the roar of traffic -- to feel the pulse of the community -- to sit here in this sermon-writing study reflecting on passing pleasures and everlasting values -- the privilege of it all is more than my little heart can hold in. For me every day is Thanksgiving Day! November promises a lot of nice things for us at FCC. And so does December. And so too, January 1975 -- and on down the calendar. Come! Enjoy the abundant life with us. It is a great time to be alive!

With gratitude slipping out the end of my pencil -- and joy overflowing within, I am, Your Novemberish friend.

November 5, 1975

Dear Fellow East Tennesseans:

The sunrise this A.M. was tremend! Magnif! Extraord! The clouds were a confusion of purple and blue rimmed by a blaze of Big Orange that faded blush pink into the hazy distance. We watched Ol' Sol do his thing for the umpteen-millionth time. His production was staged with the farthest range of the Smokies as a jagged backdrop. It was framed by a ruddy maple in our patio on the right -- and by a gum on the left that didn't know whether it was supposed to be brown or green or blue.

When God set the match to the sun and sprinkled the stars against the inky sky and then dipped his bristle-brush in the rainbow to paint the sunrises and sunsets and the seasons -- how he must have smiled as he worked! His masterpiece is not yet done. He has not laid aside his palette and tubes of umber and emerald, of ocher and amber, of sapphire and scarlet. And ours is the privilege of looking over his shoulder and smiling with him as he continues his work on his <u>magnum opus.</u>

The Creator was especially lavish when he laid out the lines of East Tennessee and pushed up its mountains and marked its rivers and planted its forests! And I am so grateful to live and to move and to have my being in what must truly be one of the most beautiful places in all creation.

Beyond that I am thankful for the high privilege of serving as the pastor of a warm and loving and caring Christian fellowship which, by chance or by Providence, happens to be in East Tennessee. That's a combination hard to beat. What a scene! And what kindly thoughts with which to crank up a new day! Ah! I feel good all over -- inside and out -- from toupee to toe!

The next 30 days in our Church Family Life are special. Though few of us harvest more than a couple dozen tomatoes and a bushel or two of beans -- still, in this autumnal season we love to raise our voices with the congregation:

> Come, ye thankful people come,
> Raise the song of harvest home;
> All is safely gathered in,
> Ere the winter storms begin.[114]

November scatters the attitude of gratitude throughout the community. Do plan to share that "good all over" feeling with us over the next several weeks. And especially on Sunday, November 16. That's when "We Gather Together" with all the church family for turkey and dressing, etc. I'll be up early that day. Watching Ol' Sol do his morning calisthenics. Absorbing the kaleidoscope of clouds and colors, of leaves and lawns, of houses and highways. Thinking of the loves and labors, the triumphs and tragedies of my people. Anticipating the hours of conversation and worship and fellowship to come. Offering to God my personal thanksgiving for life and health, for family and friends, for church and community, for faith and hope, and most of all for love -- without which everything would be a grand emptiness.

I love you all. I love you each.

November 11, 1988

Dear Thanks Givers:

The gratitude-attitude swells to full-fruitage in November. This month of giving thanks is the season when "Thank you" has an overplus of content. That casual two-word phase of appreciation is no longer casual. It carries a bit more freight. And it not only carries a bit more freight (of appreciation) it also delivers more goods (of generosity)! Show me a person who is generous and I will show you a person who is grateful. Generosity and gratitude live under the same roof. And this eleventh month of the year is for celebrating this happy marriage of receiving and giving.

This gratitude-attitude mood washed over me Monday. I was meeting a new friend for lunch. Skipped up the porch at Green Pastures rather briskly. Remembered that a few months back I was down in my back. Hobbling decrepitly. Muscle spasms. So -- for the health and strength to skip up to the porch at Green Pastures rather briskly, I am grateful.

The bells of St. Ignatius Martyr Church tolled the hour -- high noon. Twelve basso-profundo bongs echoed through the South Austin neighborhood. St. Ignatius Church has been there lo these many decades: lifting the fallen, helping the hurt, guiding the young, encouraging the seeker. I am grateful for St. Ignatius Church, and for the bells of St. Ignatius Church, and for the ears to count their pleasant bongs! That's how things are in November.

At the table across the room a pair of elderlies studied the menu. Probably sisters. Their faces showed a mutuality of trust and love. The less elderly of the two ordered their meal. Their combined years must have totaled 170 -- maybe more! Set end to end and stretched backward in time their 170-plus years could have reached all the way to 1818: the era of Andrew Jackson -- Texas was part of Mexico -- King Cotton ruled Southern agriculture. The lives of these two ladies in their eighties 'minded me of others with whom I have been privileged to share a home, a place, a church, a meal, a concert, a trip. I am grateful for elderly people. And I am grateful for un-elderly people, also!

The meal was "too"! Just "too"! Linen, silverware, china, crystal, flavorful bits of everything served with a flourish. The table was enhanced with a pink/orangey rose fresh-clipped from the church yard. We relished the food, the setting, the conversation. It was "too"! And November's mood made it even better than "too"! I am grateful.

The gratitude-attitude of this eleventh month of the calendar is itself a gift! It adds depth, color, value, delight, passion to things that ordinarily we overlook: the ability to walk briskly, church bells, older persons (and younger too!), tasteful food, a flower. The gratitude-attitude lifts the soul to sing with the Psalmist: "My cup overflows! Surely goodness and mercy shall follow me all the days of my life; and I shall dwell in the house of the Lord for ever"! (Psalms 23:5b-6 RSV) I am grateful!

Blessings on you and yours as your world is enhanced with November's gratitude-attitude. It is God's gift to you. What you make of it is your gift to others.

Thanksgivingly yours.

November 10, 2000

Dear November Friends:

Too many! Too, too many! So very too many! Too many what? Too many "Thank You!" notes not written! Many too many! Our intentions are good! But the road to "Hell is paved with good intentions!" Unwritten "Thank You!" notes. Unspoken gratitudes! Unexpressed thanksgivings! So, our tombstone may well read: "She had good intentions while on earth. But she was too busy. Now she has a timeless eternity during which to write on the chalkboard of Hell: 'I am thankful!' a zillion times and more!"

The eleventh month on the calendar is the "gratitude attitude" season. Thirty mornings to wash the sandman's grit out of our eyes, to sip a cup-of-coff, to whisper: "Dear God, Thanks!" Thirty evenings to lay the head on a fluffed-up pillow and to whisper those three words again: "Dear God, Thanks!" This gratitude attitude should not just be scattered like leaves on the autumn breeze. Rather, this gratitude attitude should be focused. For instance: We love our families: mothers, fathers. Unwritten "Thank You!" notes! Unspoken gratitudes! Unexpressed thanksgivings! But now it is too late. Our mothers, our fathers sleep with their mothers, their fathers. Our sisters, our brothers -- most of them are still with us. Now our good intentions are to do for our siblings what we should have done for our parents. Our daughters, our sons -- how they would brighten at a word of appreciation from us. And how they would treasure our yellowed "Thank You!" notes once we are for them only cherished memories. Our granddaughters, our grandsons. Our dearest friends -- both near and far. Our teachers. Our doctors. Our fellow workers. A long list!

Forest Lawn Memorial Park is a cemetery in Glendale, California. Hubert Eaton designed Forest Lawn as a setting where hurting hearts could be helped through their grief into gratitude. The Great Mausoleum-Columbarium at Forest Lawn is a castle/fortress/church structure of thirteen levels. In that Mausoleum are chapels, hallways, cloisters, chambers for urns, large rooms for crypts, stained-glass windows, statuary, fountains, gardens. Most of the plaques on the crypts in the Great Mausoleum-Columbarium bear only the names, the birth dates, the death dates of the persons resting within. Such as: "Jane Doe - April 21, 1896 - August 16, 1959." One such plaque is most memorable. It is burnished brass. The ends of the plaque are curled like a scroll. The birthdate, the death date, these have slipped beyond recalling. But the sentiment and the signature on that burnished brass are brightly remembered: "Dear God, Thanks! Ed Wynn."

Gotta go now! Gotta lotta "Thank You!" notes to write before this gratitude attitude season ends! Before the ink in my pen dries up! Before the sand in my hourglass runs out! Before I am sentenced to an eternity of writing on the chalkboard of Hell: "I am thankful!" a zillion times and more.

Sincerely and gratefully, I am Your November Friend and Minister.

11

🌿

Christmas

December 13, 1972

Dear Christmas Friends:

We move from one crescendo to a second and then to another and to one more! It is almost as though George Frederick Handel, composer of the *Messiah*, had written the score for rendering the lyrics of our church life. We climb from peak to higher peak! How can we ever outdo last Sunday's service of worship? It had everything -- youth, vigor, that hauntingly beautiful instrumental trio, uplifting prayers by our elders at the Table, a touching piece by the harp that reached to the depths of the soul, that climactic effort by the choir: "Gloria in Excelsis," a well-received non-sermon by the pastor, a lingering sense of a "presence that disturbs us with the joy of elevated thoughts" (à la Wordsworth).[115] It was a thrilling experience! Can we move from that high peak to a higher one yet? Come find out next Sunday! Our Chancel Choir will be presenting their Christmas gift of praise to God in the form of a very fine cantata. Christmas is "The Greatest Show on Earth" -- and the church is doing its share to make it even more so!

We will follow the crescendo of inspiration at next Sunday's worship service with a crescendo of warmth and intimacy as we sit around tables in the fellowship hall and enjoy good food and good company. Already we have received 180 reservations. And we are preparing food enough for 275! Come! Come! Come!

But that's not all. On December 24 we will give our worship service to our children. Ah! That, too, will be a crescendo of inspiration! Just ask any parent of any child in the children's Christmas Cantata. As everyone knows, children in a Christmas program can make no mistakes. **And even the mistakes they do make are right!** That will be a very precious and special hour. And what those children do for us will be worth far more than what a Christmas sermon could do. Yea! Even more than 10,000 fine Christmas sermons!

Friends -- this is no time to be a grouch, a critic. Even old Scrooge is transformed in December. So -- put on your happy clothes, your glad rags -- and join us as we sing and laugh and love our way through this most wonderful time of the year -- moving, as it were, from one crescendo to a second and then to another, and so on and upward!

Joy to the world! And peace! Etc.

December 3, 1975

Dear Christmas Friends:

Norman Vincent Peale put it in these words:

> Christmas waves a magic wand over the world,
> and behold, everything is softer and more beautiful.[116]

Indeed! When Christmas comes -- even the gruff, hard-nosed taxi drivers of New York City are softer!

This December feeling -- from whence does it come? This tenderness around the family table, this friendliness that follows us around town, this desire to please other people -- how do you explain it? This sentiment that wraps presents and bakes fruit cakes and sends greeting cards and hums carols and throws parties -- what is it? Answer: This is the pushing upward into our consciousness and outward into our attitudes and actions of the ultimate truth about life -- to the effect that <u>love is the heartbeat of creation</u>! Indeed!

Friends, my prayer is that December 1975 for you will have about it:

> The texture of lamb's wool -- like that of the lambs that snuggled next to their mothers on that first Christmas night;

> The wonder of the shepherds who hurried to the stable to see the child wrapped in swaddling cloths;

> The light in the eyes of the wise men who laid their gifts beside the manger, and knelt to worship,

> The love of God who so loved that he gave…!

With hope in my heart and a carol on my lips, I am, your pastor and friend.

December 4, 1987

Dear Christmas Friends:

December stacks up like a giant Dagwood sandwich. All kinds of super good things are layered into these 31 days:

> A bushel of greeting cards from friends -- old and new, near and far.
> 'Leventeen measures of music -- popular, fun, sentimental, inspiring.
> A dozen shopping trips: ten for buying -- two for exchanging!
> Several chunks of office parties and evenings out and visits away.
> Much family togetherness, around the table, the fireplace, the tree.
> A jingle of bells, a dash of reindeer, a frosting of snow, a slice of
>   fruitcake, a bowl of eggnog, a smidgen of nutmeg.

All this -- and much more -- is shoved into a merry-go-round calendar. What a joyous ride it is from the first day of December to the last!

Question: How is this most wonderful time of the year held together? What makes all the bits and slices and chunks and smidgens of the recipe meld? Is there a focus for the season? What ribbon runs through it and around it and ties it into a happy package of faith and hope and love and joy and peace? Answer: The creche of Bethlehem, of course! Love tiptoed down the stairs of heaven and placed a baby wrapped in swaddling cloths in a straw-filled manger. A bright star hung above that stable. A choir of angels sang: "Glory to God in the highest, and on earth peace among men with whom he is pleased." (Luke 2:14 RSV) Shepherds stood in the shadows. Kings laid gifts at the feet of the peasant infant: gold, frankincense, myrrh. And ever since -- for over 1900 years -- the celebration of the birth of Jesus has made December the crown of the year, the Mt. Everest of the calendar. Why? Because in Jesus we have found the true life -- the life abundant! His manner, his humility, his honesty, his passion for justice, his compassion for the underdog, his insights into Ultimate Reality -- these have illumined our shadows, thawed our coldness, softened our hardness, gentled our strength, brightened our drabness.

Your calendar may look like the parking lots at the shopping malls -- every slot taken, with other automobiles playing hide-and-seek for a space. Your schedule may be like Santa's bag -- it runneth over! You may feel that December offers too much to take in! It does! Therefore you must choose:

> If you choose a slice of baloney for your "Dagwood's Delight,"
>   you will have to leave out a cut of roast prime rib.
> If you load up with Styrofoam and tinsel,
>   you will have to do without silver and gold.

If you overindulge: partying, celebrating, carousing,
  you will have to forfeit leisure and sobriety and health.
If you follow the Pied Piper of Madison Avenue,
  you will not have time to follow the shepherds to Bethlehem, to sing
  with the angels, to kneel with the Wise Men at the creche!

These 31 days of December are frenzied. Do not make the error of thinking you can merely "sandwich" the Christian dimension into this season as though it were only one of many other ingredients. It is **the one thing required**! It is the <u>sine qua non</u> -- that without which all the others would fall apart! So then, make the birth of Jesus central, not incidental! Make it focal, not peripheral! Make it primary, not secondary! Come! "Let us go over to Bethlehem and see this thing that has happened, which the Lord has made known to us!" (Luke 2:15 RSV)

For the sake of the Christmas gospel, I am, your pastor and friend.

December 1, 1989

Dear December Friends:

It had been a super-caloric, extra-cholesterol, fantabu-licious dinner -- right down to the last crumb! The guest complimented the centerpiece, the china, the stemware, the silver, the linen. She raved about blue-cheese salad dressing, the bran muffins, the wine. The broccoli was el perfecto! The scalloped potatoes -- magnifico! The chicken royale was superlatif! But the guest's ultimate praise was for the dessert -- calorie-laden/cholesterol-burdened/butter-soaked crust filled with custardy Karo and covered with parched pecans! Not yet fully cooled. She relished her last bite, dabbed the napkin to her lips, turned to the hostess and exclaimed, "That was sooooo goooood! Did you make it yourself?" The hostess smiled and gave her a slightly syncopated answer, "Weeeell...I made it possible!"

Weeeeell...we didn't make the Church. For the Church is God's good gift. Still, though we didn't make the Church, we do make the Church possible!

A bride and groom stand at the head of the aisle. The father of the bride gives her an awkward embrace -- then places her hand in the hand of the groom. The minister offers a prayer. The most familiar words in the English language are repeated: "I, John, take you, Mary, to be my wife..." -- "I, Mary, take you, John, to be my husband..." Rings are exchanged. Another prayer. An embrace. The recessional! The couple walk briskly up the aisle to a new life as husband and wife. We don't make Christian marriage. That is God's good gift. But we make it possible!

A youngster in a muslin gown steps into a pool of clear, warm water. The minister speaks a word about bright eyes and high hopes and serious commitment. Then the words of the baptismal formula: "...upon your confession of faith that Jesus is the Christ, the Son of the living God, and in following his great example you are now baptized in the name of the Father, and of the Son, and of the Holy Spirit. Amen." He lowers her into the clear, warm water -- and then lifts her up again. We don't make Christian baptism. That is God's good gift. But we make it possible!

After the Communion hymn the Elder offers a prayer of thanksgiving. The trays are distributed to the waiting Deacons who pass them to the Congregation in the pews. Each member receives a bit of bread, a sip of wine. We remember God's grace to us in Christ -- a measure of kindness beyond measure! Sins are forgiven. Gratitudes are expressed. Resolves are made. Spirits are lifted. That's Communion. We don't make the Lord's Supper. That is God's good gift. But we make it possible!

Family and friends gather near a closed coffin over an open grave. There are flowers. There are embraces. There are tears. There are Scripture readings. There are prayers. There are the words of committal: "Forasmuch as Almighty God has received unto himself our departed friend, we, therefore, do tenderly commit her body to the ground -- earth to earth, ashes to ashes, dust to dust -- in sure and certain hope of the resurrection!" We don't make the hope of the resurrection. That is God's good gift. But we make it possible!

Phillips Brooks summed up the Christmas Gospel: "O holy child of Bethlehem, descend to us we pray."[117] We sing it again and again -- humming along as we shop -- joining in at school parties -- when we "Hang the Greens" -- around the Christmas Day dinner table. We don't make Christmas. That is God's good gift. But we make it possible!

Summer camps for teenagers -- Flowers for folk in convalescent homes -- Fellowship meals -- Bible studies -- Anthems -- A service of remembrance on All Saints' Sunday -- Christian Education from cradle roll to graduate school -- A caring presence before surgery -- Groceries for the hungry -- Children lisping "Jesus Loves Me" -- That's the Church. And we don't make the Church. That is God's good gift. But we make it possible!

December is upon us. That means Advent and carols and reunions and Handel's *Messiah* and a star at the top of an evergreen tree and *Silent Night* and a manger surrounded with shepherds and wisemen and angels, etc., etc., etc.! It is a great season! Join your family of faith and hope and love as together we make Christmas possible: "Glory to God in the highest, and on earth peace among men with whom he is pleased!" (Luke 2:14 RSV)

December 18, 1992

Dear Christmas Friends:

The birth of the Bethlehem babe divided the calendar between B.C. and A.D. -- Before Christ and <u>Anno Domini</u>. That birth and the life that came with it made an immense difference for the human family. The infant born in a stable became the carpenter of Nazareth, the teacher of Judea, the prophet of Galilee, the Christ of Calvary. He touched our world softly. He lifted children. He showed us the Kingdom of God in our midst. He leaned over to help the hurt, to encourage the sick, to liberate the oppressed. He gave us hope. His commitment to justice and compassion and peace has inspired us to similar commitments. What an immense difference the birth of the Bethlehem Babe has made! For history and forever! For others and for us!

Jesus and His teachings have moved the human family from brutality to gentleness, from greed to generosity, from callousness to compassion, from alienation to reconciliation, from hostility to harmony, from hell to heaven. His work continues in and through His disciples who put into action the song of the angels who welcomed His birth: "Glory to God in the highest, and on earth peace, good will toward men!" (Luke 2:14 KJV) And with Him we still pray: "Thy Kingdom come, Thy will be done, On earth as it is in heaven!" (Matthew 6:10 RSV)

Christmas is here! We celebrate the birth of the Bethlehem Babe! And with the shepherds and wise men we rejoice for the good things that have happened -- and that continue to happen -- because of that birth. "Joy to the world! The Lord is come! Let earth receive her King! Let every heart prepare him room! And heaven and nature sing!"[118]

Shalom! Feliz Navidad! Joyeaux Noel! God Bless Us All! Amen!

December 6, 2002

Dear December Friends,

When Jesus was twelve years old, Joseph and Mary took him to Jerusalem for the Feast of Passover. While there, the family probably made a side trip to Bethlehem. May have had tea at the infamous inn that had no room for them a dozen years earlier. See Joseph as he points to a corner in the shed and says, "Son, we did the best we could -- which wasn't much. Made a bed of straw. Your mother wept! We wrapped you real good. And right there -- see -- right there in the feeding trough -- that's where we laid you down. Here. Give me your hand. Feel that wood. This was your crib! Some shepherds shared their cheese and bread and wine with us. And some strange-speaking Easterners stopped in. They left some gifts for you: gold, frankincense, myrrh. When your mother was able, we took the road south -- to Egypt. We had it rough. It was six months before we came back through here."

Well, in the 2000 years since, we have sterilized the stable and dressed up the principal characters á la Hallmark Cards. We want to send the very best! Velvet robes, sturdy shepherds, jeweled princes, a chorus of Handel "Hallelujahs!" But the Hallmark version is gilded Styrofoam. Joseph's description was 24 karat! And it was that description that influenced Jesus to speak these autobiographical lines: "I was hungry and you gave me food, I was thirsty and you gave me drink, I was a stranger and you welcomed me, I was naked and you clothed me, I was sick and you visited me, I was in prison and you came to me." (Matthew 25:35-36 RSV)

This December, reach out "to one of the least of these." (Matthew 25:40 RSV) Pick up the tab for a meal or two. Give a coat. Speak a word of welcome. Pay for some medicine for folk who can't afford to. Sponsor a prisoner on furlough. That's the stuff that doesn't make it onto a Hallmark greeting card. But it's nearer to what really happened in Bethlehem 2000 years ago!

Notes

[1]Wordsworth, William. (1800). "Lines Written in Early Spring." Available at https://poetandpoem.com.

[2]*Webster's Seventh New Collegiate Dictionary* (1969).

[3]Kerr, Walter. (1962). *The Decline of Pleasure.* New York: Simon and Schuster.

[4]Livingstone, David. (1874). *The Life and African Explorations of David Livingstone: Diaries, reports, letters, journals.* St. Louis: Valley Press. Reprinted in 2002 by Cooper Square Press.

[5]Kim, Thomas (1674 Alt.). "Praise God from Whom All Blessings Flow." [Hymn]. *Favorite Hymns.* Cincinnati: The Standard Publishing Company, 1933.

[6]Gamble, James Jr. is said to be the chemist who discovered how to make the soap float. Gable Jr. was the son of co-founder of Procter & Gamble Company.

[7]Bushnell, Davis. (1982, June 21). "Wells Has a Dandelion Whine: The Weeds Won't Grow for Him." *People.* Retrieved March 18, 2019. Available at https://people.com/archive/adrian-wells-has-a-dandelion-whine-the-weeds-wont-grow-for-him-vol-17-no-24.

[8]*Laura Lansing Slept Here.* [Movie]. (1988). Used with permission from Turner Classic Movies. www.turner.info@turner.com.

[9]Roosevelt, Eleanor Roosevelt. (1960). *You Learn by Living: Eleven Keys for a More Fulfilling Life.* New York: Harper & Row.

[10]Brooks, Phillips. (1886). "Going up to Jerusalem." *Twenty Sermons,* p. 330.

[11]*The World's Best Poetry.* (1904). Edited by Bliss Carman, et al. Philadelphia: John D. Morris & Co.

[12]Tennyson, Alfred Lord. Horton, Robert F. (1900). *A Saintly Life.* New York: E.P. Dutton & Co. The actual quote is, "What the sun is to that flower Jesus Christ is to my soul."

[13]Reference to playing golf.

[14]Browning, Robert. "Cristina." *The Complete Poetic and Dramatic Works of Robert Browning.* Cambridge Edition. Editor: Horace E. Scudder. The Project Gutenberg EBook, Project Gutenberg License www.gutenberg.org/license. January 17, 2016 [EBook #50954].

[15]Buechner, Frederick. *Telling Secrets.* San Francisco, Harper. (1991). Reprinted with permission from Frederick Buechner Literary Assets, LLC, Cambridge, MA. The remaining part of the quote in included here. "The owner of the car turned out to be, as I'd suspected, a trust officer in a bank, and not long ago, having read an account I wrote of the incident somewhere, he found out where I lived and one afternoon brought me the license plate itself, which sits propped up on a bookshelf in my house to this day. It is rusty around the edges and a little battered, and it is also as holy a relic as I have ever seen."

[16]Shakespeare, William. (c. 1598), "The Merchant of Venice," IV, 1. *The Complete Works of Shakespeare.* Kittredge, George Lyman (Ed.). Boston: Ginn and Company. (1956).

[17]Attributed to Phillips Brooks. American Episcopal clergyman and author. (December 13, 1835–January 23, 1893). Riggins III, George S. (1990, December 5). *God's Not in a Hurry.* [Sermon]. Delivered at Forest Road United Methodist Church.

[18]Browning, Robert. "Andrea Del Sarto." *The Complete Poetic and Dramatic Works of Robert Browning.* Cambridge Edition. Editor: Horace E. Scudder. The Project Gutenberg EBook, Project Gutenberg License www.gutenberg.org/license. January 17, 2016 [EBook #50954].

[19]Tennyson, Alfred Lord. "Flower in a Crannied Wall." *A Victorian Anthology, 1857-1895.* Edmund Clarence Stedman (Ed.) Cambridge: Riverside Press. (1895).

[20]Horton, Robert F. *Alfred Tennyson, A Saintly Life.* New York: E.P. Dutton & Co.

[21]Rodgers, Richard, and Hammerstein, Oscar II. (1943) *Oklahoma!* [Musical].

[22]Authorship uncertain, some attribute to Grace E. Easley.

[23]Fawcett, John. (1782) "Blest Be the Tie That Binds." [Hymn]. *Favorite Hymns.* Cincinnati: The Standard Publishing Company, 1933.

[24]Swedish proverb.

[25]Lord, Walter. (1967). *Incredible Victory, The Battle of Midway.* New York: Harper & Row.

[26]"Hallelujah Chorus." (1741). From Frederick Handel's *The Messiah.*

[27]Keats, John. (1795-1821). "A Thing of Beauty Is a Joy Forever." Bliss Carman, et al. (Eds.). *The World's Best Poetry. Volume VI.* Fancy, 1904.

[28]Gladstone, William. (1809-1898). "The Shaping Power of Expectation." [Sermon]. Dr. Ernest T. Campbell. Delivered at Riverside Church (1971, July 18). Digitized by the Internet Archive in 2012 with funding from Princeton Theological Seminary Library. Available at http://www.archive.org/details/sermonshapingpow00camp.

[29]*The Persian Wars.* (500 B.C.). Herodotus, Greek historian. "Neither snow nor rain nor heat nor gloom of night stays these couriers from the swift completion of their appointed rounds" is full quote and the "Motto" of the USPS.

[30]The Place of a Thousand Drips is a roadside waterfall in the Great Smoky Mountains National Park located on Roaring Fork Road (Hwy. 321). The waterfall cascades to an 80-foot drop.

[31]Wooden, John. Bylined: Tom Siler. *Knoxville News-Sentinel.* (May 18, 1973).

[32]Niebuhr, Reinhold. (1933). Shapiro, Fred R. (2014, April 28). "Who Wrote the Serenity Prayer?" *The Chronicle Review.*

[33]Kethe, William. (1561). "Doxology." [Hymn]. *Favorite Hymns.* Cincinnati: The Standard Publishing Company, 1933.

[34]Attributed to Mark Twain.

[35]Johann Tetzel was a German Dominican friar and preacher. Tetzel was known for granting *indulgences* on behalf of the Roman Catholic Church in exchange for money; *indulgences* supposedly allowed a remission of temporal punishment due to sin, the guilt of which had been forgiven—a position heavily challenged by Martin Luther.

[36]Lee, Henry. (1800). *A Funeral Oration in Honor of the Memory of George Washington.* New Haven: Read and Morse.

[37]Woodbine Willie was Geoffrey Studdest Kennedy, an Anglican priest and poet. He was a chaplain in World War I and got his nickname from handing out Woodbine cigarettes to the soldiers.

[38]Author unknown.

[39]*Dallas* was a very popular TV show during the late 1970s and early 1980s.

[40]Overstreet, Bonaro. (1955). "Stubborn Ounces." *Hands Laid Upon the Wind.* New York: The Macmillan Company. Reprinted with permission from W.W. Norton & Company, Inc.

[41]Stanphill, Ira F. (1950). "I Know Who Holds Tomorrow." New Spring Publishing Inc. (ASCAP) (adm. at CapitolCMGPublishing.com). Reprinted with permission.

[42]Barrie, James. (1915). *The Little Minister.* New York: Charles Scribner's Sons.

[43]Fawcett, John. (1782). "Blest Be the Tie That Binds." [Hymn]. *Favorite Hymns.* Cincinnati: The Standard Publishing Company, 1933.

[44]Hardy, Thomas. (1919). *Poems of the Past and the Present,* "On an Invitation to the United States." London: Macmillan And Co., Limited St. Martin's Street.

[45]Burns, Robert (1759-1796). "To a Mouse." *The Norton Anthology of Poetry.* Allison, Alexander W. et al. (Eds.). New York: W. W. Norton & Company, Inc., 1975.

[46]Attributed to John D. Rockefeller. In correspondence with the Rockefeller Archive Center staff, they indicated that they have been unable to authenticate this precise quotation; however, the Archive Center welcomed the publication of this quotation and regards the sentiment as an accurate reflection of the ideas of John D. Rockefeller.

[47]Fawcett, John. (1782). "Blest Be the Tie That Binds." [Hymn]. *Favorite Hymns.* Cincinnati: The Standard Publishing Company, 1933.

[48]*Jacob's Ladder,* African-American spiritual.

[49]Rodgers, Richard, and Hammerstein, Oscar II. (1949) *South Pacific.* [Musical]. Used with permission.

[50]Carnegie, Andrew. (1889, June). "Wealth," *North American Review,* Vol. CXLVIII. [The actual quote is, "The man who dies rich dies disgraced."]

[51]Leacock, Stephen. (1911). "Gertrude the Governess." *Nonsense Novels.* The original text said "flung himself upon his horse...."

[52]Thoreau, Henry David. (1854). *Walden and On the Duty of Civil Disobedience.*

[53]John Keats, "When I Have Fears." *The Norton Anthology of Poetry.* Allison, Alexander W. et al. (Eds.). New York: W. W. Norton & Company, Inc., 1975.

[54]Paraphrased from John 9:4 KJV. "I must work the works of him that sent me, while it is day: the night cometh, when no man can work."

[55]Alfred, Lord Tennyson. "Crossing the Bar." *The Norton Anthology of Poetry.* Allison, Alexander W. et al. (Eds.). New York: W. W. Norton & Company, Inc., 1975.

[56]Booth, General William. (1912). Available at http://blog.salvationarmyusa.org/nhqblog/news/2012-05-09-ill-fight-100-years-since-booths-final-address.

[57]Berra, Yogi. (2002). *What Time Is It? You Mean Now?* New York: Simon & Schuster.

[58]Weatherhead, Leslie D. (1956). *Prescription for Anxiety.* London: Hodder & Stoughton Ltd.

[59]Johnson, Lyndon B. (1963, November 27). Address before a Joint Session of the Congress. Washington, D.C. Public Papers of the Presidents of the United States: Lyndon B. Johnson, 1963-64. Volume I, entry 11, pp. 8-10. Washington, D.C.: Government Printing Office, 1965.

[60]*Gloria Patri* or the Lesser Doxology. (3rd-4th century). [Hymn]. *Chalice Hymnal*. St. Louis: Chalice Press, 1995.

[61]Salmagundi -- a dish of chopped meat, anchovies, eggs, onions, and seasoning.

[62]Armistice Day, the 11th hour of the 11th day of the 11th month of 1918 when World War I ended. Arms were laid down and hostilities on the Western Front ended.

[63]There's a Wideness

[64]Fosdick, Harry Emerson. (1946). "The Constructive Use of Fear." [Sermon]. *On Being Fit to Live With: Sermons on Post-War Christianity*. New York: Harper & Brothers.

[65]Davenport, Abraham. (1780). "Day of Judgement." Davenport's response to a call for adjourning the Connecticut State Council because of fears that the deep darkness might be a sign that the Last Judgment was approaching, as quoted by Timothy Dwight, Connecticut Historical Collections 2d. ed. compiled by John Warner Barber, p. 403, 1836.

[66]Oxenham, John. (1908). "In Christ There Is No East or West." [Hymn]. *Favorite Hymns*. Cincinnati: The Standard Publishing Company, 1933.

[67]In 1986, President Reagan and First Secretary Gorbachev met in Reykjavik, Iceland, for a second summit about the arms race.

[68]Homer, Charlotte G. (n.d.). "Come to the Feast." [Hymn]. *Favorite Hymns*. Cincinnati: The Standard Publishing Company, 1933.

[69]Paraphrased from Williams, Hank. "Hey, Good Lookin'." Recorded on March 16, 1951. Castel Studio, Nashville.

[70]Alfred, Lord Tennyson. "Epilogue: To the Queen." *The Complete Poetical Works of Alfred, Lord Tennyson, Poet Laureate*. New York: Harper & Brothers, 1884. Original words are, "O loyal to the royal in thyself."

[71]Dickens, Charles. (1859). *A Tale of Two Cities*. New York: Books, Inc., 1936.

[72]Stevenson, Robert Louis. (1896). *Vailima letters: being correspondence addressed by Robert Louis Stevenson to Sidney Colvin*, November, 1890-October, 1894. Letter to Sidney Colvin, 23 August 1893, in Sidney Colvin (ed.) New York: Scribner's, 1909.

[73]Attributed to Lyndon Baines Johnson.

[74]Browning, Robert. "Andrea Del Sarto." *The Complete Poetic and Dramatic Works of Robert Browning*. Cambridge Edition. Editor: Horace E. Scudder. The Project Gutenberg EBook, Project Gutenberg License www.gutenberg.org/license. January 17, 2016 [EBook #50954].

[75]Shakespeare, William. (c. 1605). "Macbeth," V, 5. *The Complete Works of Shakespeare*. Kittredge, George Lyman (Ed.). Boston: Ginn and Company, 1956.

[76]Attributed to von Humboldt, Alexander. (1769-1859).

[77]Kipling, Rudyard. (c. 1895). "If." http://www.poetryloverspage.com/poets/kipling/ kipling_ind.html

[78]Shakespeare, William. (c. 1605). "Macbeth," III, 4. *The Complete Works of Shakespeare*. Kittredge, George Lyman (Ed.). Boston: Ginn and Company, 1956.

[79]Glenn Cunningham, Olympian 1932 and 1936.

[80]*Book of Common Prayer* (c. 1549).

[81]Browning, Robert. "Andrea Del Sarto." *The Complete Poetic and Dramatic Works of Robert Browning*. Cambridge Edition. Editor: Horace E. Scudder. The Project Gutenberg EBook, Project Gutenberg License www.gutenberg.org/license. January 17, 2016 [EBook #50954].

[82]Shakespeare, William. (c. 1599). "Hamlet," III, 1. *The Complete Works of Shakespeare*. Kittredge, George Lyman (Ed.). Boston: Ginn and Company, 1956.

[83]Van Dyke, Henry. (1907). "Joyful, Joyful, We Adore Thee." [Hymn]. *Chalice Hymnal*. St. Louis: Chalice Press, 1995.

[84]Bliss, P.P. (n.d.). "Hallelujah, What a Savior!" [Hymn]. *Favorite Hymns*. Cincinnati: The Standard Publishing Company, 1933.

[85]Wordsworth, William. "My Heart Leaps Up." *The Norton Anthology of Poetry*. Allison, Alexander W. et al. (Eds.). New York: W. W. Norton & Company, Inc., 1975.

[86]Babcock, Rev. Maltbie D. (1901). "This Is My Father's World." [Hymn]. *Favorite Hymns*. Cincinnati: The Standard Publishing Company, 1933.

[87]Lincoln, Abraham. (1863, November 19). *The Gettysburg Address*.

[88]Matheson, George. (1882). "O Love That Wilt Not Let Me Go." [Hymn]. *Favorite Hymns*. Cincinnati: The Standard Publishing Company, 1933.

[89]Balzac, Honore de. Paraphrased from *The Alkahest*.

[90]Wesley, Charles. (1739, alt.). "Christ the Lord Is Risen Today." [Hymn]. *Chalice Hymnal*. St. Louis: Chalice Press, 1995.

[91]Pott, Francis. (1861, from Latin 1695). "The Strife Is O'er." [Hymn]. *Chalice Hymnal*. St. Louis: Chalice Press, 1995.

[92]Attributed variously to Chalmers, Alexander (1759-1834), Immanuel Kant (1724-1804), and Joseph Addison (1672-1719).

[93]Wordsworth, William. (1770-1850). "Michael." *The Norton Anthology of Poetry*. Allison, Alexander W. et al. (Eds.). New York: W. W. Norton & Company, Inc., 1975.

[94]Wesley, Charles. (1739, alt.). "Christ the Lord Is Risen Today." [Hymn]. *Chalice Hymnal*. St. Louis: Chalice Press, 1995.

[95]Pott, Francis. (1861, from Latin 1695). "The Strife Is O'er." [Hymn]. *Chalice Hymnal*. St. Louis: Chalice Press, 1995.

[96]*Book of Common Prayer* (c. 1549).

[97]Pascal, Blaise (1623-1663). Several sources quote this as, "The heart has its reasons which reason knows nothing of."

[98]Balzac, Honore de. Paraphrased from *The Alkahest*.

[99]Ackley, Alfred H. (1933). "He Lives." [Hymn]. *Chalice Hymnal*. St. Louis: Chalice Press, 1995.

[100]Martineau, Harriet. (1802-1876). "We do not believe in immortality because we can prove it, but we try to prove it because we cannot help believing it."

[101]Old proverb.

[102]Paschal greeting in the Orthodox and Catholic churches.

[103]Wesley, Charles. (1739, alt.). "Christ the Lord Is Risen Today." [Hymn]. *Chalice Hymnal*. St. Louis: Chalice Press, 1995.

[104]Wesley, Charles. (1739, alt.). "Christ the Lord Is Risen Today." [Hymn]. *Chalice Hymnal*. St. Louis: Chalice Press, 1995.

[105]Wesley, Charles. (1739, alt.). "Christ the Lord Is Risen Today." [Hymn]. *Chalice Hymnal*. St. Louis: Chalice Press, 1995.

[106]Handel, George Frideric, *Messiah,* composed in 1741.

[107]Watts, Isaac. (1707). "Alas! And Did My Savior Bleed." *Favorite Hymns*. Cincinnati: The Standard Publishing Company, 1933.

[108]Watts, Isaac. (1707). "Alas! And Did My Savior Bleed." *Favorite Hymns*. Cincinnati: The Standard Publishing Company, 1933.

[109]Irenaeus. (c. 202). Early Church Texts. Available at https://earlychurchtexts.com.

[110]Bryant, William Cullen. "The Battle-Field." *An American Anthology, 1787–1900*. Edmund Clarence Stedman (Ed.). Boston: Houghton Mifflin, 1900.

[111]Ackley, Alfred H. (1933). "He Lives." [Hymn]. *Chalice Hymnal*. St. Louis: Chalice Press, 1995.

[112]Keats, John. (1795-1821). "A Thing of Beauty Is a Joy Forever." Bliss Carman, et al. (Eds.). *The World's Best Poetry*. Volume VI. Fancy, 1904.

[113]Wordsworth, William. (1770-1850). "My Heart Leaps Up." Francis T. Palgrave, ed. *The Golden Treasury*, 1875.

[114]Alford, Henry. (1844). "Come, Ye Thankful People, Come." *Favorite Hymns*. Cincinnati: The Standard Publishing Company, 1933.

[115]Wordsworth, William. (1779-1850). "Lines Composed a Few Miles above Tintern Abbey." *The Norton Anthology of Poetry*. Allison, Alexander W. et al. (Eds.). New York: W. W. Norton & Company, Inc., 1975. The poem actually says disturbs "me."

[116]Frequently cited quote by Norman Vincent Peale.

[117]Brooks, Phillips. (1868). "O Little Town of Bethlehem." *Chalice Hymnal*. St. Louis: Chalice Press, 1995.

[118]Watts, Isaac. (1719). "Joy to the World." *Favorite Hymns*. Cincinnati: The Standard Publishing Company, 1933.

www.ingramcontent.com/pod-product-compliance
Lightning Source LLC
Chambersburg PA
BHW081425090426
740CB00017B/3183